Praise

"A raw and compelling portrait of a mother who was the first woman to break into the all-male fortress of TV news, back in the dark ages of the 1960s. . . . It is also a personal confession of life with a mother almost obsessively driven in her career. . . . The book is a mix of solid reportorial digging with a son's sometimes heartbreaking insights."

—Lesley Stahl

"Beautifully observed and richly reported, a family tale with a twist—because it's written about the kind of family that normally wouldn't let secrets make their way outside the security fence. A tough and loving book by a gifted journalist."

—Peggy Noonan

"Anyone who was a big fan of Nancy Dickerson will hate John Dickerson by about page 40. But by the time you reach the end of his poignant, sometimes funny, but always wise and human memoir-biography, you will love them both. John for his insight and compassion, and Nancy for the price she paid to blaze the trail for Katie Couric and Greta van Susteren."

—Al Franken

"Riveting. . . . You cannot turn your eyes away."

—Elsa Walsh, *The Washington Post*

"A compelling and nuanced portrait. . . . The book is rich with details about the political and the powerful in the '60s and '70s as television news came of age."

—*The Boston Globe*

"A unique and authentic view of Nancy Hanschman Dickerson . . . that will shape future studies of this phenomenal woman."

—*The Washington Times*

On Her Trail

My Mother, Nancy Dickerson, TV News' First Woman Star

JOHN DICKERSON

SIMON & SCHUSTER PAPERBACKS

NEW YORK   LONDON   TORONTO   SYDNEY   NEW DELHI

SIMON & SCHUSTER PAPERBACKS
An Imprint of Simon & Schuster, Inc.
1230 Avenue of the Americas
New York, NY 10020

SIMON & SCHUSTER PAPERBACKS and colophon are registered
trademarks of Simon & Schuster, Inc.

For information about special discounts for bulk purchases, please contact Simon & Schuster
Special Sales at 1-800-456-6798 or business@simonandschuster.com.

Designed by Dana Sloan

Manufactured in the United States of America

1   3   5   7   9   10   8   6   4   2

Photo on p. ii reprinted by permission of the Robert Phillips Estate

The Library of Congress has cataloged the hardcover edition as follows:
Dickerson, John, date.
On her trail : my mother, Nancy Dickerson, TV news' first woman star / John Dickerson.
p.   cm.
Includes index.
1. Dickerson, Nancy (Nancy Hanschman). 2. Television journalists—United States—
Biography. 3. Women television journalists—United States—Biography.
PN4874.D44 D53 2006
070.92—B22   2006048492
ISBN 978-0-7432-8783-8
ISBN 978-1-5011-3067-0 (pbk)
ISBN 978-0-7432-9834-6 (ebook)

To Anne

Acknowledgments

First, my wife, Anne. The book never would have happened without her. She read it, shaped it and talked through my millions of theories. She has been loving, nourishing and supportive for the sixteen years she has fallen asleep to the sound of my typing. My brother Michael and sisters Elizabeth, Ann and Jane have always been unconditionally loving and protective, particularly at the challenging times. They were generous with their stories and edits and never tired of my endless questions, which will probably continue long after the book has been published. My father was generous and patient with this book. I know it was hard at times. He acted with all of the grace, care, dignity and wit that I have always admired.

As the son of a talented woman, I've benefited from knowing several others. Margaret Carlson has been my guardian angel, a mentor and a tender, smart reader of this book. Peggy Noonan gave me pointers on writing Mom's eulogy and has been sending wise and restorative e-mails ever since. Emily Bazelon offered sharp edits and clarity during my regular moments of confusion. Ana Marie Cox gave smart and bracing critical advice. Michele Orecklin and Ginia Bellafante also provided encouragement and guidance when this was all just a notion. Ann King is just wonderful in every way.

I had two talented assistants on this book. I handed over the entire mess of journals, newspaper clippings and photographs to Jennifer Guastaferro. She handled the twenty boxes with care, discretion and unmatched organizational precision. Elisabeth Higgins Null is just a force. She chased every lead, blinded herself going through Library of Congress archives and tracked hard-to-find sources. Her extraordinary diligence paid off with some great gems. She never let a moment pass without a thoughtful notion, insightful observation or a good word to keep me going. Her spirit is inspiring.

My agent and friend, Elizabeth Sheinkman, stuck with me throughout, kept this book alive and patiently listened to my theories about the other books in my head. My editor Ruth Fecych at Simon & Schuster was patient, sharp-eyed and encouraging throughout. She has an elegant touch. Thank you to my publisher, David Rosenthal, who took a chance on this book and whose enthusiasm helped me cross the finish line.

My extraordinary colleagues at Slate got to know me in the middle of this book and never complained when, no matter what other topic we were discussing, I found a way to bring the conversation back to this project. Particular thanks go to David Plotz for his questions and design help, and Jack Shafer for the chats about journalism history. Editor Jacob Weisberg lured me away from *Time* and then made good on his every promise, including giving me room to work on the book and editing my pieces with skill and passion.

I worked with many lovely and talented people during my fourteen years at *Time*. Judith Stoler and Neang Seng always took good care of me. I owe particular thanks to those who made the extra effort to teach me how to do this thing we do: Priscilla Painton, Jack White, Bonnie Angelo, Joelle Attinger, Jan Simpson, Jonathan Beaty, Sam Gwynne, Adam Zagorin, Jay Carney, Matt Cooper, Michael Duffy, Dan Goodgame, Nancy Gibbs, Richard Stengel and the late Hugh Sidey. Walter Isaacson pushed me as a journalist, encouraged and ran my first story about Mom at *Time* and then wouldn't stop pestering me until I wrote this book. His successor, Jim Kelly, has been a good friend and was a great boss.

Thank you to my teachers along the way: Neal Tonken, Richard A. Robinson, Harold Kolb and Anthony Winner. My first boss, Joe Quinlan, was a great teacher and also a deeply generous soul.

I have been blessed with extraordinary friends in life: Paschal Fowlkes, Katherine Dore, David Brown, Elizabeth Goodman, David Onek and Kara Dukakis, Brandon Ince and Alex Ince, Jim and Marion Kingdon, Lucy Owen and Jim Burns, Amelia and Adrian Wooldridge,

Penelope and Alex Privitera, David Gregory and Beth Wilkinson, and T. Brittain Stone, my first writing partner. On the road I've met more wonderful friends who also sustained me through this effort: Campbell Brown, Anne Kornblut, Frank Bruni and Mike Allen.

Thank you to my stepmother, Tandy Dickerson, for her friendship and for rescuing some of Mom's most precious possessions from being inadvertantly lost forever. Mary Matalin was an early and encouraging booster of this project. Dr. Beth Dzaman contributed priceless psychological and literary insights. Francine Proulx was a great help and I learned immediately why she was invaluable as Mom's right-hand woman. Donna Halper was generous with her time and was an extraordinary resource on the history of women in broadcasting. Thank you to Nancy Cole and Elena Brodie at the NBC archives and Marilyn Altman at "Peacock North"; Donald A. Ritchie, Associate Senate Historian; and Sister Therese Mackin and Sara McAlpin, BVM, at Clarke College. Lynsey Eilers took care of the kids while I was sequestered in the basement and made every day sunny and bright. Thank you to Chris Lehmann for his edits on the proposal that turned into this book. Al Franken plugged my book, was encouraging and said kind if breathy things about Mom every other week on his radio show while I was writing this. Additional thanks to Janice Grenci at the Library of Congress; Stephanie Slewka, who introduced me to Ray Scherer; Lisa Oberhofer at CBS; David Keough at the USAWC/AHEC Historical Services; John Solomon at On The Media; John Wells at International House; Nicole L. Bouche at the Unversity of Washington; Claudia Anderson and the staff at the Johnson Library; Laurie Austin at the John F. Kennedy Library; Meghan Lee at the Nixon Library; Steve Greene and Sahr Conway-Lanz of the Nixon Presidential Materials staff; Mary M. Huth at the University of Rochester; Gwen E. Pattison at the National Archives and Records Administration; Mary Jo Randall and Patricia Martens of the Wauwatosa Historical Society and Ken Schlessinger at the National Archives at College Park.

The songs of Bob Dylan and Ani DiFranco were either in my head or on my stereo throughout this project. They were as necessary as my laptop.

To the Phillip family, particularly Mary Ellen, thank you for the laughs and all the love. Though he's gone, Uncle Ernie needs to be celebrated near any sentence that includes the words *love* and *laughter* since he had so much of both. Thanks to Jack and Jackie McDonnell for letting me jump on the running board for so many years and to the rest of the McDonnell clan but particularly Kevin.

John Whitehead has been a loving, generous and inspiring friend. He made Mom very happy and during her sickness he was a marvel. Thanks to the Ladies' Lunch group and Kathy Greenberg for showing Mom such friendship. Thanks to Mom's nurses: Frans, Trudy, Ultima and Marlene, and most especially Elena A. Basco, angel. Betty and Leonard McKeehan have been fabulous grandparents, frictionless in-laws and, like their daughter Amy, boundless purveyors of support and love.

To Brice and Nan: thank you for interrupting each writing day with books and somersaults on the big bed. Daddy always comes back.

Since this book is one big acknowledgment to Mom I would only add here that she is definitely not responsible for any of the errors or lapses—particularly in grammar or spelling. She tried very hard on those accounts.

On Her Trail

Preface

The first time I ever heard my mother sound nervous, she'd been dead for two years. I was at the LBJ Library in Austin, Texas, listening to a recording of her telephone conversation with President Lyndon Johnson in February 1964. He had only been in office for three months. I wouldn't be born for four more years.

The White House operator begins: "Nancy Dickerson is on line two."

"Yes, honey," says the president to Mom.

"The next time I need a new swimming suit I'm going to consult you," she warbles.

Why is she talking about swimming suits?

"What's that?" Johnson doesn't know what she's talking about either.

She says it again. "The next time I need a new swimming suit I'm going to consult you."

She sounded so young. I'd listened to Johnson for hours on C-SPAN, which seemed to have a special channel just for his phone conversations. I'd bought cassettes of Johnson's greatest hits for long drives. But I'd never heard her on the tapes.

Silence. The recording captures even the regular blip of the reels turning on Johnson's tape machine. He's not responding. I cough, as if I were on the line with them. I want her to drop the swimsuit business and move on.

Johnson resets the conversation and saves us all. "How are you honey?"

"Fine, thank you," she replies, jittery.

She starts to pitch: "The reason I'm calling is this: We want to do a story this week without interviewing on television, nothing like that, but we want to follow Jack Valenti all over with whatever he does and take pictures. And he said—I just talked to him—he said, 'No, I'm not going to do it. Every time I see your camera coming I'm going to run the other way,' and I said, 'Well, we'll run after you.'"

She's trying to make the piece sound fun. With her faint Midwestern accent and precarious cheer, it sounds like she's in a musical and might break into song at any moment. She's also talking very fast, producing entire sentences that sound like single words. Now I'm nervous.

"No, we don't want to do that," says Johnson slowly. He is gruff, but not irritated. "We don't want to take pictures of employees. You'll have more jealousy here than I can deal with now. I've got enough of it between the old ones and the new ones and there's not anything he's doing that's important enough for your camera. And if it was, it oughn't to be on camera."

She tries again, but Johnson shoots her down. He's fighting to integrate his staff—like his special assistant Valenti—with the holdovers from the Kennedy administration. He doesn't want her making his task harder. Before the call ends, Mom is able to extract one approval. He will let her film the First Lady and their daughters for the *Today* show.

"That's fine," he says.

"Very good. And you let me know if there's ever anything I can do for you. Okay?"

"Thank you, honey."

He hangs up. The tape burps and the next call starts. Johnson talks to Secretary of Agriculture Orville Freeman about a cabinet appointment. I exhale. I'd been rooting for her so hard, I'd forgotten to breathe.

I went to the LBJ Library searching for scraps of my mother. She had been famous once. She was the first woman news correspondent for CBS television. The textbooks refer to her as the first woman of television news. A few other women had gotten there first, but she was the first one people remember: the first star.

Young girls imitated her in the '60s and '70s, interviewing their stuffed animals with the vacuum hose as their microphone. When big things happened, Mom was there, for CBS and later for NBC. She was the first to speak with John Kennedy after he was inaugurated, and she was at Andrews Air Force Base when his body returned from Dallas. She stood on John Glenn's lawn in 1962 and reported on his wife's reactions to his famous orbit. She was on the mall in Washington with Martin Luther King. Lyndon Johnson regularly called out to her by name when he wanted to make news.

All of this happened either before I was born or after my bedtime. By the time I was old enough to know what the news was, Mom's career with the networks was over. She was still on television once a year or so, but she wasn't like Walter Cronkite, or John Chancellor. They were a big deal. We watched them every night on the news. But people kept telling me what a big deal she was. My fourth-grade teacher asked me to get her autograph. The mother of the shortstop on my Little League baseball team asked if she was my mother and when I said yes, she got so excited, I thought they might have to call a doctor. "How neat for you to have her for a Mom."

Not exactly. I cared more about riding my bike and playing touch football. She was fine, I supposed. We lived in a big house and famous people came to call, but I was never sure why that mattered, or why she did.

By the time I was thirteen, I wasn't confused anymore. I was angry. I hated her: I thought she was a phony and a liar. Everyone still thought she was a big deal, but I thought she distinguished herself at home by being petty, rigid and clumsy. My parents divorced that year and I took my electric clock and brown comforter and I escaped. I moved in with my father. Mom stayed at Merrywood, the mansion where she and my father had raised five children, entertained presidents and smiled on cue for nearly twenty years of celebrity photographers. I would never live with her under the same roof again.

At the Johnson Library, I returned the matchbox-sized tapes of LBJ's phone calls to the desk. Mom and I had become close before she died and I wanted to spend a little more time with her memory, but I was late. I had a plane to catch and I still hadn't checked out of my hotel. I hurried back to the Driskill in downtown Austin. Mom was thirty-two, my age, when she first stayed there in 1960 to cover Johnson's run for the White House. I grabbed my battered bags and raced to the airfield used by the private planes. In the parking lot, I made a mental note of where I'd left the rental car. I'd be back in a few days.

"Jesus, Dickerson, we've been waiting for you," said someone as I ran out to the tarmac. I dropped my suitcase at the snout of a Secret Service bomb dog and ran toward the 727 that read "Bush Cheney 2000."

The flight attendants smiled and handed me a cup of warm-enough coffee. They had seen this mad dash before. My more punctual colleagues in the press were already poking at their laptops and reading the day's schedule. I took my usual seat and straightened out the ruffle of press badges that I wore around my neck. The plane started down the runway. I touched the worn leather box in my brief-case that held Mom's rosary—my preflight ritual. Where were we off to? I looked at my schedule: Michigan. Election day was just two months off.

I walked out on Mom, but almost twenty years later, I was following in her footsteps.

Chapter One

There were many Nancy Dickersons. I'll start with the first one I knew. On July 5, 1968, Mom started the day at Saks Fifth Avenue before the store opened. Three times a week she arrived with the morning shift for her appointment with Mr. Eivind, the Norwegian hairdresser. She said hello to the ladies arranging the compacts at the makeup counter. She knew them well.

After Mr. Eivind had shaped and set her brunette hair, Mom raced in her blue Mustang convertible—the top up to keep the freshly done work intact—and pulled into the NBC studios by 8:00. She had been repeatedly named among the best coiffed women in America for a reason. She was disciplined.

She would have two hours to write her script and prepare the stories she would deliver on *The News with Nancy Dickerson,* from 10:20 to 10:25, the first NBC newscast anchored by a woman.

She sifted through the Friday papers. On the front page of the *New York Times* was a story about a Dallas bar that had refused to serve an African diplomat because he was black. Alec Rose completed a 354-day sail around the world. The wires were reporting that Allied ground forces found three major caches of enemy munitions as they swept the provinces around Saigon.

By 9:00 she started typing out her script. Her long nails made almost as much noise as the typewriter keys. By 10:00 her colleagues could hear her practicing to the ping of her regulation NBC stopwatch as it switched on and off.

Twenty-four hours later I was born. Dad was in Fort Lauderdale closing a business deal so my eighteen-year-old about-to-be-half sister Elizabeth had to drive Mom to the hospital. Dad took the first flight he could find and arrived just before the blessed event.

Mom was 41. Viewers were shocked when they heard that *the* Nancy Dickerson, whom they had just been watching, had given birth. They had seen her every day and weren't aware she was pregnant. She and her bosses at NBC had stuffed me under the desk, careful always to shoot her from the chest up. Any signs of pregnancy or blatant womanhood would distract viewers from the news.

In the summer of '68 Mom was in the middle of covering the presidential race, and so my birth was reported in that context. "What's in a Name," read the headline of a *Washington Post* item. "Lyndon Hubert Eugene Richard Ronald Nelson seemed like a nice name to NBC's Nancy Dickerson, who was looking for something safe to call her son. Now she thinks it's just as well that she and her husband decided to call him John Frederick instead. 'Because,' she said with a sigh, 'we never even thought of Spiro.'"

Three weeks after I was born, Mom was in Miami covering the Republican convention. That confused viewers even more. *Didn't she just give birth?* She had, but she gave up on her experiment with breastfeeding and went off to cover the story.

Nancy and Wyatt Dickerson, my father, were leading an exciting life. Mom was not only one of the country's most famous newscasters, she was a celebrity. Dad was the CEO of a successful conglomerate. His company, Liberty Equities, developed real estate and owned businesses that manufactured everything from industrial pipe to processed foods. A butler polished the leather in their Rolls-Royce and they flew off for beach weekends in a private plane. They lived in a very big house and their liquor was excellent. In Miami, Dad stayed in their apartment at the exclusive Palm Bay Club while his superstar wife stayed in grungier digs with her press colleagues.

In the pictures from this era, my parents appear in conspicuously hip clothing—Dad wore turtlenecks with his blazer and looked like the Man from U.N.C.L.E.; Mom wore minis and pink lipstick. Their lingo matched the fashion of the times. "Come on upstairs. The party in 4-A is really swinging," Wyatt Dickerson is quoted as saying in a

Women's Wear Daily article about the society scene around the GOP convention. "It started in Virginia Gore's apartment, but it was a dud and we moved it down to Julie and Bill McKelvy's."

Groovy.

While Mom and Dad were partying, I was drooling in my crib back in McLean, Virginia. An army of uniformed servants watched over me and the other four Dickerson children. Like all successful couples of their time, my parents outsourced a lot of the child maintenance. In many of the candid shots of me as an infant or toddler I'm with at least one woman in white stockings and a white nurse's uniform. I was a very ugly child. I had a misshapen head and skin the color of cooked flounder. My bruised head and the uniforms of my caretakers made it look like I was raised in a ward of some kind.

When my older siblings and I look at pictures after Thanksgiving dinner, we try to guess the names of the nurses. Carolina, Louise, Veronica and Renata. Regular people tell stories about crazy aunts who collected Jello molds. We tell stories about Winston, who drove a cab during the day and cooked for us at night. He'd been a cook for the railroad so he couldn't prepare dinner for fewer than five hundred. He had to run out the back door one day when a girlfriend came looking for him with a razor in her shoe.

It is our ritual. We get together and return to the subject of our family the way other families return each year to summer homes. But the family legends we trade over turkey don't help me reconstruct my early days with Mom much. They suggest she wasn't home. At age five, my brother somehow started a tractor that had been brought in to build the new pool. If he'd known how to drive it he could have started a nice addition before anyone found him.

For a period, I expressed myself on the wall next to my crib. I was Jackson Pollock and my diaper was my palette. My siblings consulted with the nanny and all of them decided to sew my pajamas shut with shoelaces and a diaper pin. (I have only just forgiven them.)

Veronica is the first caretaker I can remember. She was a solid woman. I would run to hug her and bounce off. Every day, Veronica and I would visit a family of fluffy white rabbits she was raising in the abandoned poolhouse at the edge of our property.

I had fallen in love with rabbits in my storybooks. To have live, warm ones to pet was a special heaven. In the fall, I played hide-and-seek with them in piles of leaves. I let them pounce around in my warm coat. I named them: Mike, Liz, Ann and Jane. Not very creative; those are my siblings' names.

One afternoon, I asked Veronica if I could make my daily visit, but she told me the rabbits had run away. I was very upset, and I insisted we must search for them. Veronica seemed uninterested. I left a box by the back door lined with newspaper and scarves in case they were cold when they returned.

They weren't coming back; Veronica had put them in the stew.

I didn't find this out until much later. My older brother and parents told the story with a chuckle because apparently eating your family pet is funny. Today nannies are fingerprinted and have FBI-style background checks. What kind of parent leaves their children with a nanny who cooks their bunnies?

Most people have too many pictures of themselves eating spaghetti as a child. For some reason, parents feel compelled. It's almost a national requirement. It's the same with the naked tub shot. I have thousands of pictures of my children in these poses. There are no such pictures of me. Staff did the feeding and cleaning and it wasn't proper for those caring for me to go snapping photos behind the scenes. The few snaps I do have were taken by my grandparents.

Instead, what I have is publicity photographs. I appeared in the *Washington Star* and *Oakland Tribune.* Mom's star was fading—she left network television for independent production before I was two—so I didn't get nearly the exposure my older brother and sisters did. They made *Vogue, Parade,* the *Saturday Evening Post* and the *Washington Post* back when she was really famous. But I am represented in a few profiles of her. I was a necessary stop in the tour between the garden room, painted to match the Oval Office, and the library with its walnut paneling. The photographers tilted my fontanel the right way or caught me from the right angle so I look much better in glossy prints than I do in the scary candid photos.

"Luncheon with Nancy Dickerson begins with the impressive drive to her house," reads a profile in the *Oakland Tribune* in 1970. "The butler answers the door and Nancy walks into the gorgeous foyer, with its sweeping view of the Potomac below. Toddling along with his mother is 20-months old John, truly an angel child . . . a friendly, smiling, fair-haired carbon copy of his father, Wyatt. After an embrace and a one-sided conversation, John is carried away by his English nurse, for his afternoon nap. At his mother's cajoling, he blows kisses from the stairway."

Here I am in a *New Woman* profile: "Before setting down in the study, we go up the broad, thickly carpeted stairs and down the paneled hallway to John's room. John is two [*sic*], and his mother picks him up out of his crib and introduces me. Then she winds up his big tick-tock clock and we tiptoe out, hoping he will not roar when he discovers he has been conned into a nap. He doesn't."

I was a very accommodating child, blowing kisses, nodding off on cue, and I didn't call Mom on it when she told her profilers I was just two. I was three and I'm sure that like my three-year-old son now, I was very anxious to make sure people got that right. I might have had a wobbly head but I wasn't an idiot. At age forty-four, Mom fibbed about my age to make herself seem younger. Presumably, if Mom had stayed famous, future profilers would have been shocked by the disconnect between my behavior and my supposed age. How big a lie would they have let her tell? *His crib seems cramped for a six-foot boy, but he doesn't seem to mind.*

I was dressed for these photo shoots as if my parents were entering me in some kind of pageant. In one profile, I'm wearing a cap with a chin strap, short pants with straps over my shoulders, a capelike coat and red leather sandals with white socks. Outside the picture frame, you can sense the line of boys preparing to beat me silly.

This is the way you dress your child when you're paying someone else to dress him. To be fair, it's also the way you probably should dress your children when they're going to be kissing the president. My brother won this honor and he couldn't look more adorable in his hard red shoes, blue kneesocks, short pants and blazer as he plants one on Lyndon Johnson's cheek. In the picture that captures that moment, Johnson is down on his knees in the Oval Office and Defense Secretary McNamara and Secretary of State Rusk look over the spectacle from the doorway.

Mom's career on television may have been slowing while I was growing up, but throwing A-list parties was the part of her profession that endured and we needed to look nice when senators and cabinet officers were coming. At age four or five, I wasn't old enough to take full part in the production, but I wanted in on the excitement, so I followed Mom through her preparations.

Party day often started with a trip across the river to Washington to visit Mr. Eivind, the hairdresser. I got to play with the adjustable chairs while Mom was being tended to. At the end, when surveying his work in the mirror, she swiveled her head to the side while keeping her eyes fixed forward. It's the look most people give you when they think you're pulling their leg. "My eyes are sharper when I look from the side," she said, sucking in her cheeks a touch to show her high cheekbones.

It was more fun to watch her when she did her hair herself. She teased it with flat metal combs tapered to a point like a knitting needle. When I was older I'd play dressing-room Ninja, throwing them at the Styrofoam heads on which she stored her hats. If your aim was true and you really winged it, you could drive the end in all the way to the tines. She'd stick a couple of those comb ends into her hair, and by the end of the flurry of arm movements, it looked like she'd just pulled her finger from the wall socket.

When her hair was done, I followed her down the hall as she got dressed. Her dressing room off the bedroom had twenty feet of suits and gowns and silk shirts puffed with tissue paper to keep their shape. I had two pairs of shoes—loafers and sneakers. She had a wall of them, at attention in their shoe trees. Dad had far less real estate but seemed to emerge from his dressing room as if the tailor had just recut his suit for the evening.

In the back of the house were three more closets of colorful Dior, Cardin and St. Laurent outfits. She would pluck a dress, drape it across the other hanging clothes and stand back to think. Then she would repeat the drill with another and then another. This was very boring, so I ran through the dry-cleaning sheaths into a deep corner. When my friends and I played hide-and-seek, it was into these back closets that I would disappear. The cedar walls smelled like a fire burning somewhere.

Chapter Two

The first time I remember seeing Mom on television was in 1977 when she hosted a documentary called *We Will Freeze in the Dark*. We had just gotten a Betamax and we taped the program. This was a very big deal. We had no record of Mom's television shows from the previous seventeen years, even on film.

The show started with the terrifying image of two men in official uniforms carting off the refrigerator while the stunned family watched in low light. There was an energy crisis and Mom wanted to scare us and the rest of her viewers. It was very cool to be associated with a person who was on that little box. I told all the other third-graders about it at school the next day. They hadn't seen Mom, but they were pretty sure that nobody in the government took away refrigerators. They thought I was telling stories. They told the teacher and she assured us that all the refrigerators were safe. I told them I could show them a tape. They didn't want to see. I dropped it. We went back to eating paste.

When Mom wasn't at work she was at work on me. She out-sourced the care and maintenance, but she worked very hard to fix me. She had specific views about how children should be raised. As with many aspects of her life, she took her parenting cues from the Kennedy family. Rose Kennedy had told her she read to her children at the dinner table, so on the nights Mom was home, she read to us. She read from the newspaper, or took out the *Tell Me Why* book to teach us about how the telephone worked or explain why cranes didn't tip over under a heavy load. When her friend Joan Mondale, the wife of the Minnesota senator, wrote a book about modern art, we had readings from it. We learned to recognize form, shape and texture.

The dinner seminars were a part of raising us to achieve the Kennedy family ideal. We were to get straight A's, attend Ivy League universities, excel at sports, understand politics and have perfect hair and teeth (though thank God we weren't forced to have *their* teeth).

My brother could keep up, but I always felt left behind. It was like listening to Shakespeare. By the time I caught up to one sentence everyone had said several more. One afternoon in Mom's office I declared, "I want to talk at dinner. Everyone is always talking and I don't get a chance to talk."

"You're right," she said. "You should be allowed to speak." Mom had been the youngest and felt like she had a special duty to protect me and make sure I had my due. Plus, she was probably happy that I was awake enough to want to contribute. So that night she introduced me.

"John has asked to say something because we never give him a chance to speak," she said quieting my father and brother. "That's very important. Go ahead, John."

We were eating in the small breakfast room, which seemed, to my nine-year-old eyes, to have lights bright enough for surgery. I liked the idea of free speech in theory. I wanted a piece of the action, but I hadn't prepared my remarks.

"I like race-car driving," I told them. "It's a fun sport."

There was an awkward silence.

Clearly they didn't get the whole "fun" element of racing. They went back to talking about Carter's efforts to curb inflation. I watched the rest of the conversation in silence.

This did not help me get into the family swing. My parents worried I might be slow. I know because they told me. They didn't sit down and say: "John, it's your head—it's misshapen. We're sorry. And stop drooling." But they came close. When I was seven, they told me I was repeating first grade. I was in Mom's bathroom watching her prepare for a party. Dad came in. They both spoke to me at the same time; I remember backing up against the windowsill.

"It's not a bad thing," Mom told me.

"You just need a little more time," said Dad.

It was a big bathroom but it felt like the ceiling was pressing on my head. I resolved to color inside the lines more often.

Most of the time I was a very happy boy, maybe too happy. Before I'd started school I could amuse myself for hours playing with Mom's elaborate strands of jewelry. I would sing simple songs at the top of my lungs and dance and twirl. This delighted Mom and Dad. I was an easy, giddy boy. But then as I progressed through the early grades they worried that I'd gotten stuck. Would I always be a simple child? They were certain I'd wind up sitting in the park wearing a wool cap in August, muttering into my elbow.

"I gut thron in the lake for fieting," I wrote home at age nine from Camp Mishawaka. I should have been thrown in the lake for the spelling. One paragraph in a school report on "Gin Rummey" (*sic*) reads as though I've been drinking gin: "You can have 3 cards that go in ordr in the same groop. For instans 8,9,10 of harts." Grammar was a distant land that I had never visited. Mom wrote out nine sentences with blanks into which I was to write either "me" or "I." Another composition begins: "The silver dollar is made of silver." At least I had a grasp of the obvious.

Mom thought I was going off the charts, and she was going to approach me the way she might attack a news piece: through research and networking. She was working on documentaries at this point rather than daily news, which meant she had stretches of free time to cart me around to specialists.

First, she started a folder. It was green and labeled "John Frederick Dickerson." That she used my middle name was proof of just how righteously she was going to attack this problem.

"Mrs. Mathey, this is a plea for help," she wrote my fourth-grade teacher. "We feel that John does not read well; we know he does not spell well. He tells us that he does not have homework. We would like you to assign him more."

When the extra schoolwork didn't put the letters in their place, she dropped my guitar and piano lessons and sent me to after-school tutors. They made me fill pages writing the same word over and over again. I never got much better. I threw letters at words and hoped something would stick. I also took up forgery. My teachers asked me to have my parents sign my spelling tests but I did that only once. There were a lot of red marks on those tests, and that only led to tense conversations at home. So I learned to duplicate Mom and Dad's signatures precisely. I became so good at it my classmates hired me to stand in for their mothers or fathers. They'd bring in a cancelled check or trick their parents into signing a piece of paper. We'd meet in the bathroom and I'd set up shop on the edge of the sink. They didn't give me money. I was paid in glory. But there was a flaw in this scheme. When you're a bad speller, you sometimes misspell the names of your friends' parents. It was not a growth industry for me.

Mom and Dad never found out about the forgeries, so they had no chance to learn just how clever I was. As their worry grew, they took me to doctors. An ophthalmologist outfitted me in cumbersome glasses.

"His posture is contorted," he said, "and he has slow eye movement and sensitivity to light."

I should have been up in the bell tower yanking the rope.

"He may be a victim of the educational process."

I've hung on to that rationale for most of my life.

When I was eleven, I went through a series of tests at Children's Hospital.

The ride over was tense. Mom frowned as she gripped the steering wheel. She hated to drive and Children's Hospital was across town. We drove past abandoned buildings and hoodlums blowing bored smoke on doorsteps. She locked the car doors.

Surely something was wrong with me for her to be going to this effort.

"It's not that there's anything wrong with you," she told me.

Yup, something was wrong with me.

"We just think you are a little behind where you should be."

I can't remember exactly what kinds of tests they put me through, but I remember waiting in the doctor's office, staring at the puffy cartoon characters painted on the wall. They were all smiles. I didn't trust them.

The doctor walked in and closed the door with a hush. He wore a white lab coat and pointed to his clipboard.

"Here we can see that he's in the twenty-fifth percentile for his age. We should watch that." He pointed to a blue ballpoint dot on a graph labeled "Boys: 2 to 18 Years Physical Growth NCMS Percentiles."

I was the blue dot. I got that. I looked at them both trading information about the "he" who was sitting silently in his chair right in front of them. The nodding and serious tones and pointing to unreadable charts made it clear: Something was definitely wrong with me.

I left the office scared and worried. A kid in school had a lazy tongue that made him talk like he had a mouth full of marbles. Is that what I had coming my way? Children's Hospital was the place they treated the kids with cancer. Everyone knew that. Baseball and football players were always there visiting sick kids who'd lost their hair.

"Do I have cancer?" I asked.

Mom must have said no.

The mystery tour of doctors' offices finally took me to the more familiar examining room of our family doctor, Dr. Cawley. Surely he'd tell me what was going on. He looked like Captain Kangaroo, and I admired him for being able to hold down both jobs. It was no fun to be poked at again, but wriggling on and off the white paper on the examining table was a ritual that was at least familiar. When they put me under the cold lead X-ray blanket and told me not to breathe, I nearly passed out. The light went off, the nurse came back in the room and I was still holding my breath. I was taking no chances with the cancer.

"He has mild scoliosis," said Dr. Cawley. "It's something we'll have to watch."

Yup, I was dying. Things named scoliosis must make your fingers shrivel up or clog your ears before they kill you. That kind of word meant something horrible because it was so hard to spell and everyone pronounced it differently.

Would my brother Mike take my baseball cards? Who would take care of the dog?

Mom was trying. She was fulfilling the social requirement of motherhood—to look after your children's health and prepare them for the world. Some of her friends didn't even do that much. Even women who didn't work outside of the home neglected their children. She wasn't going to do that. If her son was a bad speller she was going to put her head down and find the solution. That's what the powerful men she admired did. No one admired the hand wringers. So off we marched to the doctors and the teachers. But there's a difference between working to solve a child's problems and connecting with that child. She did all the right things from the outside but none of it brought us closer together on the inside. It had the opposite effect. Those dire visits and whispered conversations with doctors and teachers told a confused bad speller with a curved spine that he was somehow broken. I was still trying to figure out where I'd failed. And I didn't like being told I'd done something wrong.

Criticism was apparently not something my ego could withstand at that age. A report card: "It is difficult for John to accept graciously his fallibility and he may disagree in a negative tone of voice with the assessment of his work." I worked out my frustrations in my artwork, which consisted mostly of batteries of gorily efficient American GIs attacking teachers, members of my family and giant lizards with awkwardly shaped feet.

Mom's desire for perfect children hit my brother Mike the hardest, during a time that is traditionally hellish. He developed obscene but perfectly normal acne as an adolescent. Each morning his face got an evaluation. Some days she'd say, "Today looks better," but more often than not he would get a harder appraisal of what his classmates called his pizza face. "Your face looks awful. Have you been using the new soap?"

Starting in the third grade, Mom made me write a paragraph every afternoon before going out to play. I would sit at the long dining room table, smelling the polish and bearing down on the wide-ruled pages of my composition book. I wrote about my father's muscles, Abraham Lincoln and World War II. When I was finished, she would release me just as my friends were sitting on the curb letting the sweat cool from their games of tackle football.

"Hemingway's mother made him sit down to write a paragraph each day," she would say over her reading glasses.

I had no idea what a Hemingway was or why his mother was so mean to him.

Chapter Three

<hr>

Merrywood, my childhood home, had a full-court gymnasium, a swimming pool and a tennis court, but I was jealous of my friends' bedrooms. They were full of delicious mayhem: GI Joe limbs crunched underfoot; Redskins paraphernalia hung over lamps; and posters of Darth Vader and Farrah Fawcett lined the walls. In my room there was little evidence that a kid lived there. Framed Ben Shahn prints hung on the wall and my clothing was always folded away. My one act of aesthetic rebellion was to draw war scenes on the inside of the tiny door at the back of my closet that led to a plumbing valve. I could sketch my mayhem and only the plumber would see.

I went away to camp in 1976 at age eight and came back to find that my room had been taken over by the USO: everything was red, white and blue. My two beds were fitted with matching bedspreads celebrating America's bicentennial. My stuffed animals were gone and my L-shaped desk, dresser, bookshelf and night table were painted Kool-Aid red. The carpet was blue shag and the curtains and box valance were striped like the flag. My bedroom looked like it was running for office.

Our house was a museum. Only the most out-of-the-way storage rooms in the basement and attic were disorderly. Everything anyone could see, including our rooms, was perfect. The antiques were constantly polished, the totems arranged at the right angles on coffee tables, and the spine of every book aligned one inch from the edge of the shelf.

This formality was balanced by extraordinary freedom. Dad was overseas a lot and Mom was off giving speeches and raising money for her independent productions. When they were home they went out a lot at night. By the time I was an adolescent, my older sisters had moved out. My brother and I amused ourselves dodging and terrifying those hired to care for us.

We had the kind of freedom other kids would have collected box tops for. Merrywood was huge by the standards of the 1960s, when Dad bought it. The childhood home of Gore Vidal and Jackie Kennedy, it belonged on Masterpiece Theatre. Perched on the Virginia side of the Potomac river, it had thirty-five rooms and sat on forty-nine acres. The freestanding four-car garage with servants' quarters above was bigger than my current house. To get into such a grand house now, I buy a ticket and stand in line.

The house allowed for a lot of mischief. It was big enough to have firecracker wars at one end and leave Mom undisturbed in her office at the other end. So that's what we did. We threw pennies and marbles and clumps of Crisco. The latter made a spectacular greasy asterisk on the wall when my brother threw a handful at my head.

When you live in a house where everything has to be kept just so, you learn to cover your tracks. We glued together small Chinese bowls we'd smashed, flipped over stained pillows and scrubbed away water stains on coffee tables with mayonnaise and ashes.

When we got bored destroying the inside of the house, we went outside.

The estate had a few abandoned buildings ripe for terror, discovery and deep puncture wounds. There was a broken-down collection of abandoned poolhouses, a deep empty fountain and a musty one-room Cape Cod once used as a dog kennel.

One day, my friends and I laid siege with bows and arrows to a neighbor's abandoned tennis shed that somehow still had all of its windows intact. When we left, only a few of the panes dangled. No one came to stop us. Mom and Dad were at the office. The housekeepers were busy keeping house. No one knew we were there.

Like other primitive tribes, we evolved from bows and arrows to firearms. At twelve, I went away to camp in the remote woods of Minnesota, where proficiency with rifles was considered a life skill.

That gave me just the reckless knowledge I needed. My first day back home, I shot a thrush with a BB gun while it sat on the bird feeder. The poor bird clutched the branch—I am certain it did—swung around and fell into the dirt.

The guilt almost caused the end of the gunplay, but then I got a better rifle. A year later, my father gave me the Winchester .22 that he'd been given at the same age. McLean, Virginia, was still rural farmland then—so we could fire at will. Someone, a parent maybe, should have told us not to shoot toward the Potomac River. We lived across from the C&O Canal. Those rounds travel about a mile and could have hit anyone walking their dog.

Sometimes at the end of the day we'd see Mom through the French doors walking up to her home office. We'd put the rifle down for a minute. Then we'd go back to shooting at planes on their descent into National Airport.

During my preteen years, Carolina and Manuel Vitorino were charged with keeping us out of the emergency room. Carolina was a healthy, well-fed woman with wiry red hair and pale pink skin. Manuel was skinny, the color of a walnut shell, and wore a blinding coat of jewelry, imitation gold necklaces with medallions and unwieldy metal watches that whirred around his bony wrist. They lived in the suite of four rooms at the back of the house for six years. Carolina performed a thousand beneficent intercessions. She bathed me and fed me and dressed me and smeared Vicks VapoRub on my chest when I had a cold. She is in many of the pictures from those years, sometimes just her fleshy arms poking out of a starched white uniform.

"You have a nice face," she would say each day before touching it. Her hands were cold and smelled of bleach.

Mom had studied Portuguese in college and she and Carolina had sweet hit-and-miss conversations. Most of Mom's phrases had to do with seeking out monuments or getting an umbrella by the seashore. Carolina would gamely try to respond and then, if there were any actual communicating to be done, Mom would revert to English, retaining her approximation of a Portuguese accent. (This led to the mangling of Carolina's name, which we all spelled and pronounced as Cordelina.)

When I had nightmares, I ran down the hall into the Vitorinos' bedroom and climbed between them for comfort. During the frequent weekends when my parents were away, the Vitorinos invited their friends over. They ate Bacalhau, a ghastly Portuguese fish dish served with the head and fins. Once, one of their friends sucked the eyes right out of the head. The room erupted into laughter and my brother and I ran for the door. We stopped to look back. The man opened his mouth and showed us the eye on his tongue like a runny antacid tablet.

Carolina and Manuel took me to the state parks to play by the Potomac River. We ate dangerously rare beef grilled on the rusty rails of the public barbecues. Then, before the E-coli could kick in, I clashed with swarms of Portuguese boys over the half-deflated soccer ball.

This is how I learned how other people lived. The Dickersons didn't have family outings with leaky thermoses and creaky folding chairs. My older sisters had gone on traditional vacations growing up because my father was working his way up when they were born. They shared beds with Dad in cheap hotels and complained about traffic in the hot car. On the vacations that I can remember, my brother, Mom, Dad and I all wore blue blazers on the plane and flew to places like Palm Beach. When we camped it was in Africa, through Abercrombie & Kent outfitters. Our tents were like little houses. Each night we ate on tablecloths and cocktails were served to us before a blazing fire of acacia leaves.

Chapter Four

Some time around age nine, I was old enough to start opening the door at Merrywood parties. I greeted senators, Cabinet secretaries and a series of coaches of the Washington Redskins as they arrived. I learned Mom was famous not because of anything I saw her do on television, but because famous people came to our house.

As her footmen, my brother and I were Mom's apprentices. "Even I was a supporting cast member," remembers my father with a slight and approving laugh.

She held an orientation session before each party. "Shake their hand firmly and look them in the eye," she said taking my hand. Mom expected us to treat those nights as seriously as she did, but we sighed and rolled our eyes.

"These nights are just as important as my work," she reminded me. "They are my work." She explained to me—in some vague way that I'm sure made no sense at the time—that politicians could make secret deals and whisper confidences after dark in ways they never could at the office.

"That was one of the first lessons I learned coming to Washington," she said before a short tutorial in access journalism. "I can ask questions tonight and get answers I'd never be able to get other ways and then I can use them on the air."

Her lessons didn't take. At least, not then.

"Do we have to answer the door for *every* guest? What if someone is *really* late?"

She bent down to paste back my cowlick and push the hair behind my ears.

I flinched at her fussing.

I've always been intrigued by the children who enter a parent's profession. Eli and Peyton Manning are both professional football quarterbacks, as was their father. As kids, they threw the football with him for hours in the front yard. Given that I grew up to be a White House correspondent, you'd think that I was prepared from the bassinet for the job. Mom must have had us running little drills, shouting questions behind a rope line and naming the steps it takes for a bill to become a law. At least she could have taught us that lobbyists and fund-raisers run the world, not those who get elected to public office. We had no such tutoring. The door-opening lesson is the only one I can really remember.

Some of the other lessons my brother and I learned about Washington we figured out on our own. We knew most of the guests didn't give a damn about us. We opened the door and welcomed them in and they looked right past us. We weren't very happy to be there either, but shouldn't we all have agreed to do a little human commerce there on the front stoop? You could tell the politicians who were comfortable in their own skin because they stopped to say hello.

We got to see the transition as the powerful in Washington put on their party game faces. We were met with the whiff of the argument spouses had just had as the car rolled to a stop, or by the distracted senator who was thinking through some sticky piece of legislation. Maybe some people were just cranky because they hadn't had their first drink. Whatever was going on, we were at best a surprise, and at worst an annoyance because we interrupted whatever they were trying to resolve in their heads before the hard work of the party began. My sister Jane says that Ted Kennedy was so imposing as he barreled by her that he gave her nightmares.

I learned to hold women's coats at a distance. They had applied a last dose of perfume just before leaving home, so I had to keep from getting too close or I'd get marked. I speared the umbrellas or canes in the front hall closet stand and draped the coats on one of the several dozen polished wood hangers. Furs were tricky. They were heavy and hoisting them up on the rail took some arching and heaving. The bristles got up my nose.

I don't ever remember trying to get out of tending the door. That kind of insubordination would never have been tolerated. My father once spanked me for not brushing my teeth, so the corporal punishment made bucking the system impossible.

We were told the exposure was good for us. "This is what parents do for their children," my mother explained. "My parents were never able to do this for me."

I had no idea what she was talking about, but I knew we were supposed to feel grateful. Years later, I was horrified to see her networking in action for my benefit. She wrote the publisher of the *New York Times,* asking if they had a post-college internship for me. Prefacing her request, she said, "Twenty years ago at Merrywood you met John Dickerson."

There was something about those nights and even my role in their production that made me feel I was a part of something exciting. It was the closest I ever got to the world Mom really loved. On those nights, our museum of a house, where toys were never scattered and where collections of rooms went undisturbed for weeks (except by the dusting maids), felt like it was fulfilling its purpose.

My parents' last great party was on January 17, 1981. Ronald Reagan was the guest of honor. His inauguration was three days later and that Saturday night was his Washington coming-out party. My parents were still married and at thirteen, I was still living at home. A year later, neither would be true.

The evening was a great social coup, and it was also perfectly timed because Mom had just started Television Corporation of America. The production company's grand name matched Mom's ambitions for it. For the first time since her independent productions in the early '70s, she had her own company and enough money to make her own documentaries. The party would help her relaunch her career.

Mom had started working on the guest list months before. Partisanship wasn't an issue. Power was. Her folder for the Reagan party included a *Wall Street Journal* article from which she culled the right attendees: "The Inner Circle: Old Friends May Play a Very Important Role in Reagan Presidency."

As the 17th drew near I helped by tracing circles with the bottom of a silver tankard. She used them to make a schematic of the tables on a large piece of poster board. After scribbling and erasing and sifting names, she produced the final seating arrangements.

As the place cards were laid out, maids fussed through the rooms plumping the cushions. By late afternoon, caterers and florists and musicians clinked glasses and unsnapped their cases. The house smelled of beef stock. Mom moved among them, her hair already set for the night. Her Chanel blue jeans had been ironed to a crisp, and her thin legs barely broke their crease when she walked. She made a final tour, micro-managing everything. She checked to see that the furniture had been dusted, confirmed the seating charts and terrified the staff.

We knew to stay out of her way so close to curtain time. Her adrenaline was up, and she'd already begun to display the broad theatrics that would be necessary for the big night. She could throw her arms open in a wide embrace of a bartender she barely knew, but, if irritated, she could inflict casualties.

"Mrs. Dickerson, we cannot fit forty-eight people," said one of the caterers tentatively. He was retreating almost as he said it.

"Mr. Silvio, the guests will be arriving in a few hours. We agreed to forty-eight. We will seat forty-eight tonight, Mr. Silvio, and you will make it glorious."

That was the end of Mr. Silvio. He wasn't fired on the spot, but I knew she would later concoct some elaborate end for him—the way the villains use piranhas for James Bond.

She moved toward the florist. The bearded man was rushing from room to room primping the flowers and breathing heavily.

Mom had a duplicate of her written order and she checked the front hall arrangement against it. It did not meet her expectations. Her instructions had not been vague: "Flowering plum or quince— quite tall to reach up and look like an early flowering of the cherry blossoms at the Tidal Basin. Bouquet also to include pussy willows and forsythia and perhaps some daffodils—it should be a very happy joyous looking bouquet."

The bearded man was not looking happy or joyous. It was January. Half of what Mom was asking for was underground. They exchanged some frantic gestures. He had clumps of moss in his hands and he looked like he wanted to feed them to her.

She promised to deal with him later and moved to the dining room. "Where are the place favors?"

This was my chance. I had been hiding in the living room, in my gray flannel trousers, white shirt and loafers. I was trying to summon the nerve to jump the yellow couch without getting caught.

The living room was Merrywood's most sacred formal space. No playing in there. There was a certain irony in that, since its walls were lined with portraits of children. My parents collected 18th-century works painted by men who roamed the countryside with their nearly completed canvases. Only the faces were left blank. When the artist got a commission, he filled them with the features of the little darling sons and daughters of his patrons.

The leap was a hard trick. The couch was wide, and once you cleared it, you had to get your momentum under control or you'd smash into the ficus tree. I had failed before—I had crashed; got caught; been forced to make glum promises not to do it again. Now, on party day, pulling off the high-stakes caper would be extra delicious.

I looked through a crack in the high cherry doors. She was pressing a poor fellow about the place favors, Lucite pyramids with a Reagan quotation about a "shining city on a hill."

Go. I was off making the mad seven strides in good time despite my slippery loafers.

"John Dickerson, stop that this instant."

Wait, what about the place favors? How did she move so fast?

I was already committed and the result was familiar. I tumbled through the doors that led into the garden room, thudding against the piano. The pictures on the top of the Steinway collapsed on cue.

I got up and began righting the frames in their careful order. "Okay, okay, I'll fix them," I yelled back to her.

"No more foolishness. That is enough of that." Perhaps she could tell from how frantically I was working that I'd gotten the message. She headed up the front hall stairs, the mimeographed floral instructions crinkling in her hand as she stomped.

I knew the pictures in those frames were important to her, even if I didn't know why. Now I realize, as I must have half-realized then, that they were the house's most public shrine to her fame. In one, Mom stands with John Kennedy in the Oval Office, days after his inauguration. The youngest president in history has his hands in his pockets and an acquisitive look on his face. Perhaps he was thinking of the dates they'd had when he was a single congressman. Was he noticing how much my mother looked like his own wife, with her brunette bob, eyes set wide apart and high cheekbones? Mom stands in a Chanel suit, newly minted news correspondent for CBS, her mouth open in midsentence, her hands clasped before her.

She later said, "Sex to Jack meant no more than a cup of coffee." How did she know? Did she ever have coffee with him? I have no reason to think so, but in that picture the president looks like he's about to start the percolator.

Another photograph showed Mom dancing with Lyndon Johnson in the East Room of the White House in 1967. She was one of his favorite reporters, but the picture suggests his admiration wasn't just intellectual. He greeted her on air with familiarity: "Hello, Nancy." The herald became so famous, strangers yelled it out to her on the street.

There are also pictures of Mom with Nixon and Ford. They are devoid of sexual energy, much like the men themselves, though Ford is holding the most admirable highball cocktail.

After fixing the pictures, I returned to the kitchen. On party days, my brother and I ate our lunch and early dinner among the chafing dishes and flurry of staff that had arrived at noon with the purple Ridgewell catering trucks. Manuel and Cordalina ran the show. Below them, a cast of regulars: bartenders who showed me magic tricks and cooks and waiters who knew just how Mrs. Dickerson liked the dishes arranged on the table and just how frequently to pour the wine.

Twenty minutes before the party, my brother and I took our positions at the front door. Mom was upstairs typing the final draft of her toast and my father's. She also came up with questions for the table.

At the appointed hour, my brother and I peeked through the gauzy curtains hanging over the front entrance windows looking for new arrivals. In the summer, we could hear the crunch of the pale beige gravel in the driveway.

The only moments of temporary relief during door duty came

when one of the waiters we had charmed swung by with a silver tray of Portuguese croquettes, lovely little warm breaded poppers filled with gooey sausage gravy. We weren't supposed to eat them; they were for the guests. But I'd snatch one, run into the black and gold bathroom by the front door, blow on the croquette until it was cool, pop it into my mouth and race back to my duties, wincing as the molten filling seared my tongue. Michael and I did this in shifts, but sometimes the door work interrupted, and I had to stuff a half-eaten croquette in my pocket while I looked Dr. Kissinger in the eye.

The president-elect and Mrs. Reagan arrived that night already looking like they'd been in office for months. Frank Sinatra had the bad luck of arriving behind his old California friend. The president's Secret Service cars and police cruisers snaked all the way up our half-mile drive. Ol' Blue Eyes had to walk partway down through the bushes and sneak in the back door.

A scrum of reporters trampled where I'd picked weeds out of the pachysandra and photographers jostled to capture the new First Couple. My parents waited on the front porch without overcoats, their breath blowing clouds in the cold. My father wore his tuxedo, tailored on Savile Row in London, lined with light blue Hermès silk. Mom wore a pearl white Givenchy gown made just for the occasion. Around her neck, befitting the fashion of the time, she wore a white feather boa. Just that morning, I had trailed it behind me like jet exhaust as I ran down the upstairs hall.

I was on the porch too. I had work to do.

The Secret Service agent who opened the limousine door winked at me. I was a certified junior Secret Service agent, a post I'd won after getting in their way for most of the day as they cased the house.

"Welcome to Merrywood," Mike and I said to the Reagans. The pictures taken at the time show Michael's hand at the base of my back, moving me into position. Five years older, he got to wear a tuxedo. I was in our more regular uniform of blue blazer and gray flannel trousers augmented by a pocket square and red vest.

"Well hello there," said the future two-term president as he shook my hand. "Thank you." (In the mail, weeks later, my first signed presidential photograph arrived capturing the moment. I've kept mine off the piano and hidden in my home office.)

High-octane parties make some people nervous, but that's where Mom was most comfortable. She didn't swan through the room or make a grand entrance down the elegant front stairway. She was generous and easygoing, more so than in regular life.

Guests asked her how she was; I remember her saying, "All the better for seeing you." She loved that line because she had first heard it in Ireland. She loved her Irish heritage. It's amazing I'm not named Seamus.

Mom never let the energy in the room flag. She led newcomers by the elbow to make a first introduction. Into each conversational cluster she dropped nimble talk before moving on to fertilize another. And all the while she made sure the waiters hit each corner of the room and that the bartenders kept tipping their silver jiggers of gin.

Even though the Reagan party was just before the divorce, at a time when Mom and Dad were having frigid, sheered-off exchanges at our family dinner table, they switched on the charm for guests. Like dance champions who couldn't stand each other backstage, they were great when they hit the front hall.

"Nancy and I want to welcome you to Merrywood," my father said before dinner was served. "So would my wife." The line got a big laugh.

By the time the guests were seated we were upstairs, stinking of perfume, our guts swollen from the croquettes and our right hands tanned from the Brasso polish on the front door knob. In my bedroom, I could hear Mom's laughter break through the conversations.

The Reagan party was the kickoff to an age of promise for the city. It had gone through a terrible social drought. Watergate had been a downer and during the dreary Carter years, the Georgia crowd stayed home, turned down the thermostat and frowned. Reagan promised the return of Washington's party culture, through which so much good business could be done. For the permanent Washington class, the conservative president with a Hollywood past meant no more cardigan sweaters. Top hats and tails were back.

After the meal, as the staff rolled up the red Chinese carpet in our front hall to create a dance floor, Mom stood with her champagne glass:

"Everyone knows the president-elect has the last word—but it's a prerogative of the house to break protocol . . . the first inauguration I went to was President Eisenhower's first and I've covered every one since. There is always a feeling of hope when a new administration comes in, but this time it's different in its intensity. (I must say, Nancy, Governor, for two people who campaigned so vigorously against Washington, after twelve hours you owned the city.) I've never seen Washington so anxious to welcome anyone.

"In the recent past we've had some massive hand-wringing around here and a feeling that the problems were too tough to handle. You've changed all that around—as difficult and complex as the problems are, there's a feeling now that there are solutions and you're going to find them—and once again make this a 'shining city on a hill.'

"Now, if I can break protocol once more—with your permission, Nancy—Governor, would you dance with me?"

Chapter Five

The Reagan party recaptured for an evening the glamour and stature of Merrywood and the Dickersons, but seven months later, my parents separated. A year after that, I moved out to live with my dad. The disintegration felt sudden, but it was the product of a long slow corrosion that took over all of us. As graceful as Mom might have seemed to the outside world, my brother and I saw only a string of flaws. She couldn't leave a preposition dangling without us starting a chorus of corrections. She was clueless about sports, our friends, music and anything else we cared about. She got carsick when she drove, thought answering machines could get computer viruses and could not carry a tune, though she fearlessly tried.

For our most regular laughs at her expense, we returned to the commercials we had done as a family in the mid-1970s. For three years, starting when I was seven, the four of us made an annual trip to Florida to make commercials for various products I'd never heard of before—and didn't hear much about afterward. We'd work under hot lights, turning Mom's fading fame into cash. Mom needed to do commercials because as the economy had slumped, the local news stations that had bought her one-and-a-half-minute independent news reports from Washington could no longer afford them. Commercials kept her in the public eye and augmented the money she made giving speeches and narrating infrequent documentaries.

One of these commercials was for ProPower orange drink. My father, brother and I sat in a kitchen in tennis clothes looking toward the swinging door through which the woman of the house was at any minute going to bring breakfast and ProPower orange drink.

In real life, my brother and I started the day with the maid.

Anyone who knew Mom would have chuckled to see her near spatulas and soup spoons. She could make one dish: warm toast with peanut butter topped with pats of butter. At the right temperature, little yellow puddles would form in the waves of peanut butter made by the spreading knife.

Otherwise, Mom's kitchen adventures had a Lucille Ball quality—though without Lucy's game, adorable lack of self-consciousness. Once she emptied a pot of boiling peas into a colander—that was sitting on the counter.

Her role as a cook was summed up by my brother, teased at age seven by CBS correspondent Paul Niven, who told him he doubted his mother cooked.

"What does your mother cook?" Niven asked.

"Scrambled eggs," Michael replied, defiantly trying to defend his mother.

"Ah, when does she cook them?"

"Christmas."

The viewers who saw the ProPower commercials didn't care about Nancy Dickerson's culinary deficiencies. She was a working woman and a provider, the modern model for all households, and therefore just the kind of woman who would be drinking a modern breakfast drink.

Her lines were simple: "ProPower has as much vitamin C as orange juice, the calcium of milk and the fiber of a piece of toast."

Wearing her tight tennis skirt, Mom strode into the kitchen and declared: "ProPower has as much milk as vitamin C and as much bread as orange juice." We nearly snorted up our ProPower.

Take Two: skirt freshly adjusted, door swings open and here's Nancy: "ProPower has as much toast . . ."

Take three: The swinging door bangs her in the noggin.

Take four: Door settled, she's in full stride, gunning for victims: "ProPower has as much vitamin J as orange juice, and the bread of toast."

She would have compared the orange drink to the salty flavor of country ham if the director hadn't intervened.

ProPower actually did taste like it had milk in it, which is probably why it didn't stay on the market very long. Anguished and embarrassed, Michael and I were told to look like we loved our ProPower, so we took increasingly larger gulps at the start of each take. But after so many takes, our stomachs grew moody.

"You don't have to drink it each time," said a helpful lighting guy. "You can just sip it."

Mom's ProPower gaffes provided Michael and me with a reliable set of laughs. In adolescence we collected her faults and played them back to her over and over. We thought Mom was uncool. All parents are uncool, but at some point, they instruct the kids to stop acting like cretins and accept some authority. We might have been told to behave, but we didn't listen. We kept going after Mom.

At a young age I was apparently quite good at making people feel miserable. My teachers said so. "While John's gregarious nature attracts others to him," wrote my third-grade teacher at Potomac School, "he is not sufficiently aware that his impulsive 'put down' comments to his peers are hurtful and inappropriate."

We were punishing her, maybe bullying her. Her neglect (or inattention) bestowed on us the freedom that other children had to earn, but we were confident we'd made our own way without her. When she was around, she was an intrusion. I've had to remember this hard lesson when a story keeps me away from my own children. When I come home from traveling for a few days, my son Brice runs into the other room. If I grab him to give him a kiss, it makes the situation worse. I'm doing it for me, not for him. He's reacting as Mike and I did: Get away. That I know I'm repeating Mom's mistake doesn't make me want to grab him any less. If I really want to fail spectacularly, I'll come home and direct him to take a bath or pick up—screaming follows. Unless I've had the most well-adjusted day, I'm likely to want to force him into submission.

So I have learned to adjust. If I sit on the lawn for a half hour reading while he plays nearby, eventually he comes over to me. Then we roll down the hill together until we're covered in grass. Mom's schedule never had a window large enough for such natural moments. It didn't have that window because she didn't schedule them. "Even this morning they were with me in my room as I packed," she told one magazine reporter about her time with her children. She dropped everything for the emergencies, the doctor's visits and the moments of duty, but that was it. She didn't know about the rest of her children's lives because it was like a dog's whistle to her. She couldn't hear it. If we weren't on her list or it wasn't the approved togethertime between when she came home and when the servants took us for our baths, she wasn't hungering to connect with our world.

When we were all home together, Mom watched the evening news while taking fast notes on her spiral steno pad. Dinner had to wait until she had watched all the networks' newscasts. She insisted that there were subtle differences in their coverage. We mocked her earnestness.

"Reagan is still president on the other network too!"

"Mom, where have I seen this story before? Oh yes, just ten minutes ago on ABC."

When CBS picked Dan Rather over Roger Mudd in the sweepstakes to replace Walter Cronkite as lead anchor, she paced around the library, outraged. The news broke just after she'd come home from work. Mudd was the more serious journalist. She thought Rather was flashy and well groomed, but not serious.

"It is the triumph of style over substance," she said to no one in particular.

We didn't share her level of concern. My sister and her new fiancé were discussing their upcoming wedding. Mike and I were playing backgammon.

"They pick him and all he's done is go out and get a haircut and a blow job."

That got our attention. That's what they called going under the hair dryer at her salon, but her proclamation gave us years of laughs when we told it at high volume, mimicking her straight posture and announcer's voice.

We had perhaps our greatest laughs at her expense when she played tennis. It must have been hell to be so graceful at work and so clumsy on the court. To overcome her natural shortcomings, she applied more grit, which was her simple formula in life. With each new ball she squeezed her racket harder. Her arm stiffened, her knuckles got white and the chances for a successful hit diminished. The errant balls sailed and she gripped harder.

At some point, either my brother and I became too good or the taunts became too much—she imported a group of tennis partners who would not mock her.

Mom's authority diminished as we continued our free rein. At some time around age eleven, she tried to spank me for lying about a phone message I'd forgotten to give her. She worked on my behind until her arm got tired. From my posture over her knee, I just laughed. During one bout of teasing my eighteen-year-old brother held her over the balcony. If he'd let go she would have dropped into the front hall. We were laughing. She was terrified.

She was stoic in the face of much of this cruel imitation of wit. Her favorite phrase, "Oh, honestly," was usually accompanied by some head-shaking to show that she could play along and that it didn't hurt that much. If you're going to be a man's woman you have to show that you can take a joke, particularly about yourself.

There was a time when my father wouldn't have let us get away with inflicting these paper cuts. He had rules and he enforced them. When my brother Michael left his hands on the dinner table after repeatedly being told not to, Dad took his knife by the blade and fully intended to bring the handle down on Mike's hand. Fortunately Mike moved the offending digits and the knife just cracked the table.

But Dad let us go on teasing Mom because by 1980 their marriage was dissolving. We watched the unraveling every night at dinner. For a stretch, we ate in the formal dining room among the oil paintings and antiques. Mom and Dad sat at opposite ends of the long polished table, and Michael and I sat across from each other in the vast middle.

The atmosphere was tense. My parents didn't talk. They debated. Not policy and news of the day, but each other's failings and miserable choices. Their discussions had clear winners and losers. Argument was combat. Criticism of your opponent, often for the absurdity of their views, was a perfectly reasonable weapon even if the target happened to be your spouse. Even if I didn't understand what was being debated, their rough body language was easy enough to interpret. The subtle digs and sometimes not-so-subtle snarls were propelled by plenty of wine.

"You're just dead wrong," I can remember my father saying regularly.

"If you're so smart," Mom would say to him, "why don't you run for president?"

No topic or piece of trivia was too inconsequential for debate. They sparred over their recollections about places they'd visited or who first introduced whom to Frank Sinatra. I watched the bickering match from an increasingly far remove. While they exchanged volleys, I fiddled with the brass latch that kept the table leaves together, moving it in and out.

Chapter Six

One evening in 1982 at age thirteen, I snuck down the back staircase to see what wonderful—please let it be R-rated—movie might be on our newly installed Home Box Office. I found Faye Dunaway playing Joan Crawford, a mess of rage and flyaway hair scrubbing the bathroom floor and yelling at her mopey daughter. It was a gaudy and wonderful freak show. One moment, Dunaway was a smiling public actress, and the next she was a private ogre terrorizing her two young children with her wild mood swings. She tore her daughter's clothes from the closet and flung them on the floor. "No more wire hangers," she famously screamed.

Mommie Dearest is a luridly bad film, but as I watched it, I had a revelation. Across the country at Stanford, Mike had a similar epiphany: We had seen that movie before.

A few days later, we giddily traded reactions on the phone. Mom wasn't nearly as bad as the cartoon portrayal on the screen but that didn't matter. We weren't taking the parallel seriously. It was just another way to have a good laugh at her expense. But also at some level we knew about life with a gap between public and private personas. We too had to duck our mother's stormy reaction to perceived slights and an inflexibility maintained almost for its own sake. We never had any wire-hanger moments, but we knew what it was like to be pulled onstage and asked to perform for smiling friends.

Being displayed for Mom took something from us. Whatever

37

pleasure you might take in an accomplishment could be immediately diminished by having to repeat it for her in front of an audience. It was worse for my brother; he had more to brag about. Mom sent copies of his grades to her friend Jack Valenti, LBJ's close aide who went on to head the Motion Picture Association of America. She was proud of her son. To us, it looked like she was proud of herself.

Working the front door, we felt like we were being used. Nancy could have a fantastic career and pleasant children too! Other people took care of us, so we became plug-and-play kids, ready to be displayed at the appropriate moments.

That made me suspicious of her and all those guests she showed us to. If anyone took a moment or two longer on the front stoop to act interested in us, we were pretty sure he or she was doing it to get closer to her.

All of the Dickerson children rebelled at about the same age when our natural desire for independence clashed with Mom's demands that we fit into her schedule. Though she wasn't with the network anymore when I went through my spell, she was almost as busy trying to make it on her own while keeping up a network star's social schedule.

When Mom was around, it was an intrusion and it meant some demand had to be fulfilled. We were called in to watch the news, to talk about what we had done that day or to answer for some frivolous show we had chosen to watch in the rare moments when we could watch non-news TV. It was like she was back from months at sea and insisting we all get together and share the same bathroom.

As the marriage disintegrated, my parents started to feed Mike and me little bits that they hoped would help tear down the other spouse. Before we left for a party one night, my father—who refused to go—said, "I don't want to see you parade around those kids." Ah ha! Now we knew what was being done to us, even if we really did want to go to the party and throw ice cubes at each other with the rest of the kids. Mom made grave references to Dad's past money troubles.

I liked being let in on secrets. There seemed to be more and more going on behind the scenes in our house. My father's bathroom shared a wall with my bedroom, and if I put my ear to the wall, I could hear them fight. When that didn't work, I could listen at the heating vent. When the heat was on, you had to switch ears to keep from getting burned.

If there was an early influence that pushed me toward journalism, it may not have been anything my mother taught me overtly or encouraged me to recognize. I may have gotten hooked on looking for the real story by trying to figure out the crude drama my parents were acting out in front of me. At times, I didn't have to work that hard. The signs of my parents' impending split became so obvious it made the papers. Elisabeth Bumiller, who later covered the White House for the *New York Times* at the same time I did for *Time*, wrote in the *Washington Post*:

> *Last night, Nancy Dickerson was the host with {Gore} Vidal at the Virginia estate, bought by her husband C. Wyatt Dickerson. His name was not on the invitation, which had furthered gossip column speculation that all was not bliss for him and his wife. But both were there.*
> *"No," said Nancy Dickerson, "we're not getting divorced."*
> *"Does it look like it?" added her husband.*

For the party and the press, they put on a good show because it was helpful for their public life and Mom's new production company, Television Corporation of America. She was working on its first project, a documentary on Watergate. She didn't want distracting gossip.

Four months later, in August 1981, Mom picked me up from a month away at summer camp and on the way back from the airport pulled in to the scenic overlook on the George Washington Parkway.

"Your father has moved out of the house," she said, crying behind her tea saucer–sized sunglasses.

"Where?"

"He has an apartment.

"Okay."

"We still love you. Both of us. Your father and I may have disagreements but we both still love you. Do you know that?"

"Yes."

I didn't say much more. It is possible that I have blocked out some horror or empty pit of loneliness that I felt at hearing my family was breaking up. I've thought about that moment countless times over the years, and the act of writing about it has made me turn it around in my hands like an autographed ball: If I felt more pain than I remember, it's either the result of dedicated and steadfast suppression or my reaction was, in fact, as I recall it: I wasn't that broken up about the divorce. My parents did their thing, and I did mine.

It must have been hell for her. They hadn't been a unified team for a few years, but having their glamorous partnership—well-documented and necessary to keep Merrywood going—dissolve in full view further eroded the dwindling public stature she clung to so hard.

Mom tried to press books on me like *The Kids' Book of Divorce,* but I didn't turn to them for answers to my nonexistent angst. In fact, the divorce was exciting. It allowed me to act like an adult. Both my parents claimed to have been responsible for the other's success. Both blamed each other for the other's decline. They traded charges and countercharges over who was at fault and who might have been having an affair with whom. I was let in on the details. I gathered facts and I disseminated them.

When my brother went to Stanford that summer of their divorce, he left me with instructions. "Be careful of Mom befriending you with false intentions," he wrote. "She will only let you be if it is on her terms. Don't be afraid to tell her if she is bullshitting you. I am sorry if my alienation with Mom is causing you pain. . . . I am happy to be on my own. I don't need her guilt trips. I have no respect for her at all. I am sorry, but that's the way I feel."

When my aunt Mary Ellen came to town just after the split, suddenly I was able to join in a delicious adult rag session.

"Your mother always did her own thing for herself," she said. "I suppose your father got tired of that."

The two sisters from Wauwatosa, Wisconsin, had always had a tense relationship. My aunt, Mary Ellen, had stayed home, raised four children and took care of her mother. She was annoyed by the holiday breeze-ins of her younger sister that drew the neighbors over to see the famous correspondent. I loved Mary Ellen. She was on our team and had all those easy qualities Mom didn't possess. She was funny and sharp and a little bawdy. Her husband Ernie and their kids laughed so often and so loudly that when I was a little boy I thought it had something to do with where they came from: In the South they have an accent and eat fried chicken. In the Midwest they laugh.

"She has to control everything," I said. At thirteen, I was learning all kinds of ways of talking about human behavior. I started hunting through Mom's desk to keep playing a role in that adult drama. I thought nothing of snooping through her office for her journals. I climbed the shelves in her lingerie closet and found some typewritten memos to herself about Dad's every sin.

I stayed with Mom but took up my father's cause. He was all the things she was not: confident, smooth and able to understand me. He had a tiny little townhouse in Georgetown where I occasionally spent the weekend. We'd watch movies, go out to dinner and talk for hours about anything. He had none of the awkwardness of those parents who use jargon and slang as they try too hard to be the kind of parents you want to be around. He could tell funny jokes, or tell me more about American history than my teachers. He'd boxed and shot marbles as a kid and he could whistle loud enough to be heard ten blocks away. When we went out to dinner one night he scolded two drunken men at another table for cursing repeatedly and loudly—a small show of authority that could have backfired, but the strong words from this wiry, compact, forceful man shamed them. They spent the rest of the night mumbling. Before I was born a farmhand he'd fired had come to their house one night during dinner and called him out. The man had to be carried away afterward. I wanted to be like Dad.

At Merrywood I buried myself in my newfound interest in computers, and I did only what was necessary to get a ride to and from school and a regular allowance. Even then, I pushed the limits.

Mom had always been arbitrary with money, or so it seemed to her children. She had closets full of clothes and yet scrutinized every piece of clothing my sisters bought when they were teenagers. "Why do you need *this* bra?" she'd asked, checking its price tag. If she disapproved, she made them return their purchase. My youngest half sister, Jane, hated the inquisitions so much she started stealing clothes from the lost-and-found at her school.

Mom wanted to teach us the value of money. But mostly that meant telling us what everything cost—even our Christmas presents. One year, I tore open the wrapping of one present to find the remote control tank I'd been asking for. Mom let me know it had cost fifty dollars (though, strictly speaking, it had been given to me by Santa). By the end of the day she had made this point so often, I named the tank "Fifty."

When we lived alone together after the divorce, it was inevitable that our clashes would be about money. Her role as appropriator was the best way to control me, and as I asserted my independence, Mom was determined to bring me in line. She stopped the flow of funds and hid the .22 rifle and the pellet gun my uncle had given me. "I only had one disagreement with her over the years and that was over her treatment of you," says Marie Ridder, our neighbor and Mom's longtime friend. "She favored capital punishment." Each morning as she drove me to school before heading to TCA, her production company, she would go over my spending habits.

"How did you spend the nine dollars I gave you last week?" she asked one morning as we pulled up to school.

"I told you. I spent five on the movie, two on popcorn, one on a drink," I said quickly.

"That's only eight," she said slowly. "What happened to the other dollar?"

"I don't know, but I need ten dollars for the class trip."

"John, you can't . . ."

I'd heard the patronizing tone before: It was the dinner-table voice of so many of my parents' fights with each other. It was time to go and I did, slamming the door shut behind me.

"Come back here this instant," she yelled through the closed car door.

I kept walking up the stairs.

She leaned on the horn. I kept walking, up the long steps to school.

All my seventh-grade classmates were watching and snickering. I had just transferred to the fancy Sidwell Friends School, and it was agony to be known as the kid with the insane honking mother. I got to the top of the steps and looked back. Mom was still blowing the horn, her mouth twisted in anger. I stood there ready to dig my foxhole. The horn continued. She was not going to blink. I relented and walked back to her car. I still didn't get the ten bucks.

I was too embarrassed to bring home my friends from Sidwell. When I finally did, I regretted it.

One of my black friends, a scholarship student, kept his winter jacket and wool cap on during the meal. Mom was visibly agitated.

"Won't you take off your hat?" she asked with a strain in her voice.

My friend mumbled a little.

"Please, won't you take off your hat." She mispronounced his African name.

I corrected her. I had no idea what was going on, but I could see she was terrifying him. I didn't know why, though now it seems obvious to any thinking person, that he was very uncomfortable and Mom was making him more so. Our kitchen and breakfast room were probably as big as his entire apartment. Mom asked questions of both of us like we were onstage at assembly and rang a hand bell to summon the cook into the dining room. She must have looked to him like she belonged to another species.

"Mom," I said. I didn't know what protest I was making, but I knew I had to stop whatever was making my friend so uncomfortable.

"Well you should take off your hat for dinner," she said as if reading from an etiquette book.

My friend put his hand to his head but kept his cap on.

She wasn't trying to make him feel at ease. She was trying to get him to follow the rules. And when he didn't, she couldn't get over it. It consumed her. Later, she sat me down.

"John, I don't think you should be spending so much time with him. He wouldn't even remove his hat at dinner."

She called my father to make the same point. I was angry that she was trying to tell me who my new friends could be, but I also hated that she was such a snob. I had never really understood how wealthy we were—or appeared to be anyway—until I got to Sidwell. In public school no one talked about it and I never much took note of the disparities. At the fancy private school, though, it was a big topic of conversation. Suddenly my classmates started asking me if it was true I was chauffeured to school in a limousine and given my allowance in hundred-dollar bills. On the school's football team, the comments were more acute. Coaches say things they shouldn't—they talk about your parents' cars and the size of your house. They think it toughens you. They called me "Richie Rich" for a while. Nicknames work so well because they rob you of whatever sense of yourself you're trying to create. Mom was doing that well enough on her own, making me "John Dickerson," presentable child. Then, to have her behave with all of the formality and rigidness you'd expect of Richie Rich's mother only made me angrier. I had to get out.

I tried to stay away from her. I played sports and became a raging computer geek, not a traditional mixture, but somehow I made it work. I learned how to program computers and started to write my own games. (Computer code required only limited spelling, thank goodness.) I stayed up all night typing line after line of code. I went to bed when the sun started to rise.

I had designed the perfect sanctuary. Sports were approved because the Kennedys played sports. Working on the computer was okay too because, after all those years of horrible spelling, I was showing intellectual prowess. Mom allowed me to disappear into my room for hours, and I had a pretext for not interacting with her.

My computer habit meant that I got to have a television in my room. I wasn't allowed to watch any shows, but as long as I used it for the computer I could keep this special privilege.

The détente worked for a while. She was distracted with her Watergate documentary, timed to come out on the tenth anniversary of the break-in. But then the truce broke down. One Friday, Mom was in her bedroom watching some kind of variety show or pageant on the best television in the house. I could hear the emcee's voice between the flourish of trumpets and the scatty enthusiasm of show tunes. She started down the hall, her sweat suit swishing as she walked. She sat on my bed.

I pretended not to notice her. I could barely contain myself when she peered over my shoulder while I was working on my computer. I could feel it on my neck.

"I want to watch the *Broadway Cavalcade*," she said, reaching for the television dial.

"But I'm using the computer," I said, shocked.

She turned the channel. The television picked up the audio but no video. To get picture reception you had to throw a switch on the silver box taped to the back of the set.

"I was in the middle of doing something," I said, my hands still on the keyboard. I wasn't going to help her out.

When Mom got truly angry her pauses and movements became deliberate. She smoothed her hands slowly across my bicentennial bedspread.

"How would you like it if I came down to your room and changed the channel while you were in the middle of watching the news?" I asked.

Her jaw set, and a little walnut formed while she bore down on her gold-capped molars. "I bought you this television and I'll be damned if you're going to use that tone with me."

She lunged for the television. Mom was not athletically graceful, so I was a little startled when she wrapped her arms around the set and yanked it off the desk. My father once tore the phone out of the wall when one of my sisters talked back, and it became the standard in our family for the ultimate retaliation. If you really screwed up, a phone got ripped out of the wall. But hauling off a television was another matter. Mom poked herself on the rabbit ears and knocked over the end table as the plug shot from the outlet. She left the room with the cord trailing behind her, stomping back to her room where the emcee could still be heard on her television introducing the next act on the *Broadway Cavalcade*.

Mom made it clear our relationship was conditional. Whether it was gifts given with the price tag on, or details about just how inconvenient it was for her to drive me to school, she expected regular payment in obedience and gratitude. So it was with the television, the only thing in my highly formalized bedroom that I truly considered to be my own. Everything seemed subject to change no matter how arbitrary the reasoning.

Ultimately I had no power, or at least none of the adult power I thought I had gained from reading those secrets about her life and her feuds with my father. When my sisters and brother had their issues with Mom, they bucked against my parents' more or less united front. But I had what they didn't: an out. I decided I would find a way to leave Merrywood and move in with my father. To work out my frustrations one night I took her publicity photograph and put it in a Plexiglas frame on the floor under the window in my bedroom. I knew where she had hidden the pellet gun my uncle had given me, and I stole it back. I started firing ragged holes in the picture.

"What are you doing?" she asked from the doorway.

"Nothing." I fired again.

"Is that my picture?"

"Yes," I said squeezing the trigger again.

Chapter Seven

A few weeks after Mom's burial in October 1997, the cardboard boxes arrived from New York and I started discovering another Nancy Dickerson. As the only journalist in the family, I became her archivist by default. I thought that meant I would get Mom's books and those presidential photographs from the piano, but more than twenty boxes were delivered to *Time*'s Washington bureau, where at age twenty-eight I had been working as a reporter for two years.

I pulled out calendars and guest lists and seating arrangements from scores of parties along with folders of news clippings on issues like abortion and welfare—research for future speeches she never gave. I found her wedding registry, a cracked white leather book, the pages lined with her neat script. Secretary of Defense McNamara gave my parents a silver bowl and Walter Cronkite and his wife sent twelve thistle tumblers. Bonnie Angelo, a colleague of mine at *Time*, gave my parents brandy glasses. Mom had drawn a careful even line through each name after she had written a thank-you note.

A bursting Bonwit Teller shirt box read "Johnson wedding." She'd been to both Lynda Bird's and Luci Johnson's weddings and had kept a thick sandwich of stiff cardboard invitations of all the parties and showers she'd attended in their honor. Each wedding guest had been given a heart-shaped satin box full of rice. She still had hers. The grains had clotted into petrified logs. Now we were passing into bag lady territory.

There were several "John Dickerson" folders filled with doctor's bills, permission forms and letters to tutors and teachers. Another held the notes I would leave her as a boy when I was away working. "Nobody LIX John," read one. "Why won't EU Giv os owr wae!" There were half a dozen or so with crayon pictures I'd left her and the message "I love you." When she was away I would leave those for her by her door and on the bottom of a few she would type her reply and leave it by my door: "Mom says I love you too."

I cut open another box and found the divorce papers in which the belongings of twenty years of marriage were divided up. All the accusations, claims and counterclaims were typed in triplicate.

Finding familiar items like her favorite fountain pen or oldest rosary brought on obvious moments of pathos. Discovering so many things that I really should have known about was even harder. It wasn't the unanswered questions that bothered me. It was the unasked ones. I had seen a few profiles of her over the years but I was pulling them out of the boxes by the handful. I found no box of family recipes for chocolate cake or worn thimbles. Those would have been a shock. But I did find corny poems and love letters. She had kept hundreds of publicity photographs capturing the fashions she followed so closely: from kid gloves in the '60s to headscarves in the '70s to the feather boas of the Reagan era. She usually pulled it off, though the headscarves were a mistake.

It was embarrassing how little I knew about this woman we'd just buried. I had tried too late. As she tried to recover from a stroke, her past was our therapy. We'd sit with piles of red leather scrapbooks; I'd turn the pages to see if the pictures of her with LBJ or Murrow or Nixon might scare up a comment or a smile. I felt like I was turning her convalescence into a Lifetime movie.

In the back of one of the boxes I found a brittle cassette tape of one of her broadcasts from the '60s. She didn't talk very well the last year and a half of her life. She slurred and her sentences ran out of gas in midstream. I played the tape on the office mailroom boom box and her voice came back. She predicted that Gene McCarthy would come out against Johnson over the Vietnam War. On another tape she hosted a "Salute to Congress," a variety show on the White House lawn that President Johnson threw for his old colleagues. Presidents are more likely to give Congress the one-finger salute these days.

The cleaning crew in my office never knew what to do with the late-night reader in the room full of cardboard. Sometimes I'd sit behind the maze of boxes to read a letter or look through an old script. If they couldn't see me, they'd assume no one was there and turn off the lights.

During the day, I was covering President Clinton's impeachment proceedings for *Time*. I spent the mornings at the House Judiciary Committee hearing room and then shuttled between interviews. At night I would come back to the office, which smelled like yellowed newsprint, and go through Mom's papers. I found pictures of her walking under the same vast oil paintings I had that day, her bag over her arm and a small notebook in her hand. In the margin of a book on the Senate called *The Citadel*, she'd drawn herself a map of the Capitol so she could find her way as a young reporter. I was getting lost in the very same warren. If you take a wrong turn in the basement you can end up in a boiler room or the storage pen where they stack the flags sent to constituents who ask for one that has flown above the Capitol.

As I read, she became both more real and more distant. Her intimate diaries brought me closer, but to process all the new information I had to put her into categories like any other subject or politician I might study. I made the same instinctive sorting with Mom: Wisconsin years, Washington Girl Friday, star and then the years I knew: Diva and Elder Stateswoman.

Then I discovered young Nancy, writing journals after she was supposed to have gone to bed on Cedar Street in Wauwatosa. When today's news personalities write their bestselling memoirs they spend a lot of time back in the hometown. Tom Brokaw glorified Yankton, South Dakota; Tim Russert, Buffalo; and Charles Osgood and Russell Baker wrote about Baltimore. In Mom's 1976 autobiography, she did the opposite: she blew through Wauwatosa, Wisconsin. There's no talk about an influential teacher, or the drunk but lovable uncle or moment of epiphany at the five-and-dime. "In the summer we played kick the can in the street and put up a lemonade stand," she wrote. "It was a lazy relaxed childhood, but as far as I was concerned, nothing ever happened there." She sprang perfectly groomed and formed from Anywhere, U.S.A., which barely deserved mention.

Her brassy sister, Mary Ellen Philipp, still recites that one sentence through gritted teeth. Two years older than mom, Mary Ellen did what women of that generation were supposed to do: She married a Milwaukee lawyer not long after college, settled just thirty miles from where she had grown up and had four children. "Once I got married I was pretty much stuck there," she says somewhat ruefully.

Mary Ellen thought Mom's politics were too lefty and thought she behaved as if those who'd stayed behind in Wisconsin were only concerned with leaky basements and soggy diapers. "Wauwatosa just wasn't important to her," says Mary Ellen. "There were no important people there."

To say there was nothing doing in Wauwatosa would have been a compliment if it had come from one of the city elders. In 1927, when Mom was born, it was a sober, sensible town of flat-faced buildings lined up on a grid of streets dotted by elms and maples. The Germans had settled there at the turn of the century, and by the Great Depression, it had one of those middle-class affirming suburban labels, calling itself the "City of Homes."

People were supposed to stick around town. Girls learned to cut bolts of fabric and sneak chocolate-covered cream at Lefeber's drygoods emporium and were expected to take their daughters there to do the same. The wealthy didn't flaunt it, and there weren't too many truly poor people. The fathers went to work in new efficient factories that made useful items like galvanized tubs. Or they put on a uniform to drive a bus or light the gas streetlamps. The mothers didn't work outside of their aprons. They shopped, made dinner, kept house and watched that the children didn't eat too much candy.

My grandparents, the Hanschmans, lived in a two-story house on Cedar Street. Down the way lived a Methodist minister and a deafmute family. The milkman made his rounds in a horse-drawn wagon and the iceman left sawdust on the carpet after he'd put the weekly twenty-five-pound block in the ice box.

Mom recorded no discussion of the current world or national events in her journals as a little girl. Around the dining table, her parents talked about card games and their neighbors, but not all that much about the second World War that was starting in Europe when

Mom was in junior high. "They never had a substantive discussion that I can remember," Mom used to say.

Like most everyone else in America during the war years, if you wanted the news you read the paper or listened to the radio. FDR updated the country on the progress of the war with his fireside chats. Edward R. Murrow, whom Mom would later idolize, reported on the war from bombed-out London. There were only seven thousand televisions in the United States in 1945 and the Hanschman household wouldn't have one until after Nancy left for Washington in 1950.

As a young girl she collected clothes, chased boys and let even more of them chase her. There seemed to be no end to the chances for young Nan to put an apple blossom in her hair and go out in a new dress she had made herself.

A childhood friend, Cis Reuteman, makes regular appearances in the boy-meets-girl-meets-boy adventures of Mom's journals. I called her up in Wisconsin. She'd just had hip surgery.

"Didn't you talk about anything other than boys?"

"Well, we talked about the other girls too."

"No, I mean the world."

"We hated the Germans and Japs, as we called them back then, but that was it," she said. "We didn't think beyond who we were going to date for the weekend." Mom didn't need to be in the Model United Nations, I just wonder why a world war made no mark in her life.

Mom snuck out from church and eased the car out of the garage before starting it—all to secretly meet up with the boys. On the weekends, she went with her friends to the lake. "We'd pile six of us into a car and sometimes with a case of beer," said Reuteman. "We'd all get so drunk no one could see straight. That's how stupid we were."

Mom was getting more interesting all the time.

The scrapbooks do show glimmers of her future career. Mom was the editor of her junior high school newspaper, the *Hawthorn Echo,* but her classmates don't remember her bylines. At a convention of school newspaper editors in Chicago, she organized the bellboys into a makeshift union and made them march down the hallway. She had an early talent for corralling men.

Boys are the central characters in the thirteen-year-old Nan's journals. She wrote in thick lead pencil on Morton's Salt notepaper, each page no bigger than a playing card, or in the wilted spiral-bound pages of University Composition books. There are the boys she left behind: "He said he didn't want to like me but try as hard as he could he couldn't forget about me (I just eat that stuff up)." There are the boys to be reconsidered, like the track star: "I was so disgusted with him, but then I opened the paper one morning before church and saw his name plastered all over it and immediately changed my mind." And there are the boys that take a little work: "I haven't had a date with him for three weeks and all the girls are loving this: 'Just think, here's one man she couldn't keep.' They thrive on stuff like that . . . for once I was at a loss for what to do. Luckily I didn't have to do anything."

At age thirteen she asked her father to buy her an erector set.

"Nancy, an erector set is a boy's toy," said her father.

A week later, she was connecting metal girders and stringing cables on the living room carpet. She had convinced Mr. Fitzgerald across the street to buy what her father would not. "She could always get men to do what she wanted," says Mary Ellen. The favors exacted from her peers were more modest. "Allan Wood said he would give me three Cokes if I would wear a sweater and skirt this week to dancing class," she wrote. "I got the three Cokes."

I knew Mom could manipulate men, but I'm surprised by how good she was at it at such an early age. It's an important reporter's trait. Even men flirt with male sources when they're working a story. They either peddle facts to show how smart they are, or join in the towel-snapping that boys usually save for the locker room. This is usually my preferred route. If you can get a source laughing without looking like a clown, you can lower the tension. The most embarrassing thing is the sucking up. You've never seen true sycophancy until you've watched a group of grown men talk about sports or politics around George W. Bush. All the fast breathing and excited interjections . . . it's downright embarrassing.

By age fifteen, Miss Hanschman was receiving October letters from college boys trying to grab a place on the Christmas holiday date calendar. One addressed the letter to "the star student, social queen, and most influential girl in Wauwatosa." Some tried to book her for the Christmas dance *and* New Year's Eve parties. "If the above dates are open and you aren't averse to a little good clean fun," wrote one boy in 1942, "send the good word back by carrier pigeon or the grapevine. . . . I'll be there no matter what the draft board says."

When Mom became famous, the number of her old boyfriends grew. The men left behind in Wauwatosa all claimed to have dated her. "Everyone she ever knew went out with her," Cis Reuteman remembered. "Wrong. Even now, I have to go around saying to people: 'You never went out with Nancy.' " I don't know. There are *a lot* of men in those journals, and they are even now reaching out to me. As I was just finishing this book, I opened the e-mail account readers use to respond to my *Slate* stories. "Dear Mr. Dickerson, I dated your mother at UW [University of Wisconsin]. I thought I would say hi. Bob Rogers." Hi, Bob.

Young Nan was also competitive, another trait she kept her whole life. "Today we voted for the five highest girls to be queen of the dance," she wrote. "I was second highest. Sally Wood, to whom I'm not speaking at present, was first."

Mostly though, the young version of my mother is more impish than mean. In a letter to her older sister, the seventeen-year-old Nan delights at her skillful undoing of one of Mary Ellen's old boyfriends. She walked in on him at a party while he was canoodling on the sofa with another girl.

"You should have seen his face when he saw me," she writes her sister of "Brick," who, like everyone in Wauwatosa under thirty, seems to have a Labrador's nickname. "But then we both commenced to be as sweet as sugar."

The confused new girlfriend was wearing a gift that Mary Ellen had given Brick.

"It was the scarf you gave the old boy!" Mom wrote. "That was all I could take. So, I waited 'till Brick was in hearing distance and said (to the girl): 'why don't you take your scarf off and stay a while?' Say, that's such a pretty scarf. Gee, I like that scarf a lot!"

Not content to embarrass the new girlfriend about the scarf, Nan heads to the record collection. She put on "Don't Sit Under the Apple

Tree," a record that Mary Ellen had also given the two-timing Brick.

The girl who typed that letter was going to be a reporter. Reporters do what they do for one of two reasons: They're reformers or they've got an itch to know what's going on. Sometimes they're both. Reformers are easy to spot. They can't sit still if they think someone is getting away with it, whatever it may be. They're tattletales but the ones who survive are more than just scolds. They make other people's lives safer, water cleaner and government less corrupt.

The other type can't sit still because they're gossips and they want to know what's going on. Once they know, they want to tell people. They're easily bored. If they are not in a place where there are things worth knowing and then telling (maybe in a whisper), then they want to get out of town and go where the action is.

Mom may have just enjoyed being a tattletale when she wrote Mary Ellen, but it's clear she loved being in the center of that drama and knowing the little secret about what was really going on. She was in control. As she wrote her sister I can see her giggling into the family typewriter as she punched its keys.

My grandparents don't appear much in the journals, which makes sense because in a lot of ways, Nan and Mary Ellen raised themselves. Their mother, Florence, contracted tuberculosis when they were in elementary school and spent a year in a sanitarium. Aunt Peggy, her sister from Duluth, moved in to take care of the girls, but she was only twenty-two. She was a friend and roommate more than a stand-in mother. They snuck candy together and watched double features. Mom got so excited before going to any Shirley Temple movie that she threw up, once on the patron sitting in front of her.

Florence Hanschman, my grandmother, was frail when she returned home. Doctors had removed one of her lungs, and she spent most of her time resting on the upstairs porch where the air was better. The girls didn't dare creep up to see her; Florence had told them if they got close they would get sick, too.

My grandmother was obsessed with health, hers and everyone else's. She had small cold hands and always urged people to wear coats. When she got nervous she made herself sick. She insisted her daughter not let her nerves do the same. "Whatever you do," she wrote Mom later, "don't let it get you sick—your health is so important and only you can take care of it. It is a lonesome business being sick."

When Mom started high school, my grandmother was strong enough to attend mass at St. Jude's every day. Nan and Mary Ellen also went to perform perpetual health devotions for their mother. They prayed for their father too. Like many of the men of the time he stayed home and let his wife do the churchgoing. "The nuns think I'm in trouble," my grandfather later wrote Mom about a rare visit to church, "but they just don't know what a swell guy I am."

Fred Hanschman, who died before I was born, was a swell guy. He ran a contracting firm that built bridges, factories and part of Soldier's Field in Chicago. He was a man's man, a former All-American football guard who liked to have a joke with the boys. He was German but acted Irish. Florence was Irish but acted German. In pictures his laugh takes over his whole face and Mom beamed whenever she talked about him. She kept two tiny gold footballs in her bedside table that he'd won for playing on back-to-back college championship teams. Fred spent his leisure time at the ballgame or the card table. When he was around, or with the boys, he was goofy. "I never use a shot glass," he used to boast to my older cousins, "I just turn up the bottle and count the glugs." He was apparently full of these odd-lot witticisms. When he left Sunday dinner at Mary Ellen's he would tell her children: "If I never see you again: 'hello.' "

In his letters to Mom, he banters in the same mischievous voice I find so surprising in her journals. He indulged her and encouraged her mischief, even when he was trying to be strict. "There are several articles (wearing apparel) that seem to have vanished from Cedar Street," he writes Mom when she goes off to college. "Of course these may have accidentally fallen into your grips while packing—but you should be unpacked by now and ought to have found them. The rest of the family are up in arms about it and that ain't music to my ears. Frinstance: scissors, gloves, and Mary's Argyle socks which Betty Mueller gave her. Those kinds of tricks honey never leave a good taste. So why don't you check over your stuff and return what belongs here so that we can start operating again. There goes the noon whistle. So much for that, and don't laugh!"

Fred was charming and warm, but he was also a man of his time.

He had clear views about what women were supposed to do. They took care of the house and the churchgoing and didn't play with erector sets. When Mom ran home to announce she'd gotten 100 on a test, he answered, "Oh." She repeated that story to us a hundred times. It defined her childhood. Not only did she think there was nothing going on in Wauwatosa, but even her father, whom she was most anxious to please, couldn't connect with her. It seems inevitable that she would look for an audience that would appreciate her. "We grew up to be emotionally cold," says Mary Ellen. "There wasn't a lot of hugging. And because there was a lack of emotion in our household, you spent your emotion on other people or on community projects."

The lack of attention and support in her own upbringing inspired Mom's most confusing act of parental boosterism. "Isn't it great to be John Dickerson?" she would ask me as a child. This was supposed to paper over any of my insecurities in a quick swipe. It baffled me. How was I to respond to this question? Yes? Against being what other kind of person would I have been able to make the comparison? It was as meaningful as if she had asked me if my portfolio had an even mix of stocks and bonds. I ask my son the same question just to watch him give me a funny quizzical look that must have been the same kind I gave Mom.

I expected the young Nancy to be the one raising her hand to remind the teacher to hand out homework. I didn't expect the girl in the saddle shoes and Peter Pan collars to be full of easy mischief, the quality my brother and I thought she lacked. She's a clever performer; my friends and I would have wanted to pass notes to her.

What happened? What happened to the spirit of the girl who at the end of 1942 anticipates how she will write in her journal the next year: "I shall write in the third person. I'll forget about writing with modesty—bear in mind that I am only 15 years of age, really about 18–19 in measure of age and experience." But she doesn't even wait until the New Year to boast. A few pages later she writes: "I won the popularity award at Hawthorn [junior high school]—noted by the whole damn school to be the nicest." She underlines "damn" twice. Mom gave Wauwatosa only a handful of lean sentences in her autobiography because its quaint simplicity didn't fit her narrative. She spent her life trying to show how serious and substantive she was. Her young life was neither. Newswomen were assigned soft personality stories to keep them in the ghetto. She wasn't going to assign herself one with her own autobiography. It's a shame. There was so much material there to examine, but that was Mom's way: She buried who she was in order to show us what she thought we should see.

Chapter Eight

———

Mom left Wauwatosa in the spring of 1951. She didn't know what she wanted to do, but she knew she wanted to be where things were happening.

She'd mentally moved away in 1945 when she left for Clarke College, an all-girls school run by nuns in Dubuque, Iowa. Girls could go out one night a week and then only until ten. But if Mom wasn't able to indulge her mischievous side, she did open up her mind. "How much do we really know about this World War II and about its underlying causes?" she wrote in a book review for the college literary magazine. "Oh yes, we read newspaper headlines; we digest censored articles written by foreign correspondents. But how many of us know the inside story of the whole thing?" The review praises the book *Beyond All Fronts*, written by an NBC radio reporter who argues that all Germans are not pro-Hitler and that the "thinkers of today" are wrong about the fanaticism of the German people. Mom not only embraces the thesis but the author's methods—preferring an eyewitness and shoe-leather account to the conventional wisdom. "It would truly be a holy and wholesome thing were all Americans to read and read thoughtfully Beyond All Fronts."

She ranked twelfth and fourteenth in her class during her time at Clarke, but after two years, she wanted a bigger stage. She enrolled at the University of Wisconsin and joined a sorority. There she could go out any night she wanted with any of the boys just home from the war; and instead of the austere rituals of the Catholic retreats, her older sorority sisters welcomed her into the Kappa house with this ditty:

> *All the boys have taken a fancy*
> *To our Kappa pledge called Nancy*
> *Sig Chis and Betas are only a few*
> *Of the boys that to her would say "I do."*
> *So with her charm, her line, and her luck*
> *She'll have enough beaus to fill this truck.*

As a sorority pledge, she lay on the floor and pretended she was "giving birth to a snake," a giggly rite of initiation into a sisterhood of bad euphemisms. They also paraded her before the statue of Lincoln in front of Bascom Hall. If she were a virgin, her new friends told her, the statue would stand up. "The difference between the two schools was akin to heaven and hell," Mom used to say.

She became a Badger Beauty, a title associated with comeliness, not buck teeth. The school mascot is the Badger. She got straight A's and by her senior year, at age 21, maneuvered her way into becoming a United Nations student delegate to Europe. In June 1948 she boarded an Amsterdam freighter with hundreds of other students, maintained a constant level of seasickness for two weeks and landed in Le Havre, France. She took a train to Paris, where rubble was piled in the streets, but she had arrived on Bastille Day and was swept into the celebration of European rebirth. She knew no one but walked down the Left Bank watching the cheering Parisians.

"Hey Nance," a voice yelled out of the crowd. It was Sammy Hope from Wauwatosa. What were the odds of that? He was as shocked to see her in Europe as she was to see him. He ran across the street and kissed her. Everyone kissed in the streets in Paris, he said, handing her a cigarette.

"You can smoke it walking down the Champs Elysees!"

And so she did, embracing her blossoming habit. They had dinner at Café de la Paix and watched the lights of the city come on for the first time since the war. She spent the evening dancing in the streets with Sammy and a cast of nameless Frenchmen.

She traded her petrol stamps for clothes, cigarettes and wine on the black market. She roamed throughout the continent with her fellow students and a few others they collected along the way, including some residents of the new state of Israel. Mom had never been east of Chicago and suddenly she was in this vast landscape. She indulged: She followed her impulses and emotions. She ventured farther than she'd ever imagined.

She kept a scrapbook from the trip marking every careful step, from the Faraglioni on Capri to bicycle tours of Geneva to Ristorante Quadri in Venice "where I choked on tripe." She toured every museum and soot-covered church but also saw Josephine Baker in Naples and La Revue de la Femme Cabaret show in Paris. She asked questions and launched brave theories and everyone seemed to welcome the fresh, excited American woman. There are lots of boys in the pictures. A love letter is pasted next to an 8x10 glossy photo of a dark-haired young man in shiny shoes. "Nancy, will you look and remember?" Another picture and letter come from a Palestinian boy named Ami. Mysterious Duccio typed a farewell note from Italy: "The only thing I may tell you is that yesterday I misunderstood you. For this reason I acted that way. Nothing else, for remains to me only the sorrow of having broken a wonderful dream and lost a true friend. Thank you Nancy of having been Nancy until now. Adieu." (They didn't write like that back in Wauwatosa.)

She stayed several weeks beyond the limit of her tour, to model for Nina Ricci in Paris. That led to a lovely full-page picture of her in *Mademoiselle* in 1948 standing in pearls and a full-length mink on a spiral iron staircase. By the end of her trip, Mom seemed to have fallen into the rhythm of the place. My spastic mother, who seemed genetically uncool, smoked and wore dark sunglasses as she lounged in cafes with morose French boyfriends in droopy socks. She stopped sending home regular dispatches, which caused her mother to wire: WORRIED NO MAIL ARE YOU ALL RIGHT WIRE LOVE MOTHER. She responded: ALL IS WELL WIRE MONEY.

But soon the money ran out and her sister wrote her, scolding her for being selfish and reminding her of her duties back home, which included making a living for herself or getting married. It was as if she was trapped in a Henry James novel: an American girl who discovers the natural and reasonable emotions of life in Europe only to be called back into the efficient, onerous and dutiful order in the United States. This struggle would become a dominant one in Mom's life: the battle between her sense of self-discovery and self-indulgence and her fears that others would think she was selfish and frivolous.

When she returned from Europe, Mom wanted to leave Wauwatosa, but her mother insisted she get a teaching certificate. So she spent two years teaching middle school, at which point she was so antsy, she was ready to walk east. According to her students she was a lovely and warm teacher. A few of the boys fell in love. "There was one boy in particular who had what we liked to call 'bedroom eyes,' " says Jerry Marchant, who taught with Mom at John Dewey Junior High.

Mom was desperate to get back to the excitement and swirl she had tasted in Europe. She had found herself there and that made Wauwatosa a place where she had all the wrong instincts and wasn't interested in any of the roles people wanted her to fill. The feeling was so indelible that forty years later, after moving to New York at age 62, it is this period she reflects back on as she tries to understand why she feels so at sea in her new city: "childhood insecurity brought on by the same lack of love and coddling that made me want to get out of Wauwatosa. I had to GET OUT."

She finally did in 1951. She didn't know what she wanted to be but, in the spring of that year, at age 24, she stepped off the train in New York and got a room at a women's boardinghouse. An older boy from her hometown who took pictures for *Life* magazine helped her get an interview for a secretarial job at Time-Life's headquarters. It was like going to a live theater show. Everyone moved a little faster and the women dressed in styles she'd never seen before. She asked as many questions as they asked her. They figured she was too green and turned her down. Forty years later, I got my first job as a secretary for *Time*.

Mom took the train to Washington, which immediately looked far more comforting than New York. Instead of high-rises and asphalt, daffodils and azaleas were blooming. No building was taller than those in downtown Milwaukee. For six weeks, she rode the trolley to and from typing tests. She made repeated trips to the Pentagon until she learned that the colonels were not so interested in giving her a job as they were in having a bit of conversation over morning coffee.

Finally, she landed an interview at the Senate Foreign Relations Committee, the most powerful committee in the most powerful governing body in the world. They needed a stenographer. She was ready for the job. Could she take shorthand? Of course, she could. She was hired as a clerk.

At age twenty-four, Mom couldn't take shorthand any more than she could cook. So, she tried to fake it. The committee staff director dictated and she tried to keep up. She tried so hard she shook in her chair. He paced. The chair started to squeak. Her loopy handwriting grew larger as he spoke faster. She caught her pen in the spiral wire binder.

"Now Nancy, read that back to me."

Silence.

At night she studied and tried to improve. Her roommate read to her from the newspaper. She got calluses, but she still couldn't keep up.

Mom was replaced. But she had been charming and eager, so they kept her on, putting her through the background check all Senate employees went through. In those reports "the applicant is described as unusually intelligent and hard working," according to an FBI interview of a former teacher at Clarke. "Also, she considered the applicant to possess an excellent character and reputation during the time she was acquainted with her, and that she never had any reason to question the applicant's loyalty to the United States." (No wonder she'd decorated my room in red, white and blue.)

Mom was embarrassed by her steno failure and worked long hours to make up for it. She showed up early to arrange the dispatches from the embassies and stayed up late typing legislation. Even Secretary of State Dean Acheson noticed how hard she was working, thanking her in a letter for her "cheerful helpfulness while on duty day and night during the course of the Mutual Security Program legislation through Congress."

For three years, Mom toiled with the typists, telephone operators, receptionists, filing clerks and duplicating machine operators. For many of her female colleagues, having a career was a way station— something you did before you got married. Once you got smiling children and a thoroughly modern kitchen you could drop the nine-to-five. Mom assumed she wanted some version of that life eventually, but she had come from Wauwatosa to do more than repeat its suburban family drama in a different zip code.

The Senate Foreign Relations Committee was an exciting place to work in the spring of 1951. The Soviets had detonated an atomic bomb in 1949, the same year the communist regime took power in China. The Korean conflict droned on. Truman had fired General Douglas MacArthur for insubordination. In a September 1952 speech, Truman marked the signing of the peace treaty ending World War II, in the first televised nationwide broadcast available to the nine million homes that had television. The president was pessimistic about the dangerous world. "Unfortunately, today, the world is faced with new threats of aggression. Many of the countries represented here are now engaged in a hard fight to uphold the United Nations against international law-breaking. There are thugs among nations, just as among individuals."

Senator Joseph McCarthy capitalized on Cold War anxieties about the spread of communism. Ohio's Republican Senator Robert Taft positioned himself for a possible presidential nomination in 1952 by blasting President Truman for ignoring Congress in setting major foreign policy objectives.

Mom got addicted to the Senate drama. Each day she could watch all the personal striving, pettiness, glory, generosity and pride of the human condition. Senators are great theater, especially when they get indignant about their prerogatives. They gave outraged floor speeches and cornered each other to exact promises and trade favors. She loved the sounds of the Capitol, the halls echoing with the click of heels on marble, the tourists asking for directions and the typewriters clattering in every office as she walked by.

Mom hadn't seen much of the country but now she was working for senators on the Foreign Relations Committee like the exotic chairman, Tom Connally of Texas, who used words she'd never heard of like *tarnation* and *hoosegow*. Once when he learned a senator was trying to force action from his committee, Connally rushed to the Senate floor and said in mock humility, "I assure the senator of California that this matter will have in the Foreign Relations Committee *exactly* the consideration it so richly deserves." Here Connally, whose leonine white hair was easy to spot from the press galleries, grinned at the newsmen and passed his index finger across his throat like the blade of a knife.

Not long after she started at the committee, Mom met the flirtatious Lyndon Johnson. He walked across a room, sat in a comfortable stuffed chair and put his feet up on her desk. He asked if he could use her phone. "I raised an eyebrow at him," Mom said in her oral history in the Johnson Library, "making it clear that even for the distinguished majority leader of the Senate that wasn't the proper place to put one's feet."

For Mom, the Senate was like an Advent calendar. There was the public show, but if you knew the right trick, you could open a little window and see behind the scenes. When Senator Frank Church downed pitcher after pitcher of water during a hearing she turned to a colleague and said, "He's putting out the fire from last night," knowingly referring to his hangover. When Senator McCarthy's face twitched repeatedly during a hearing, she joked about it later to a colleague. "Nancy," her friend responded, "that's not a tick, he's winking at you." The Wisconsin senator wasn't the only one. "Chasing women kind of comes with the territory in the male-chauvinist Senate," wrote columnist Hugh Sidey at the time, "like the springy black leather couches."

Some people come to Washington with dreams of Jeffersonian idealism. They get misty walking beneath the oil painting of Washington resigning his commission or run their fingers along the marble statues and wonder. Mom didn't come to town with well-annotated volumes of the *Federalist Papers*. She came with a love of action and power and became an enthusiast of those who wielded it flamboyantly. The more she watched, the more she wanted to be more than a spectator. She wanted to trade opinions in the debates. She wanted to be taken seriously by the powerful men she admired.

But that is not exactly how Mom would tell it. She had a more romantic story. Her idealism had drawn her to Washington. In her autobiography, she wrote that having seen the ravages of war firsthand in Europe, she returned with a yen to change the world.

It's a good story. It's just the kind of story people tell in Washington, especially those who came up in the Kennedy era when you couldn't do the laundry without having a lofty mission.

But her scrapbooks from Europe suggest Mom was a lot less concerned with "making the world a better place" than with having a good time. She wrote no anguished letters home about the Marshall Plan. There are no pictures of her rebuilding a bombed church in France. The gap between the narrative she told about herself and the Holly Golightly experience of her journals would have outraged me as a kid. The hypocrisy!

The girl who had wanted to be at center stage at Wauwatosa East high school wanted to see the world. She did. That was extraordinary and confusing and eye-opening. But she couldn't be wide-eyed about Europe around the eggheads on the Foreign Relations Committee. They were very serious men. She didn't have their advanced degrees, so to compete she made her European tour sound like a profound policy experience. When senators and their male aides agreed that Europe was America's first and most important line of defense against a Soviet advance in the Cold War, Mom weighed in with her firsthand serious observations about European currency and the appetite for American global leadership.

Upgrading the significance of her European tour also helped her justify it. It had been meaningful, not the selfish escapade that her sister and parents thought. This was a useful conversion: It kept her from feeling guilty and frivolous. Mom loved the action and romance and adventure of Europe and she convinced herself that she wasn't just doing it for herself, that all of those experiences were making the world a better place. This is a time-honored Washington trick. It's not just politicians who upgrade their golfing trips to Scotland by calling them fact-finding missions; everyone in town learns to cloak their personal driving emotions in policy rationales. The former they only admit to themselves, if that. The latter, they use for their public speeches.

Everyone in Washington needs a narrative to tell about themselves. The transience of politics demands it. In the 1950s, people in the rest of the country worked their entire lives for one company and lived in one town, but Washington was already full of the job shifting that is now a part of modern life. You introduce yourself quickly in Washington because you might not be around for long. You emphasize your best points and hide the unpopular or conflicting ones. Some of the great fiction writing goes on in resumes and politicians are forever being uncovered for having padded theirs. They do a more aggressive version of what Mom did—they tweak their credentials when they start out and by the time they've gotten stature they've either bought into their own myth or they've forgotten to airbrush the embellishments out. Even the sanctimonious crusading journalists who uncover those politicians, they also embellish and promote a self-styled version of themselves while railing against just such behavior.

Mom had to work so hard at her own story because it's clear that the men weren't anxious to listen to her. I find a letter written in November 1953 on Committee on Foreign Relations stationery:

> *Dear Commander,*
>
> *You may recall a wandering, nebulous conversation a week ago relating to American public opinion from the period when Russia came into the war on our side (June 22, 1941—Germany attacked Russia—when I say our, I mean the Allies, realizing that we were not in the war at the time) up through the middle of 1946, when she first used the veto at the UN.*
>
> *If you recall, I made a statement to the effect that "the majority of the American people felt friendly toward the Russians and trusted them," and later, added in reply to your question that "our leaders also trusted the Russians." You will recall that this was a general statement about the majority.*
>
> *You and your two private industry friends then flatly stated that I was wrong and you concluded that I wouldn't know anything about it anyway as I was "just a kid in high school" at the time. (Verbatim quote.)*
>
> *I would suggest you read the attached—not to convince you necessarily, but to inform. It occurs to me that my statement was not without factual basis and that I'd appreciate it in the future if you wouldn't dismiss my arguments so summarily!*
>
> *N.L.H.*

I don't know who the poor commander is, but included with this peppery letter is a forty-eight-page report on U.S. public opinion about the Russians that proves her point.

At the committee she learned that information was a ticket to the game. By knowing her facts and the players she could gain the same advantage in Washington that she had had over Mary Ellen's boyfriend. Information allowed her to get into the conversation with that commander and his two private industry friends (I like to think she knew those men's names but intentionally refers to them anonymously as if they're just another pair of company men in hats). Same game, new rules. "I've always been charmed by political maneuvering," she would tell the author of a 1963 piece in *Current Biography*. "It amuses me—it delights me."

Her same report on American attitudes about Russia helped introduce her to Jack Kennedy, who was serving his first year in the Senate. "May I please see a copy of the famous 'Hanschman report?'" he wrote her. I found the note on Kennedy's Senate stationery among her typed committee reports. She treated all other JFK correspondence like a fussy curator, placing it in a special protective file. Was this one not with the others because she'd filed it when Jack was just a junior senator?

Mom kept that dry survey of American attitudes on the Soviet Union even after it became Russia because, along with the phone book–sized committee reports she'd helped write, it was a trophy from her education in Washington. She discarded many of her love letters from that era, but she kept even her most dreary clerical work for the committee. Those three years as a government employee were where she gained intellectual legitimacy in a town in which anyone who wanted a seat at the adult's table had to be ready to present their credentials. Those relics also represented victories, the times when she did her work, got 100 and a man said something more than just, "Oh."

Chapter Nine

The summer after Mom died in 1997, my brother and I joined our Wisconsin cousins on a rough-and-ready old dairy farm Mary Ellen owns in the northern part of the state. We wanted to get in touch with our neglected heritage, which meant eating bratwurst, drinking Leinenkugel's beer and throwing ourselves into home improvement projects. Once we built a porch. Another summer, we reconstructed the forty-foot windmill.

The Merrywood Dickersons had stayed away from windmills and overt interaction with nature. We certainly had never vacationed in Wisconsin. Mom wanted credit for her Midwestern pluck, gumption and good-heartedness, but bratwurst ruins the figure. Fortunately I wasn't completely unfamiliar with outdoor life. Mom and Dad knew I needed roughing up so they sent me away to summer camps. I knew when a bat flies at your head it's uncool to hit the deck. They'll avoid you most of the time on their own.

We knew we shared genetic markers with our cousins when both tribes wandered out to the porch with drinks in their hand. Whether it was in Milwaukee or Washington, the grandchildren of Fred and Florence Hanschman were familiar with cocktail hour, or as other people call it, lunch.

I found a trove of Mom's past on the farm. After her parents had died, their scrapbooks were moved under the staircase in the granary. I ducked the cobwebs, cleared a seat among the bat droppings and dug in. In an expandable file there were hundreds of yellowed stories from her time in Washington during the '50s, mostly profiles with catchy headlines like "Washington's Girl Reporter" or "Who Can Keep Up with Nancy?" If Mom's parents were emotionally cold, they sure did pay a lot of attention to her activities.

There are stacks of clippings from a snowy day in January 1954 when Mom walked the four miles from Georgetown to the Capitol. Her Peugeot with a hole in the floor couldn't make it out of the embankment. Even the trolley cars weren't working. When two Capitol police officers saw the lone brunette walking down the middle of the white street, they offered to carry her over the drifts. She obliged, putting one arm around each of their shoulders. A UPI photographer was there, and the next morning the snap was on the front page of papers across the country—from the *Kansas City Star* to the *Los Angeles Times* to the *Albuquerque Journal.* The Hanschmans' friends from all those towns mailed them the clipping with descending marginalia. "Nancy seems to be making her mark!" wrote one. Mom seems to have forwarded some of the clips home, including one with a note still attached from her roommate's brother: "She looks even dainty-er than in the glow of your September martinis."

Under the musty clippings were several boxes of slides and a viewer that looked like something used for the eye test at the DMV. My grandparents had taken several trips to Washington, but they didn't take pictures of the Lincoln Memorial or Tidal Basin. They took pictures at their daughter's cocktail parties.

The Hanschmans weren't lushes, but they kept a full bar on Cedar Street and they knew how to mine its exhilarations. My grandmother sipped bourbon and bitters. My grandfather drank Scotch more ambitiously. "When the bar and walls start to move, keep your seats," he wrote his daughter on the lined orange paper of his draftsman's pad. He describes jolly nights out and the hangovers that followed. "Needless to say, I couldn't get out of low gear all day."

Mom's letters back have the same boozy references:

"Thank you for the candy, I didn't take Pootsy's because I was full of bourbon at the time." Her roommate Pootsy must have been grateful.

"I must say I had had apprehensions about the whole proceedings and had a good stiff drink before everyone arrived and that sort of bolstered me."

"I celebrated my birthday yesterday with George Farris and we drank champagne all afternoon."

Mom may have arrived in Washington fuzzy about the Mutual Strategic Alliance, but she'd come from a cocktail culture that assumed everyone liked to have a good time no matter where they were from. Her party skills were particularly useful in Washington, where the bar was definitely open. During Mom's early days, whiskey consumption in the nation's capital was three times the national average.

Senator Estes Kefauver's Senate hideaway was always littered with empty bottles. Lyndon Johnson, as Senate majority leader, could polish off a dozen or so Scotch-and-sodas in an afternoon and evening. He claimed they were half-strength but stopped early in his presidency. House Speaker Sam Rayburn hosted a daily happy hour. President Truman had at least a couple of bourbons a day. Nixon was once so drunk he couldn't talk to the British prime minister. "When I talked to the president he was loaded," Henry Kissinger told an aide when explaining why the president couldn't take the call. How did we ever get through the Cold War when everyone was so plastered? Perhaps that's how we did.

As I clicked each new slide into the projector, the bulb baked a little more dust and Mom appeared at a different person's elbow. She was in her late twenties and her parents were at a party in her P Street apartment. My grandparents seemed to be having a lovely time. It was the first time I'd ever seen my grandfather in a color photo. Fred was standing with Mom, comfortably holding his martini. The men in Washington aren't that different than they are in Wauwatosa, I imagine my grandfather thinks. It confirms his view of the wider social fraternity in which he had always believed.

At one of the cocktail parties Mom overheard her mother talking about the vice president, who was off with his family in California: "Oh, wouldn't it be lovely to see the Nixons after they return from vacation."

"Mother," Mom laughed, "you say that as if they were the Tiefenthalers who had just returned from Florida!"

Mom was so proud of her knowingness she told this story to a friend in a letter. She said that she moved back through the room, a little thrilled she'd been able to show she wasn't a hayseed like her mother. Kids will, um, do that.

It was easy to be a quick social veteran in Washington those days. It was a roaring town. "We went out every night," says Patricia McCarrick, who worked with Mom on the hill. "You didn't sleep with them then the way people do now. Within six months of arriving I probably knew five hundred people." Mom was in Europe by the Potomac.

When Mom's Senate duties were completed, she raced home to wriggle into the party dress she'd left out on her bed that morning. Almost every night the doorbell rang and off she would go with another handsome young man. "Monday, I will be with Senator Scoop Jackson for dinner," she wrote her parents in a typical rundown of one week's acrobatics. "Tuesday Senator Keating has invited me to a party he is having for the vice president [Nixon]. Thursday I see Cord [Meyer] again and Friday I'm going out with a New York Times columnist . . . I sure am getting fancy."

By 1954, Mom wanted to be even fancier, but attending cocktail parties at night and studying committee proceedings during the day wasn't going to get her a powerful position on the Foreign Relations Committee. The only way that was going to happen was if she earned an advanced degree or won election to the Senate. Staff rules did not allow a single woman to travel with committee members nor did they allow young women to make investigative staff trips on their own, as young male staff members did. If she wanted to be center stage, there was no faster way than to be a member of the press delivering a bulletin: The audience gathered around you. She'd seen how much power the members of the press had over elected officials. "I was in awe of reporters," she used to say. "Senators taught me that. They could be powerful and pompous and roar and turn around and be sycophants to reporters."

The word *sycophant* has a peculiar place in my Washington upbringing. I remember very clearly asking about that word when I heard my parents use it. They were referring to a family friend in politics. My brother later whispered to me: "ass kisser." Wow. I'd been let in on my first secret. I still can't talk to that family friend without seeing the word blink in neon on his forehead. Of all the monikers to learn in Washington, it's one of the most useful.

Mom started her job hunt with Lawrence Spivak, the NBC

bureau chief who hosted *Meet the Press,* but he wasn't impressed. The *Washington Daily News* offered her a job as a women's editor. She turned them down. She looked for openings in the newspapers, the halls of Congress and at dinner parties.

At a British Embassy party welcoming the newly crowned chief of Britain's Foreign Trade Commission, she was approached by Phil Graham, the publisher of the *Washington Post.* In a long hallway they sipped drinks and pinched hors d'oeuvres from white-gloved waiters. He handed her his business card and suggested she come by the *Post* to talk about a job.

When she went to see Graham, their meeting quickly turned into a footrace. He didn't want to hire her. He wanted to sleep with her. When she turned down his offer to start an affair, he pounced. She wriggled free but Graham chased her. He followed her down the hall and out the door. Mom recounted to author C. David Heymann the conversation she had over her shoulder as she fled:

"I thought you were married."

"I am but only metaphysically."

"What does that mean?"

"It means I am available romantically."

"But I'm not."

For several months the pursuit continued until Graham moved on.

"This happened all the time with men," remembers McCarrick. "To your mother a lot but to all of us. You learned to just move past it."

Finally, after searching for months, Mom heard that CBS radio needed a producer, a man who knew the players on Capitol Hill and who could convince them to come on their two signature radio shows, *The Leading Question* and *Capitol Cloakroom.* Mom certainly knew the terrain, so she applied. They wanted a man, but they wanted the contacts even more. She was hired. "Right off the bat she seemed to know everyone who was anybody," said Bill Shadel, the moderator of *Capitol Cloakroom.*

Each week, Mom had to find members of the House or Senate who would sit down for an hour to discuss the farm bill or Soviet troop levels. It wasn't an easy task. She'd get a commitment from a congressman and then he'd cancel at the last minute. Or, a subject wouldn't call at all. He'd just fail to show up.

Were they canceling on her because she was a woman?

If she got a commitment in the hallway or at a cocktail party did they take her less seriously?

Until someone was seated in front of the microphone and the tape was rolling, she lived in panic that the audience would tune in and hear "and now for a half hour of recorded music," because she had failed to produce enough warm bodies.

Congressmen weren't the microphone hounds they are today. They played the inside game, influencing their colleagues in the back room rather than on the afternoon chat show. Often, they didn't want to be known by a national audience. A politician could be for busing in the northern part of his state and rail against it in the southern part. In a few years, television would make it difficult for politicians to use these old tricks, though some still try.

Today, most members of Congress seek the cameras, building up a constituency in public that gives them stature in the cloakroom. Bookers, as Mom's successors are called, can find a warm member of Congress at any hour of the day. Some, like Republican Arlen Specter, are known for their availability. Hill staffers joke that you should never get between Specter and a camera or you'll be run down. When Democratic Senator Chuck Schumer once said "no comment," the reporters surrounding him said in unison: "a first."

Mom had to learn which senators or congressmen were too drunk to rely on and which ones would say yes only to cancel at the last minute. There was no way she could get revenge: She needed them more than they needed her.

She had to run the powerbrokers down in person to make the sale. Mom chased them and charmed them and stayed right in their face until they were about to go on the air. From her letters home to her parents, it seems the dialogues went something like this:

"Senator Humphrey," she said, following the Minnesotan out of his office. "Senator Humphrey, we certainly would like you to be on the show this weekend."

"Yes, Nancy, I would like to do it but . . ."

"I've talked to Ellen in your office and she says you'll be in town this Friday and you have time."

"That was very nice of you to check on that for me, Nancy."

"Senator, the listeners would very much appreciate hearing your views on the latest relief program for workers."

"All right, Nancy."

"Terrific. We'll see you then. It's really going to be a good show. We can count on you then?"

"Yes, Nancy."

It's possible that Mom hadn't talked to Ellen, the senator's secretary, but once she was armed with a commitment from Humphrey, she'd have her put it on his official schedule, making sure that she knew that Humphrey had given his word. It's also possible that Ellen had tipped Mom off, letting her know that Humphrey was in fact available and telling her where to find him. Mom knew one of the most important lessons in Washington: Be kind to the assistants and secretaries. They are your gateway to the powerful, and they may be powerful in their own right one day.

No reporter in Mom's position ever wants to be seen trying to get a source to talk or agree to join them on a program. When part of your job is defined by your access to politicians as much as reporting the facts, you can find yourself tap-dancing, spinning plates, making shadow puppets, doing anything to get them to say yes. This doesn't ensure that you'll give a source a pass, but it means you'll go through some serious contortions to get them to talk. You have to explain to a politician why the show needs them. To make them believe you, you also have to pitch yourself. Sources are going to act in their self-interest, but they get their first cues from you.

This little dance between reporters and sources requires more than just some facial tics. You have to put on personas. Don't use the locker-room quips you used with George Bush when you're talking to the more cerebral Senator Joe Lieberman. One of my first journalistic tasks was babysitting a Middle Eastern terrorist, so I bought cigarettes, smoked nonstop with him and acted like a shit to every waiter, cab driver and other human we came in contact with. (That I carried off this act without causing uncontrollable laughter from my source is a testament to his self-absorption and not my playacting.) When I interviewed John McCain's mother, I smiled like the little angel who grew up opening the door at Merrywood. I prayed like I was taught in Sunday school when I bowed my head before dinner with John Ashcroft at a rib joint in South Carolina.

There is nothing remarkable about this. Any metro reporter has to do this better, more often, and on a wider variety of subjects than I ever have. But this is what reporters do: We sample our personalities to make sources feel more comfortable talking to us. Or, we create a persona that makes a source deeply uncomfortable by getting in their face, hoping that in the confrontation the information we want breaks free. How exactly did Mom do it when there were no templates for her to follow? She'd sweet-talked boys in Wauwatosa, and that was easy enough to repeat in Washington, but it didn't always work. There was a big downside: Too much flirting would make people think she was frivolous. She knew how to assert herself, but she didn't want to be a pushy broad. She had to make up her public reporter's identity as she went along.

Until she figured out what her real role was, she knew that she could never look unsure. "She had a great sense of the image," remembers Bonnie Angelo, then a reporter at *Newsday*. "She didn't walk around all flibbertigibbet. She walked and talked and acted like she knew what she was doing. Even if she wasn't self-confident, you thought for sure that she was."

As a young girl, Helen Bartlett, the youngest daughter of Mom's friends Charlie and Martha, watched how Mom's body language changed as she put on the reporter's role even during dinner parties. "She would cross her arms and stand almost with her legs in a V shape almost like a guy when she was about to ask a tough question. It was like *now she's going into business*. It was her way of saying: 'Now this is something I really want to know.'"

Mom's male colleagues didn't like the competition from this new animal. In a *TV Guide* profile, one bitter male correspondent coined a term for Mom and her female colleagues at the newspapers: the stranglers. "They grab a senator by the throat," he complained, "and they don't let go until he comes through with an interview, agrees to turn up on a panel, admits he'd like to be president or, at the very least, sends them a lollipop. There isn't a man on Capitol Hill who doesn't surrender when one of the Stranglers moves in. . . . I've seen her moving around the cocktail parties and she looks like a comer to me. She's a Class-A Strangler."

What a whiny boy. The lollipop he's referring to is a peppermint one Mom received from Everett Dirksen, the Wizard of Oz–looking Republican Senate minority leader. She never knew why he sent it to her. I can't figure it out either. Sometimes senators do odd things. When I walked up to Senator Pat Roberts once, he offered me a piece of candy he was unwrapping before we stepped into the subway. It was the first time I'd ever interviewed him.

I started covering Congress about the time Mom died, which meant she was always in my head as I ran up to the press galleries of the House and Senate where a member might be holding court. During Bill Clinton's impeachment I trolled the Senate's underground train for a lone senator I could accompany on his ride back to his office. In between the wandering, I went back to the sources I'd developed and maintained: the impeachment manager who would criticize his Republican colleagues or the Democratic senator flirting with a new public criticism of President Clinton.

You develop a skill for holding a conversation while walking pretty quickly, though how she did it in high heels I don't know. If a congressman doesn't really want to talk, you have to skitter along after him as he tosses answers over his shoulder. You dodge constituents and tourists and security guards while trying to write something down on your pad that will be legible when you try to read it later. All along the way, you weigh whether you shouldn't peel off and grab that other senator walking the other way—or the advisor who'd give you something useful even if it's off the record.

If you don't want to chase them down, you can find them where they rest. In both the House and Senate, reporters can scrawl a note to a member asking them to come see you and have a page carry it into the chamber. More often than not, they will come when called.

During any big news event, the lobbies just off the chambers clot with little press conferences. Reporters follow unwritten dance steps, letting their colleagues interview a member they've called from the floor but only for a few questions. Then, one by one, we quickly join the interview until the subject has us hanging off him like charms on a bracelet.

Sometimes, when I worked for *Time,* I tried to summon members for a private talk, handing off the slip of paper on which I'd written a congressman's name quietly as if placing a shady bet. I had a weekly deadline, which meant I was worried the news I'd discover would appear elsewhere before the magazine could go to print. I didn't want my colleagues with the daily papers or wires seeing who I was talking to and scooping me.

"Dickerson?" said an older clerk I'd not met when I discreetly slipped him the paper requesting a cetrain congressman. "That's a famous name isn't it?"

"My mother used to work here."

"That's right. Dickerson. Nancy Dickerson. She was a beauty."

"Yes. Shame about her son though."

"Yeah. Didn't rub off."

Chapter Ten

The first guest Mom booked on *Capitol Cloakroom* in 1954 was two-term New York congressman Ken Keating. Keating was easy to sign up—they were having a relationship. At first, no one knew for sure, but the two of them were seen around town a lot together grinning a little too much and finishing each other's sentences a little too often.

He was married, though his wife was in the late stages of multiple sclerosis and never traveled to Washington. In a nod to the propriety of the day, Keating took Mom's roommate to some of the parties too, but no one in Washington was much fooled.

Her friend Paul Niven, a colleague who became famous for his questions on *Face the Nation,* asked her privately, "Are you and the good congressman having an affair, Nancy?"

"Keep your questions about affairs to foreign affairs please," she responded coyly.

"That's okay," said Niven, "everyone assumes you are anyway."

If everyone knew, they gave them a pass. Keating's wife's situation gave him the same kind of pass that closeted homosexuals like columnist Joe Alsop got at the time. People talked occasionally, but that didn't keep Keating or Alsop from being invited to the elite parties. These allowances did not extend past Washington or shade politicians in the glare of a political campaign. In 1952, Adlai Stevenson's divorce was a political liability for the Democratic nominee. With no wife, he was no match for Nixon and Ike, whose spouses nodded loyally at their sides. They seemed to project the message that the traditional American family was intact and so was the country.

One CBS lobbyist threatened to expose Mom's relationship with Keating to CBS president Frank Stanton. But it wasn't hurting CBS that Nancy had become friendly with the congressman and his pals, who started showing up regularly on the weekend broadcast.

You can sprain an ankle trying to tiptoe through your mother's sex life, especially when she describes her first serious Washington beau in her memoir as being "as old as my mother." My older sister Ann met Keating in the '70s when he served as Nixon's ambassador to India. She assures me he was dashing. He was a decorated war veteran and was by all accounts charming, confident and full of winning phrases and snappy comebacks. But in pictures from the '50s Keating's skin looks like pudding and he has tiny dim-sum pillows under his eyes. Of course he does—he is *as old as her mother.*

But judging Keating by his looks misses the point. He was influential and admired for his intellect. He was a serious man who took her seriously. And he was a wit. I can see why she was attracted to him. I never found any early love letters but, as Bonnie Angelo pointed out: "with that kind of proximity, who needs letters." Still, she kept the letters he sent from his foreign postings under Nixon. He wrote them after he had remarried and she was ten years into her marriage to my Dad. They joke about his "arch rival," Secretary of State Henry Kissinger, and he mocks his own talents as a diplomat: ". . . at the present time I have succeeded in driving the United States' respect and regard in India to the lowest point in history. Only China is below us, but as soon as we can get lower than China, I want to start building back so that by the year 2000 I can mount the steps of the Capitol (if I am not in the White House) and shout that we have India as our dearest and most valued friend."

There was still plenty of flirting. "It would plunge me into ecstasy if I suddenly received a cable that you were on your way," he wrote to her when he was ambassador to Israel in 1973. From his post in India: "I hope that you will feel that my danger is so great that you should get out here to protect me," he writes. After such fawning he often signs off with, "best to Dick," my father.

As long as Mom and Keating could avoid any threat of scandal, the relationship was good fun and great business. Keating was her ticket to the big show. She, in turn, was delighted to arrive on his arm at Washington's best parties or even join him for a weekend at the Kentucky Derby as a guest of the governor. When Mom needed to book the famous Washington hostess and ambassador to Luxembourg, Perle Mesta, on her radio program, Keating arranged for her to visit Mesta at her grand Washington apartment. Taking tea overlooking Rock Creek Park, Mom won her over.

When some congressional Republicans wouldn't go on Mom's show, Keating called the White House. Eisenhower's chief of staff agreed to meet with her. Mom asked that he lean on Senate Minority Leader Everett Dirksen and other GOP leaders. It didn't work. "The Republicans are so silly," she writes her parents. "They have a chance for thousands of dollars of publicity and they won't do it. A few months from now, they will have to pay all the networks for time and they will be sorry then . . . That Dirksen is really a pot. I asked him to go on and he refused. If for no other reason, I would become a Democrat." (Mom's allegiances were easy that way. She once wrote home about Vice President Nixon: "I now like Nixon as he told someone that I was a lovely girl.")

Mom started attending awkward parties at Vice President Nixon's house with Keating, who had served in Congress with him. Nixon was a jittery host, disappearing for stretches and then hopping through the room serving drinks and encouraging everyone else to have another. Then he'd disappear again. Checkers the cocker spaniel ran underfoot, and for Mom that meant she was on the inside. Sure, people could meet the vice president. But who could say they'd nearly tripped over the dog from the famous speech that had saved Nixon's career.

Mom is annoyingly vague about Keating in her autobiography. She skips over how complicated such an affair must have been for her. She describes it as a light escapade of laughs, but, in fact, it required an act of will to allow it to continue against the objections of her Catholic faith.

Mom struggled her whole life to reconcile her desires and her religion. At Clarke she attended mass each day, said her rosary and studied the catechism. Priests would visit for regular weekend-long retreats where the girls would deny themselves by eating only celery.

The priests talked; the girls crunched. Mom took six pages of careful notes at the four-day Ash Wednesday retreat in 1946. The priests did not teach theological abstractions but offered news you can use. Mom's notes read like a ten-point plan for living like Jesus and avoiding damnation.

> *The seriousness of mortal sin! . . . One sin today is also that infinitely grievous, and only one mortal sin is sufficient to cause the loss of our soul.*
>
> *We should be truly sorry for our sins not only because we fear hell or loss of Heaven, but because we have offended God. That is as horrible a thing as possible.*
>
> *Practice self denial to attain self control. We must be the master of our emotions or we will live as animals, following our impulses and desires without reason.*
>
> *FEAR HELL. Do not submit oneself to undue temptation—*
> *Have the courage not to tell dirty jokes etc. Be like unto Mary. Keep your mind pure and clean of thought.*
>
> *Be merciful—Don't always have to be in the lime-light.*

The pages list the seven capital sins and lessons on how to avoid them. She must pray to the Blessed Virgin Mary, get married and offer her married love to God and create a home as happy as that of Mary, Joseph and Jesus. Along the way she should avoid other fruitless earthy behavior like daydreaming (*stop it—wishful thinking!*).

By the time she came to Washington, Mom had lost the passion that made her write down the priest's teachings so faithfully. She had been to Europe and had been introduced to the continent's more relaxed approach to love and intimacy, but she was, by one account, still prudish—at least in public. Oatsie Charles, a famous Washington hostess, lunched in the early 1950s with Mom and Lorraine Cooper, the wife of John Sherman Cooper, the Republican senator from Kentucky. "We were discussing the enticing subject of husbands versus lovers, or at least Lorraine was," she told author Heymann. "Nancy, a practicing Catholic and still young enough to be idealistic, seemed a little put off by Lorraine's frankness. At one point Lorraine remarked, 'When we die and go to heaven, I wonder who'll be there waiting for us—our husbands or our lovers?' "

Mom ultimately did what idealistic people do when they come to the big city and what almost everyone who survives in Washington must do: She gave herself an exception. "She rationalized that relationship {with Keating} because his wife was institutionalized," says my father.

Mom covered her affair with Keating by dating a rotating cast of bachelors: Senator Scoop Jackson, Senator Stuart Symington, and Navy Captain John McMullen. Washington is still a great town for the young, stylish and single female. There's not much competition. As the authors of *Don't Quote Me,* a 1975 book about women and Washington power, put it: "To understand Nancy's meteoric rise to national fame requires realizing that glamorous women are something of a rare commodity in Washington." The downside was that when Mom went out with a member of Congress, inevitably she was asked at dinner parties about her date's views and not her own: "What does the *Senator* think?"

Her beaus helped her meet a widening circle of influential Washingtonians who not only went on her show but plugged CBS's coming attractions. I came across a yellowing stack of pages from the Congressional Record that seemed like scraps from forgettable debates. But then I noticed that each sheet contained a floor statement about an upcoming CBS news program or a quote from one of the two radio shows she produced. Mom was having her dates plant plugs for her network in the permanent record.

She never seems to have stopped moving. Her letters contain more dates, trips to Mass and frantic travel than it seems possible to pack into one week. In her letters back home, I thought she was exaggerating her social exhibitionism (who doesn't want to sound impressive to their parents) but the stories all check out. Plus, who could make up this evening at Bobby Kennedy's in June 1956:

. . . we were met by five incredibly delightful children who were looking for their rabbits who had gotten out of the cage. We all pursued rabbits for a while only to be told by the little girl that no one was as good as Teddy {Kennedy} for getting rabbits. Teddy is the youngest Kennedy boy and is real cute—he goes to college, I guess. Well Teddy finally arrived and went to the kitchen and did a Mexican war dance and got all the colored servants

*jumping out of their skin and then the accordion player got there and every-
one ended up doing wild dances—had to dance for your supper—even had
staid old Senator {John} McClellan doing the cha-cha-cha. They have
white rugs, a gorgeous blue wall and white draperies and white brocaded
chairs and gold screens—really plush—and at about 12 midnight Bobby
and Teddy disappeared for a while and came back with a little donkey who
walked all over but Ethel couldn't be bothered to stop dancing long enough to
worry about the donkey who also got out on the dance floor for a while. Very
very gay party, and the four little Kennedy kids stood on the steps with their
nurse and danced and did everything their mother and Teddy were doing.
Jack came later and I told him you mother were going to vote for him if he ran
for President and he was pleased to get the news. I had a nice long chat with
him—he really is a nice person. The sister Eunice was there and all the kids
are nice to each other—really fine family. I never heard of young Teddy before,
but he really is the liveliest item I've ever seen. Ethel is as pretty as Jackie, who
is Jack Kennedy's wife and Ethyl is really much more fun and friendly. Teddy
entered the party by yelling through the door at the top of his voice, which is
considerable, similar to a fog horn, "Who am I?" And this was a sign for the
4 kids to come dashing down the stairs in pajamas and climb up on him as if
he were a tree and they were all shouting "It's the one-armed giant!" Must
say I had a fine time. All day Sunday I slept and was worn out.*

It's quaint to hear Mom describing the Kennedy players and their
roles. Today, the romance and gaiety of the Kennedy age has been
stretched beyond all recognition. Sometimes the family's private
world feels like a sitcom where everyone makes a year's worth of
snappy jokes and witty comebacks in a half hour. In those years,
whole neighborhoods in Washington seemed to be having Bloody
Marys on the stone terrace in the afternoon, a cigar after dinner and
no hangovers. But through Mom's eyes I can see the kinetic, uncon-
strained excitement in the Kennedy cavalcade even four years before
he became president. Mom felt like a part of the new gang that
wasn't waiting their turn at politics. When Kennedy was asked four
years later why he thought he should be president despite his youth
he said, "Why not me? That's the answer. And I think it's enough."
That was Mom's answer too. If you were ambitious you could get the
system to move faster than it had before.

Chapter Eleven

T he cab driver couldn't understand her.

"Driver," Mom said slowly. "I would like to proceed to the Statler Hilton please."

Prow-ceed? Was this dame foreign? Did she have toffee in her mouth?

"Pardon?"

She repeated herself slowly but with irritation in her voice.

The cabbie looked in his rearview mirror.

The voice changed. "Oh honestly," Mom said, once again sounding like a girl who had spent twenty-four years in Wisconsin. "May I *please* go to the Statler Hilton?"

In the summer of 1956, the twenty-nine-year-old Nancy Hanschman was trying to strip the Wauwatosa from her voice. She had been working for CBS for two years but had no luck getting herself near a microphone. To improve her chances, she took voice lessons. Once a week for almost a year, Mom sat with a private voice teacher and read the front page of fresh wire copy into his judgmental reel-to-reel tape recorder.

"Oh I don't sound like that," she said, nervously lighting a cigarette.

"Try rounding the A a little more."

She wrote her teacher's jargon in exact block lettering on her steno pad—"phonation," "resonation," "articulation" and "tempo."

She practiced on the unsuspecting: cabdrivers, boyfriends and store clerks: They also got little lectures. "Women's voices tend to rise, you see," she would explain, "particularly under stress and pressure. It takes a special effort to keep the voice low and relaxed. A small high voice commenting on the news doesn't sound very important." She showed them how she practiced breathing.

When she got home she played Henry Higgins. She watched her mouth move in the bathroom mirror as she approximated the symbols she'd so hopefully copied down in her spiral-bound reporter's book. I can see her at the edge of the sink, concentrating, frowning, catching herself and then relaxing her face quickly to beat back any wrinkles the frown might leave.

"She was the most disciplined student I ever had," says Donald Graham, the voice coach. "From the first time she came into my studio she said, 'I am going to be on television.'"

She worked just as hard to improve her social skills. There were no social tutors she could hire in the yellow pages, so an ambitious young woman had to align herself with a Washington hostess. They were once as formidable as the monuments on the Mall. The Washington hostess reigned over candlelit evenings with senators, cabinet officials and ambassadors, and if you wanted to achieve success in town you had to find one who could be your patron—if you were on her guest list it meant you were powerful or about to be. By charming the people seated to your left and right, you would only become more so.

Power meant access. Washington can be a confusing city. The bureaucracy seems designed to baffle anyone who confronts it, and members of Congress design their offices so that staffers can keep them insulated. If you knew the right hostess or met people through her you could access her power structure. You could call on people and blow through the delays.

Perle Mesta was the most famous hostess of the modern era. Her multiple chins and messy smile proved that you didn't need to be glamorous to have clout, which in her case meant getting powerful people in her living room when she wanted them. Susan Mary Alsop and her husband, columnist Joe Alsop, entertained the Kennedys and the circle of Camelot. Katharine Graham, publisher of the *Washington Post,* held power for the longest period—from the Kennedy administration all the way through to the presidency of Bush 43.

Washington's political social life has shriveled to a dry nut under George W. Bush. A president sets the town's social rhythm. Kennedy was up all night, and Bush is in bed by nine, sober and with his wife, as he has been for the fifteen years before coming to office. The forty-third president grudgingly went to one of Katharine Graham's parties early in his first term and that was it. "He's been grumbling about it all day," his communications director Dan Bartlett told me.

Mom's first patron was Laura Gross, the owner of the exclusive F Street Club. Gross' husband had died and left her destitute. She asked her friends for help. She would turn her antebellum mansion into a club if two hundred of them would sign on immediately as members.

Congressman Keating introduced Mom to Gross, and Mom knew that she had found her tutor. Gross taught her how to seat a dinner party for the most fun (split the spouses, limit the bores), how to decorate (keep it simple) and how to get away with murder in a man's world (smile). Perhaps the best trick Mom learned from Gross was how to ask questions. I don't know what specifics she taught her, but all women in Washington society knew how to do this to one degree or another because the best way to treat a man was to let him do the thing he loved the most: talk. But to get him to say something interesting was how you kept yourself from nodding off into your soup. There's no better training for a journalist.

Gross explained that you didn't just plan a dinner party and hope it all worked out. Guests were like billiard balls you had to keep in motion. If they ever rolled to a stop, a hostess had to get them clicking against each other again. As the hostess you could pick the agenda and control it. Her rules meant no separate cabals at her parties. There were no side conversations and men could not clot in the drawing room after dinner for cigars while the women stayed out of earshot.

"You must strive to be among those present, Nancy," Gross told her. That was the phrase newspapers used before listing the attendees at an important Washington social function. Mom turned Gross' dictum into a newsgathering strategy and took that phrase as the title of her autobiography.

Fortunately, in Washington, policy and political fights are always waiting to break out. Gross would arm herself with questions and push her guests to answer them. If she tweaked the mood correctly, the table would be in an uproar midway through the appetizer course. During the 1952 presidential campaign, Gross sat Eisenhower to her right and Senator Taft to her left and held a Republican primary debate. The two men argued about taxes and drank more with each heated exchange (another of her tricks was to keep everyone pickled). After a while, no one knew what was being said, but they were angry. Everyone at the dinner had to deny the tiff had occurred when word of it leaked to the papers.

"Aunt Laura," as Mom called her, also taught her how to play the angles. When the D.C. government wouldn't give her No Parking signs for the front of the club, she arranged to steal some. Each week, she sent a car to pick up a deputy attorney general who was using one of her private dining rooms for regular lunches with his mistress. Aunt Laura told her driver that after returning the satisfied guest to the Justice Department, he should pinch two No Parking signs. He did and they remained in front of the club until it closed in 1989.

Hostesses didn't just plug you into the town's social grid and stand back. They were powerful in their own right—wry observers and practitioners who worked through and around the reigning beliefs about the capacities of women. They knew when to defy the rules, exploit them and believe in them.

Alice Roosevelt Longworth was Mom's other tutor. At their first meeting in 1953, the 69-year-old daughter of Teddy Roosevelt showed her how to wield a knife. "She told me she keeps a big knife under her bed in case burglars come in," Mom wrote home, "and that you use it this way and then she showed me—she is really something and has lovely skin."

Gross taught Mom discretion, and Longworth showed her the power of opinions. Longworth had an acid tongue and is perhaps most famous for her line, "If you don't have anything nice to say, sit next to me." No one was spared, not even her cousin Franklin. "He's 10 percent Eleanor and 9 percent mush," she said.

"Mrs. Longworth's parties are the smallest, and in the opinion of some, the most select in Washington," reads an issue of *Cosmopolitan* magazine in 1958. "The guest list is usually limited to ten or fourteen people. But the parties are known for their wit and liveliness. An invitation stamps one as an 'inner circle' success." An invitation also meant stepping on a carnival ride. Longworth once took Mom to a boxing match in downtown Washington. When they sat ringside, Longworth had them hold up white handkerchiefs, the family's signal, devised to notify other friends in the audience that they had arrived. When the bout was under way, Longworth rattled her bracelets with each blow and barked out "bully, bully," her father's favorite phrase.

At my oldest sister's coming-out party in 1967, the then eighty-six-year-old matron abandoned the adults murmuring on the patio at Merrywood and headed off to find the younger crowd. Crunching across the gravel driveway in the moonlight in her flowing Madame Chiang Kai-shek robe, she entered the gymnasium where two hundred teenagers were boogying under posters of Allen Ginsberg and Clark Gable. Soon, all the adults followed her. There are a lot of awkward unpublished pictures of dignitaries doing the frug but looking as if they're trying to close a sticky drawer.

Mom loved the idea of Longworth even if in public she was too conservative to appropriate the doyenne's high sense of flair. "One of the great cardinal sins is to be dull," Mom loved to say, parroting Longworth. Mom learned her lessons well, and expertly mixed her social life with her work at CBS. The breathless issue of *Cosmopolitan* in 1958 had the cover line "Food, Liquor, Parties and Politics" and featured six pages on mom. "Nancy Hanschman, radio-TV producer in Washington, is living testament to the fact that politicians are human, too—she charms them into appearing on her CBS shows." Mom hadn't made it on the air yet, but the story of a woman working in a man's world of power was novel enough. Those early profiles show her standing with nearly every important member on the Hill—Kennedy, Johnson, Speaker Rayburn—making a pitch for one of her shows or jotting down their comments in a small three-ringed binder.

Mom's sources started inviting her backstage into the private offices and the clubby political conversations. After Democrats rejected Eisenhower's nominee for secretary of commerce, Lewis Strauss, she stayed up until 2:30 in the morning drinking with Majority Leader Lyndon Johnson and his gloating Democratic colleague Clinton Anderson, who had a personal vendetta against the pompous nominee.

"Self-righteous, condescending and arrogant is no way to win the hearts and minds of men," said Johnson laughing. "And did you see old Barry?" he said, preparing to mimic Barry Goldwater, the Republican senator from Arizona. "Goddamn," he said, slamming his hand on the desk as Goldwater had when the vote tally came in. LBJ was particularly pleased with himself because he had only announced his opposition to Strauss that morning, along with a host of others he'd quietly corralled behind the scenes. In an instant, the president's man was sunk.

Mom ate eye-watering shrimp gumbo in Louisiana Senator Allen Ellender's private dining room, one of the coveted hideaways in the Capitol where the most powerful Senators let out their suspenders, entertained their mistresses or retired from the chamber into a boozy lunch. One day, she brought in her mother's cookies and insisted that everyone sample one. "Senator Church thought the cookies had a toffee taste without any toffee in them," she explained to her mother in a letter. She helped Senator Symington convince Johnson that the lemon frosting was worth going off his diet for.

Her letters home are full of inside little secrets. "These last few days I have been watching the Senate debate on McCarthy. It really is a sad sight. It is clear that he does not have two friends in the world: [William] Jenner and [Herman] Welker, both of whom are drunk or terribly high during most of this debate. He is awful. . . . Senator [Leverett] Saltonstall, from Boston, who was in a tough spot because of all of the Irish Catholics in his district, told me today that 'you just have to stop [McCarthy] somewhere' . . . Joe's lawyer tells me that Joe is a complete psycho case. He told me yesterday that Joe was doing everything possible to incur censure. I have presents for everyone except Bernice, Aunt Millie, and Betty Mueller and the Heinans. What should be done about them?"

Mom jumbled together Joe McCarthy and Betty Mueller from Wauwatosa. She zoomed around the city, as comfortable with the senators in the Capitol and at cocktail parties as she had been with her neighbors on Cedar Street. She was lively, eager and charming. She was so disarming, men could almost forget that she knew exactly what she was doing. At a dinner in the late 1950s thrown by Carl Marcy, her former boss at the Senate Foreign Relations Committee, each guest was asked to give one piece of advice to a new woman trying to make a career in Washington. Read the newspaper every morning, said one. Become friendly with people in both political parties, said another. Mom's advice was that any young woman should save enough money to buy a mink jacket so that she could go out at night and make enough of an impression to get noticed.

During President Clinton's impeachment trial, I spent several afternoons in Senator Edward Kennedy's hideaway. He gave a small group of reporters his off-the-record halftime views as the prosecutors laid out the case. The whole town seemed to have decided that the activities in the well of the Senate were a charade. We laughed about Strom Thurmond, the ninety-six-year-old senator from South Carolina who handed a piece of candy each day to the attractive women on the president's defense team. The House impeachment managers also provided regular chuckles. They looked like the sullen members of a lost tribe as they presented their case to the Senate that didn't want to hear it. They even seemed to speak a different language. House manager Bill McCollum pronounced the word *genitalia* as if it rhymed with *pedophilia*.

One of the last sanctuaries not overexposed by the twenty-four-hour cable channels, Kennedy's room was cluttered like a dowager's parlor. Behind the stacked books, you expected to find hidden tins of candy that had long gone stale and pieces of tarnished silver. The walls were packed with photographs of Kennedy's family. On the back wall, just above the small table where the senator took lunch, hung an oil painting of his oldest brother, Joe, the downed World War Two pilot. Had Mom been in this room? Surely she had.

It's harder to get backstage now, but occasionally I caught a glimpse of the little side dramas Mom saw so regularly. Before Clinton's impeachment trial began, the Senate looked for a fast way to vote Clinton innocent without appearing to shirk their duty. The hearings in the House had reconfirmed what everyone in Washington knew: A microscopic investigation of rushed sex in the White House diminished everyone.

In an act of self-preservation, the senators from both parties joined hands and devised a sanitary approach: They would hold a trial but not concern themselves with evaluating the specific pieces of evidence. The House impeachment managers would make their case and senators would ask questions without immediately having to call witnesses. This would avoid a prolonged examination of the president's specific sex acts.

After a unanimous vote on this arrangement, Senate Majority Leader Trent Lott went looking for Ted Kennedy. The two men had clashed over everything from raising the minimum wage to health care, but Kennedy had been the co-author of the compromise that Lott was so anxious for. I followed Lott as he entered an office off the Senate floor. Kennedy was there. Both men were drunk on consensus and their improbable flash-friendship. Lott gave Kennedy's wife a big kiss and they both celebrated the new deal and joked about what good friends they now were.

"How about some crawfish étouffée?" the Mississippian joked. Kennedy tried his best to duplicate Lott's toffee accent: "I want me a po'boy." The suggestion led to billows of stage laughter. "This is going to make the health-care bill of rights a piece of cake," said Kennedy.

"Piece of cake," said Lott. "Let's go do it now."

"Yes, and minimum wage," said Kennedy.

They broke up in a concert of chuckles. Before they went out to face the cameras both men composed themselves. Impeachment was no laughing matter.

Chapter Twelve

For six years Mom asked her bosses to let her go on the air and for six years her bosses said no. She typed up questions for the guests she'd booked on *Capitol Cloakroom* and *The Leading Question* to show that she knew the material. They said no. She dropped hints, like sitting in the chair or practicing in front of the microphone. They said no. She even got the guests she'd booked to suggest it. *Hey, why doesn't Nancy Hanschman go on the air?* Her bosses still said no.

Finally, in 1959 she took a trolley across the river and convinced Pentagon officials that they needed to do a story on the Women's Army Corps. It wasn't clear whether she was asking as the producer of the two radio shows she worked on or in some other capacity. The army "Coordination Record" of her pitch describes Mom in the official report as a "girl Friday to a number of CBS officials," and hints at how she may have convinced the Army they wanted to work with her. "She is connected with the Price subcommittee. . . . Mr. Price has asked her to give him questions re: women for the committee."

Clever. How does a woman with no power get some? She appropriates it from the powerful men—in this case Congressman Melvin Price, who oversaw the WAC program. Mom wasn't connected to the committee any more than I am, but she knew that the Army dare not turn down a friend of the man who determined their funding. So she dropped Price's name, and just so they didn't miss the point, suggested that he had somehow empowered her to help him come up with questions for a future public hearing of WAC officials. Mom wasn't threatening them exactly; she was using soft power. But they got the message: The questions they'd face later from Congressman Price would be easier if they accommodated the smiling Miss Hanschman.

Reading the memo from the Army archive, I laughed out loud. I didn't know she had it in her.

What? I imagine her saying to me with a smile, knowing she'd been busted. The ethics of the trick are a little shady because well, you're not supposed to use members of Congress for your career advancement. But after being told to run along for six years, it was a breadcrumb sin. I admire her chutzpah.

The Army generals said yes and her CBS bosses allowed her to go in part because the Army paid for her trip, certainly not something the network would allow today. But just because her bosses let her go didn't mean they trusted her. They treated her as if she'd never seen a news report before. One producer insisted that she promise to file pieces that did more than just call the WACs a "group of attractive women." She smiled, bit her tongue and headed off to the airfield. For five weeks, in the fall of 1959, she flew in drafty prop planes across Europe: Berlin, Heidelberg, Rome and Vienna, returning to the places where ten years earlier she had danced on Bastille Day, perfected her smoking and tied a scarf around her neck the way the Parisian girls did.

The Army boys loved showing her around. As they flew in a helicopter along the Berlin Wall they cut the engines, going into free fall. "It's just like a roller coaster," she gulped gamely. That she flew on a helicopter at all is a marvel. Vehicles of any sort made her sick. Even elevators were menacing. Riding a helicopter is like being at the end of a child's toy. You're up and then you're down. They're also hell on a hairdo. I rode on a lot of them while covering President Bush. If you were lucky enough to avoid the hydraulic fluid dripping from the ceiling and to keep your hearing after the exposure to the deafening motor, you then had to endure the sprint out of the chopper while the blades whirred at top speed. This provided immediate exfoliation and an updo. If you landed in a field, you picked dirt and grass clippings out of your ears for days.

The Army got what they paid for from Mom. Her radio reports on the air were glowing. She reported back to the Pentagon about her progress: "By now you may have heard from [WAC colonel] Gray and then you know I'm ready to enlist! It would do your heart good to hear all the superlatives about the WAC that I have." She included in her letter a medal blessed by the pope; she had picked it up while in Rome as a gift for the top WAC officer, a sister Catholic. She also included some scripts of her glowing reports, pointing out that she's deftly handled their most touchy issue: that men think the women will replace them. Her script from Heidelberg reads: "The one limitation on their assignment is that they do only those things that are 'physically and culturally acceptable to the American woman.' And *that's* the Army way of saying, no combat duty for women. It's not replacement of men. It's full utilization of the available woman and/or manpower." In the margin Mom writes to the director: "Note the way I handled this. You'd be interested to know that at least 4 officers, including General Eddleman, said the WACs did a better job than the men they replaced!"

Mom also covered unexpected spot news on her trip. Khrushchev was visiting Eisenhower at Camp David, and she was asked to capture the European reaction. She stopped people on the street and found enough English speakers so she could refer to "the reaction here in Vienna" with authority, though she'd only been there a day.

When Mom returned to Washington, her CBS bosses applauded her. The reports she had filed had been first-rate, they said. She had other ideas too, she said, and was ready to get into the recording booth to start working on them. Or maybe she could do some news analysis from Capitol Hill. She'd liked doing that from the streets of Europe. "We'll see, Nancy," she was told. Nothing happened. Soon after her return, they promoted one of her male colleagues instead. "I expected it as I am a female," she wrote her mother, "but I deserve it more than he does. Then too, the man I dislike so much has sort of moved up—not really but he has a bigger office so he acts like he is . . . I am going to go to NY and see if I can't work out something that would give me a little more time on the air." She flew to New York but got nowhere.

A male colleague explained that it was unfair for her to expect a promotion. CBS journalists were paid for each appearance in addition to their regular salary, so as a thirty-two-year-old unmarried woman, she would be taking money from a man who had to support his wife and children.

She was stuck. But her experience in Europe had confirmed her belief that if she could get a scoop they'd have to put her on the air. So, she picked the hardest target: Speaker of the House Sam Rayburn. The formidable Texas lawmaker hated television. He banned cameras from the House except during a few specified hours a year. He complained to his friend Lyndon Johnson that the damn things were ruining the business of politics. Plus the bright lights reflected off his bald pate and made him look like he had a star burning on his noggin. And so, to most requests he would say something like "No one has a finer command of language than the person who keeps his mouth shut," and move along.

But the seventy-eight-year-old was sweet on "Miss Nancy," as he called her. So he agreed to give her a rare and exclusive interview. If she scored such a coup, her dubious producers had said, they would put it on the air. "But Nancy," one said, "if you're interviewing the Speaker of the House please don't giggle."

She did giggle a little but not because she was flirty and chirpy. She was nervous. Rayburn was a giant. The longest-serving Speaker, he had led the Democrats for twenty of his forty-eight years in the body.

Most female television stars today start on a local station interviewing the town gardener about her prize pumpkin. Everyone needs a little time to get accustomed to the lights. No one's first televised interview is with one of the most powerful men in the country.

In my first television performance I forgot to breathe. I was twenty-five but I looked ten. Fortunately, I was on Court TV, which was a fledgling operation then, so probably about fourteen people saw me. I was talking about a prosecution in the BCCI banking case. While I knew intellectually that breathing is crucial to speaking, I couldn't do it. My answers to the questions petered out the minute I started, as if I hadn't inhaled since college. I knew what I was talking about. I just had drywall dust in my lungs. Fred Grandy, the host, had worked with Mom at CBS. "I'm sorry, John, we're running out of time," he said after I'd barely answered the second question. He looked like he wanted to give me CPR. Running out of time? It was

Court TV. They had nothing but time. They were just trying to hustle me off the set and bring on a less mumbly guest. The bum's rush must have brought me back to life because I answered his last question about political influence with gusto. "There's no political influence in my estimation in the prosecution of this case."

In my estimation? Who talks like that when they're twenty-five? Someone gasping for air, that's who. Someone should have slapped me. I don't remember what if anything Mom said about the performance.

Maybe she had been sympathetic. Her first time was balky too.

Rayburn roared into his office, nearly tripping over the thick TV cables. "What have you done to my damned office," he yelled at her. She hadn't exactly told Rayburn that it was going to be a filmed interview. He thought he was sitting down for a little chat with only a pad and paper. "Get all of this out of here."

"Oh, it won't take very long, Mr. Speaker," she pleaded.

He relented. On the tape, Rayburn looks like the character out of a Dickens novel who refuses to give orphans soup or a seat by the fire. His voice is gravelly and still tattooed with a Texas twang. He can't sit still and swivels in his leather chair like he has to go to the potty. Mom sits at the edge of his desk as close as she can get to stay in the shot but stay clear of his swing. She's dressed conservatively in a black suit and white blouse with a flower pin on her lapel.

"You're going to be terrific," she says, putting her hands on his.

"I'm going to make you a star," he grumbles into his shirt. "Well, if I'm not going to marry you, I might as well go on your program."

"She's asked me forty times to marry her," he says to the cameramen. "I won't do that but I'll do anything else for her or to her."

Anything else *to her*? Excuse me, Mr. Speaker? Mom either doesn't hear or moves on.

"Do I look pretty?" he asks.

"Yes."

"It is my greatest ambition in life to look pretty." He laughs a little to himself.

The real interview starts. It's perfectly fine. They talk about the coming legislative year, his seventy-eighth birthday and the 1960 political campaign. Rayburn seems so much more rich and textured than the men in office today, but maybe everyone looks that way in black and white. When he gives his last answer, she thanks him and then turns and looks at the camera: "Now back to Douglas Edwards in New York."

She had heard other people say those words but after practicing them herself so many times, she could barely get them out. She just couldn't believe it was happening. The tape records a few more tries before she gets that closing right.

In New York, producer Don Hewitt, who would later produce *60 Minutes*, called after the program: "We want you on every night." A *Good Housekeeping* profile of Mom recorded CBS vice president John Day's reaction: "It dawned on him, just as she'd planned it to, that Nancy was 'the answer to what to do next to spark up our coverage.'"

Chapter Thirteen

Seven months after her interview with Speaker Rayburn, Mom was working as a CBS correspondent. She was covering the 1960 convention live. There would be no redoing the endings of her pieces, no more warming up her sources before the cameras started rolling. Walter Cronkite was going to throw to her and she had to get it right on the first hit. There was no net. The Democratic Convention in Los Angeles was a riveting spectacle. Kennedy looked like he had the nomination in hand, but that wasn't a certainty. He'd won the most votes in the primaries, but segments of the party were unhappy: He was too young and too Catholic. The old Democratic bulls didn't want to gamble on a green candidate after being shut out of the White House for eight years. Powers in the party might convince the delegates to pick Lyndon Johnson or Adlai Stevenson. The party was also fighting over the civil rights plank in its platform. Would they support sit-ins and call for an end to segregation, or would they back Senator Sam Ervin, later of Watergate fame, who called for a more gradual approach to the "negro problem"?

The Kennedy team looked young and vibrant and stylish. They weren't relying on the Democratic Party bosses left over from the FDR machine. "This is the convention where the old guard may change," said Cronkite in kicking off CBS's coverage, "replaced by a young force that has no allegiances to the old guard." The old guard was trying to keep that from happening. Eleanor Roosevelt made a surprise appearance at a rally for Stevenson in her haphazard flowered dress.

Kennedy was too young and couldn't win the black vote, she insisted.

For the network news divisions, conventions were like the Super Bowl. Normally, the news took up a mere fifteen minutes a day. Only the rare bulletin would break into the variety shows and sitcoms. Or, the news was used like grout, to fill in the gaps in entertainment programming. The day Mom joined CBS, NBC's censors cited Jack Paar's *Tonight Show* for telling an off-color joke "about a water closet in a wayside chapel." To replace the gag in the middle of the taped show, producers squeezed in a little news filler.

The conventions offered the news divisions a chance to sell their product over a long stretch of time. If the estimated 93 million viewers watching the hours of convention coverage liked what they saw, they might demand a little more news or at least become devotees of that brief nightly newscast.

Weeks before the gavel sounded in Los Angeles, truckloads of network equipment rolled in for the event. The networks handed out press releases heralding their most spectacular James Bond gadgets. CBS boasted a "synch-signal-phase-shifter" that would allow them to seamlessly transfer from one remote correspondent to another without jerky movement or mistakenly intercepting the signal of another network. "Transi-talkies" allowed correspondents to report from the convention floor.

When CBS announced that Nancy Hanschman would be part of their convention news team, newspapers didn't focus on her professional efforts. The *New York Times* ran a piece devoted to her wardrobe and how she planned on keeping her Dior dress from being ruined by the crush of two conventions. "Her clothes are simply cut, mostly with eased skirts," said the piece. Mom explains why: "I spend my life getting in and out of sound trucks and taxis." The *Milwaukee Sentinel* ran a story on her hairdo.

Local television guides ran cover photos of Mom and anchor Douglas Edwards standing in a field of pastel-colored telephones. At the 1956 convention all the phones had been black, so it was impossible to know whether you were picking up a call from the control room, a colleague outside or a competitor. A few CBS correspondents had picked up the NBC handset and shouted emergency instructions to confused rivals.

Phones are as important to journalists as keyboards. In Mom's day, reporters kept little mental notes dedicated to the locations of the nearest phones. White House wire reporters tried to knock each other down as they ran to the line to call in a bulletin. Merriman Smith of the Associated Press was accused of doing just that to call in the bulletin that JFK had been shot. Now, the minute news breaks journalists press ever-smaller cell phones against their ears like ice packs against an ache.

Papers also ran pictures of Mom and Charles Collingwood modeling the cumbersome transi-talkies: two overnight-bag sized packs accompanied by a footlong antenna to be worn on the shoulder. The wife of a CBS sound engineer was so startled that Mom would have to wear the piercing epaulette, she tried to make a little hat for the whatsit. It was no improvement. The hat made Mom look like a Martian with mouse ears. She was smart enough to leave it on the dressing room table.

As the cameras focused on the brass bands, platform fights and movie stars in the hall, the CBS news team spent the first two days of the convention trying to get an accurate delegate count. It looked like Kennedy was going to win but no one was certain. "The old pro Lyndon Johnson isn't going to fade away," reported Edward R. Murrow. "The delegates are laden down with rumors about who it might be."

Mom idolized Murrow. The famous war correspondent with the hangdog look always reminded me of Humphrey Bogart. (They were two black-and-white men with slicked-back hair who smoked expertly. They both had a kind of symmetry in our home. When Bogart appeared on television, Dad, who had acted briefly in Hollywood, would make sure we paid attention. Mom would do the same thing when an old Murrow clip aired.) Murrow was the most famous of the CBS cast and he set the moral tone. Everyone wanted to be one of Murrow's boys, even those who hadn't worked with him in Europe during the war. Eric Sevareid and Howard K. Smith had. They were his legitimate soulmates at CBS, gruff radio veterans with exacting standards. They clashed with their television bosses, complaining that the network was trying to turn journalism into entertainment.

When Mom was named Murrow's communications assistant in 1956, he yelled, "What the hell's a communications assistant?"

"That's me," she piped up.

"Oh."

It wasn't a promising introduction, but it was a start. She'd endure Murrow's gruffness if it meant getting his approval. So she copied his every move. When she was hired as a correspondent, she sought his instruction.

She should keep her reports simple and full of news, Murrow told her. "Don't tell them everything you know," he said. "Just tell them the one thing you want them to know and tell it straight so they understand. It's not necessary to establish your wide knowledge." Fifty-one percent of a report is about the substance, he told her, but the other 49 percent is how you say it. The unreasonable demands of the CBS overlords was a common theme of their chats. The day of the highly compensated news star was a long way off. Advising Mom on her contract with CBS, Murrow wrote to her, "It is a scandal and an outrage—it is, in fact, slavery. You are sold down the river for two years, but you can be put ashore with thirty days' notice. . . . Having said this, I must tell you that it is the standard CBS contract."

He had guidance for life outside the newsroom too. "At cocktail parties, stop rushing around. Stay in one place and let people come to you." No detail was too small for a man who paid $150 for his hand-made shirts, though he spent money to look classic, not flamboyant. "Dress conservatively, Nancy," he told her. "You are attractive and you don't want them thinking you're some sexy Madonna." He even advised her to get shoes that made her feet look smaller. His message was that to be good you had to be inconspicuous and not flashy. It's a simple transaction: Go get the news and tell people. Don't let a lot of frills get in the way.

She practiced Murrow's rules as diligently as she had her voice lessons. If she just followed his paces, she'd get there. She was so diligent, she might have slicked back her hair and switched to smoking Camels, his brand. As a writer would later put it in *Good Housekeeping*: "She has a strange case of hero worship for her fellow CBS news men—Eric Sevareid, Edward R. Murrow—whom she considers 'the really elite kind of newsmen, the best in the business.'"

Murrow meant legitimacy. If he endorsed her, it would mean she was a pro, not an ornament.

Mom was so fond of Murrow that she took on his crusade against Joseph McCarthy long after the Wisconsin senator was out of office. In 1965 she returned to Wauwatosa to give a commencement speech devoted entirely to the evils and dangers of McCarthyism. She wound up stirring the audience of parents, some of whom had voted enthusiastically for old Joe. "After the ceremony, one of the fathers came storming over to Nancy and became very, very threatening," remembers Timothy Heinan, her cousin. "She stood her ground, even though she told me later, 'I thought he was going to hit me.' I thought he was too, so I stepped between the two of them, told Nancy that we had to go, and escorted her out of the school gym."

CBS's Eric Sevareid was also a friend. He had become London bureau chief by the 1960 convention, but he kept up his guidance from across the ocean. "I can't tell you how pleased I am with your success as a reporter; of course it's bloody hard work and they are probably taking every advantage of you in terms of promotion. If you can bear up under it, let them—for a time yet. Then, when you are solid in your position and an unquestioned asset to the company start fending them off."

More than career advice, what Mom cherished about Sevareid's notes was that he talked about politics with her as he would with an equal. "My God, does America and particularly Ike look pathetic these days to Europeans" he wrote. "The whole hollow facade of show-window presidency had to crack one day and now it has. You know of course that Ike has never been *real*. It's been a mannequin show done with visible wires; I always hoped that the American people would be the first to yell 'fake,' not the Russians or the Japs, and ask for their money back."

The electorate looked at the 1960 conventions not just for political theater but for clues about which new leader would guide them out of troubling times. The contentment Americans felt during the first half of Ike's term had disappeared. Riots in Little Rock, Arkansas, over desegregation of the public schools had deepened the country's divide over civil rights. The Russians seemed to be winning the Cold War. They had launched Sputnik, the first unmanned satellite, and tested several hydrogen bombs. Critics claimed Eisenhower had allowed a "missile gap" to open, and Nikita Khruschev was emboldened to boast that the Soviet Union would "bury" the United States. When an American U-2 plane was shot down over Russia, Eisenhower denied its existence until the Soviets embarrassed him by parading the pilot Francis Gary Powers before the cameras.

Mom carted her space pack transi-talkie up and down the convention floor. She'd lost the timidity of her first Rayburn interview. She'd gotten the job she always wanted and marched through the crowd propelled by fear and adrenaline. Now she had to prove she was more durable than the gimmicks she carried on her back.

Delegates jostled and churned, trading gossip and rumors. To get on the air she had to find someone newsworthy in all the suits and smoke. At the moment that meant anyone from the Kennedy operation who could give her an update on the candidate or his chances in the backroom balloting. If she found someone, she was to wave a flashlight and the cameras would find her.

It was like hunting for a lost child at Disneyland—hope spiked with each new face that walked by and then dashed just as quickly as she realized it was just any old delegate. She saw Ted Kennedy, the senator's younger brother, and nearly tackled him. She held his arm to keep him from escaping and waved a flashlight to the control room in the rafters. The camera light didn't come on in response. She waved faster. A director with binoculars spotted her signal and pointed the camera at the frantic flashlight hundreds of feet away.

Cronkite, holding a bath soap–sized device to his ear, heard Nancy was ready and gave the cue: "And now to Nancy Hanschman." The cameras cut to her. She didn't know it.

"What!" she shouted into her microphone as viewers watched her make fatigued loops of the flashlight.

"You're on, Nance," came back a loud voice.

"Oh." She hauled Kennedy into the shot, becoming the first network newswoman to broadcast from the floor of a convention.

"Mr. Kennedy, how is your brother taking all of this?" she asked about the wait for the delegate count.

Kennedy didn't have much to say, particularly about the crucial Pennsylvania delegation, which everyone was focusing on that day.

Would party bosses throw all of the state's eighty-one votes to Kennedy or Stevenson for maximum political effect, or would they let their members vote their conscience? The latter would probably split the tally between the two men, leave the nomination unresolved and squander any chance of putting the nominee in their debt.

Forty-five years later, I watched the interview in a dark booth in the Museum of Television and Radio while vacationers at other stations watched reruns of *The Love Boat* and *Hogan's Heroes.* I had never seen this footage and stared at the screen the way my son stares at the magician at birthday parties. Seeing a young version of Mom took a moment to get used to, but it was her behavior that had me riveted. It was authentic and engaging and without artifice. It was so fresh-faced I was nervous for her, hoping she'd get the question out and make some news. Our relationship had flipped. I was the nervous parent hoping she could make it through. When the Kennedy interview ended, I smiled. I was proud of her.

The convention attendees were not television savvy. Jocular men in hats walked in front of her and Kennedy. I wanted to swat them. "Hello Bill," said one rube in high-water pants. They were thinking: Who is this dame with all the equipment anyway? Is that a toaster oven she's carrying on her back? Maybe she is with Betty Furness, that lovely Westinghouse gal.

Westinghouse sponsored the CBS coverage and every fifteen minutes or so Cronkite would pitch to Furness the way he would one of his correspondents. "Thank you, Walter," the actress would say before gliding in her ball gown to demonstrate the new Gold Medallion Total Electric Home. She was a beacon of domestic bliss and tranquility. Her weightless voice made talk of keeping vegetables "crisp, comfortable and dewy fresh" in the Westinghouse center-drawer refrigerator seem like the solution to life's every last problem. She plugged the timely "people's choice" appliance sale and the "convention special Laundromat." Viewers who acted fast could get a galvanized ice tray—a $1.29 value.

The other young dames on the convention floor wore pretty costumes. Hundreds of Golden Girls had been hired by the Democrats as "walking information booths." As delegates arrived they were greeted by a line of girls in bikinis advertising a local restaurant.

Edwin Newman's color piece about events outside the coliseum was punctuated by catcalls responding to the shapely ladies.

Mom bristled at how silly she looked with her wires and packs but secretly she loved the contraption. Unlike the women reporters at the other networks, she wasn't being paid to just smile and do endless stories about the wives of the candidates. She was interviewing newsmakers. Not everyone saw that distinction. "The chains are not overlooking the importance of the distaff touch," wrote Jack Gould in the *New York Times* of the networks' coverage of the event. "CBS is starring Nancy Hanschman, but is making the ridiculous mistake of cluttering up her attractive figure with a great deal of portable equipment."

When Mom waded into the folding chairs of the Texas delegation to interview House Speaker Sam Rayburn, the Democratic leader didn't stand up. She didn't care. She just stooped over and let the packs of equipment swing to her sides like saddlebags. (Viewers did care. They wrote to Rayburn scolding him for not standing in the presence of a lady.) There weren't a lot of fancy multiple shots in television back then so you went with what you got, which in this case was an entire interview where viewers could only see the back of Rayburn's bald head. He was irritated. No one was rallying around his man Lyndon Johnson. Rayburn was one of the most powerful men in the party, and he was not in the cabal making the decisions. "If there are any smoke-filled rooms, I wouldn't mind being in them," he grumbled. The old guard was changing.

Smoke-filled rooms were real back then. Delegates met to hammer out which candidate should get the nomination. At one point in the convention footage, a CBS correspondent pointed to the door of an actual smoke-filled room. The static picture didn't make great television—directors preferred the gliding hats and jostling signs. But suddenly the door opened and the Pennsylvania delegate apportionment was handed out on a slip of paper. The correspondent read the tally quickly. Kennedy had sealed the nomination. If you hadn't been watching you'd have missed it. There was no replay.

Chapter Fourteen

O n the third night of the convention, Lyndon Johnson was sulk-ing in his hotel room. Senator Kennedy had won the nomination and the two dozen reporters camped in the hallway outside Johnson's room waited for his reaction. Mom was among them, smoking Winstons and trying to figure out a way to get an exclusive with the majority leader. In her earpiece, the CBS control kept asking for an update. They didn't want NBC to hear from Johnson first. She lit another Winston.

She knew Johnson from her ten years on the Hill. He and Lady Bird had thrown a party for her in his private office when CBS finally hired her to go on air. They'd served burgers in the shape of Texas and presented her with an enormous cake that read "All eyes are on Nancy," below a CBS eye logo. Now, at this important moment she was expected to turn that friendship into a scoop.

Mom buzzed through the Biltmore to find someone who could give her an update on Johnson's thinking or a tip on whether Kennedy had decided on a vice presidential nominee. The Democratic party had set up headquarters there, and so had every major candidate (Kennedy, Johnson, Stevenson and Symington). Kennedy girls milled through the lobby in their red, white and blue striped dresses pressing badges on anyone who stood still. Johnson girls offered taffy from Austin, Texas. Delegates from Puerto Rico played steel drums. Hawaiians rustled in native dress. In the press "bowl," hundreds of correspondents set up their typewriters and trolled through the lounges.

Johnson was furious about Kennedy's victory. Though the Texan had lost the primaries coming into the convention, he thought he might have a backroom chance to snatch the nomination. Delegates would come to their senses and realize that the Kennedy boy was just too green and could never win. A year earlier, everybody had thought Johnson would be the one to go against Nixon and now it had all fallen apart. He wasn't giving any damn press conferences, and he wasn't going to talk to Nancy or anyone else and answer a lot of fool questions about rumors that Kennedy might ask him to join the ticket.

In the anchor booth, Walter Cronkite tried to fill the airtime while everyone waited for Mom to report Johnson's official reaction. "We had expected Senator Johnson to come out and make a statement," Cronkite said. "We had been told he would join us. . . . We understand now that there has been a change of plans . . . We understand that the Senator has issued a statement instead—that he has . . . uh . . . put on his pajamas, gone to bed, and we switch now to Nancy Hanschman, who is covering him."

The men in the control room broke up. When the picture switched to her, Mom was not astride the vanquished candidate but breathlessly reading a two-sentence statement from Johnson congratulating his colleague Senator Kennedy in as few words as possible. Later, Mom learned Johnson amused his Texas friends with the story of Cronkite's introduction.

It stung. The inadvertently bawdy introduction revived the snickering about Mom and President Johnson. Rumors were already circulating that they were having an affair. "A few of the redneck cameramen used to talk a lot about how Johnson was in her pants," says Sandy Sokolow, Cronkite's producer at that convention. The slurs undermined her reputation for competency. Was she on that assignment because she was a good journalist or because Johnson liked her legs? She could work harder, and stay longer, than the men to get past the usual obstacles, but how do you beat back the rumors? How do you beat back an anecdote you'd tell yourself if it weren't about you? Do you stay home? Being close to Johnson was one of the best things she had going.

The boys snickered because Mom was breaking into their clubhouse. Yes, there had been girls around the office, but they were secretaries. "She was a freak," said Sokolow. "Females were strange in this business. We didn't know what to do with her."

Mom wasn't quite sure what to do either. Four months after signing her contract as a correspondent, she was hearing more of the snide jokes and snickering: She was pushy and irritating, and if she hadn't been so pretty she never would have gotten on the air. Even her triumphs were turned against her. To get a platform high enough to film Senator Humphrey at a West Virginia rally, she'd convinced a farmer to lend his tractor. What did she have to do in the barn to get that tractor, joked one toothy soundman?

"Nancy, do you think we should do a two shot?" a cameraman would ask.

"Do you think? I suppose we could," she would answer, thinking he was using the term for a shot that includes two people.

"Oh yes, Nancy, we definitely need a two shot," another cameraman would chime in.

"Okay, whatever you think is best."

The boys would snicker and giggle. For cameramen shooting a lone woman, a "two shot" meant a shot of her breasts.

Later Mom would ask: "Why aren't we doing the two shot?" The camera men would renew their laugh. Because she was serious and took them seriously and wanted to do it right, she'd keep asking about the two shot and prompting more snickers.

In public, Mom tried to have it both ways. She wanted a man to offer her his arm but also wanted to be known as tough enough to throw elbows herself. "I try to wear things that are feminine," she told one reporter, "so that I stand out." But Mom was doing more than just standing out. "Your Mom attracted men, which made it fun to be around her," says Pat McCarrick. "She didn't misuse it, but she used it." In one 1960 story, Mom admitted, "I'd have to be dead not to like all these men around."

But in a different profile during the same period, she got irritated when a reporter suggested femininity and not her news credentials might affect how the boys in the newsroom receive her. "I have no doubts about my reception. I've worked in Washington for years and I know all the politicians and newsmen."

In a *TV Guide* profile not long after she had waited all evening for Johnson to make his statement on Kennedy's nomination, she laughed at the male reporters who waited with her. "Jane Scholl of *Life* magazine and I were covering Senator Johnson at the convention . . . We'd been waiting in the hall for hours and hours. The Senator came out. He felt sorry for us. He invited Jane and me into his suite. We were able to rest in there and watch TV while we waited. At which point, the men raised a rumpus. They made all kinds of objections and complaints. They argued it was gross discrimination, etc., etc. The Senator came out and explained, 'But it's just two girls *resting!*' What a fuss! We weren't even in the same room with him!"

She couldn't make the case to *TV Guide* or any of her colleagues that having a little advantage by sitting in Johnson's anteroom was the only upside to the rumors of her affairs with him or the jokes about "covering him" in his pajamas or a fair balance to all those interviews the men got while Johnson was in the bathroom or dressing room. The boys weren't going to be convinced. They were competing with her and what they saw was hypocrisy: She wanted to be treated seriously like a man but also wanted the comfortable parlor seat due the lady. She couldn't have it both ways.

Mom was the first woman television correspondent for CBS News, but Pauline Frederick was the very first woman of television news. She had suffered the indignities. Her first assignment was a forum on "How to Get a Husband." Next: a market rush on nylon hosiery. She would become a specialist on the United Nations.

An article about the two of them described Frederick as "pleasant looking." That faint praise says it all: Frederick was hired for her "award-winning" talent, not her looks or glamour. All of Mom's profiles from the period led with her green eyes and have headlines like "A Correspondent Who Could Be a Fashion Model," and "TV's Prettiest Reporter." That bugged her.

"Listen, I don't just put on a nice dress and smile," she told one reporter at the time. "I work like the devil and I wish you wouldn't make it seem like all a person has to do is be pretty."

Some profilers listened, conveying the sentiment with a hint of Mom's sternness: "Miss Hanschman would prefer to be admired for the quality of her journalism rather than for her looks or for the fact that she is a woman working in a predominantly masculine profession."

Little has changed. NBC's Campbell Brown and I became friends while covering George W. Bush during the 2000 campaign. She's a natural reporter and excellent company, and I resisted telling her she reminded me of my mother for fear she would get a restraining order or have me put into therapy. Even forty years after Mom was on the air, Campbell has faced the same gender categorizing Mom did. She covered the Bush White House and anchored the nightly news, traveling from war-torn Iraq to the Palestinian territories, but as the weekend anchor of the *Today* show all those hard-news accomplishments are a disadvantage. In her early-morning spot, the largely female demographic wants a softer image, whatever that is. When she so ably covered the devastation of Hurricane Katrina she was praised as much for still looking sympathetic, soft and feminine as she was for the quality of her reporting.

Mom put up with the snickering because she was following Aunt Laura's advice: She was among those present. Even bickering with the guys in the Biltmore lobby meant she was in the mix.

After reading Johnson's statement on the night of Kennedy's nomination, Mom had a new worry. Like all of her colleagues, she was sent to find out whom Kennedy would ask to join the ticket. Today candidates arrive at conventions arm in arm with their running mates. In 1960, Kennedy's choice for number two was a mystery right up to the announcement. He'd told some it would be Senator Stuart Symington. Bobby Kennedy had told Minnesota governor Orville Freeman the job would be his. Everyone thought they knew one thing for sure: Kennedy wouldn't pick Johnson. Kennedy needed someone who could bring in votes, but the powerful majority leader was just the wrong fit. The two didn't get along and the fifty-one-year-old Texan might make the forty-three-year-old one-term senator look slight by comparison. Plus, Kennedy wasn't sure that a dominating personality like Johnson would be willing to take direction from someone who had deprived him of the presidency, especially someone Johnson viewed as less qualified for the job.

But the rumors about Johnson persisted. Mom ran into Mary Margaret Valenti, the wife of Johnson's close aide Jack Valenti, who had also worked for the majority leader. She had sat quietly in the hotel suite while the men came and went. The Kennedy camp itself barely knew who Kennedy was going to pick. Johnson was even more in the dark. Mom's disjointed notes from the conversation give a sense of the mayhem. "Rayburn called and said: 'I hope you won't take it.' . . . Symington's going to get the V.P., there's a deal . . . John Connally came in and said there was talk in the hall about an offer [to LBJ] . . . [Senator] Bob Kerr: 'there's a bullet to your head if you do and a bullet if you don't' . . . so confusing."

For weeks, Mom had been reporting that Johnson had no interest in the idea. "I wouldn't want to trade a vote for a gavel," he said repeatedly, "and I certainly wouldn't want to trade the active position of leadership in the greatest deliberative body in the world for the part-time job of presiding." She had asked him if he'd take the spot as recently as two days before, when he arrived at the convention. Wouldn't he consider the spot? "Not ever?" she asked. "No, no, never," he said. Then Kennedy won, and Johnson said yes.

Mom got the first interview after Johnson joined the ticket, and she knew what her first question had to be: "Senator Johnson, you said you wouldn't take the position as vice president." "That's right. I said I wouldn't *seek* it," Johnson said in the mock earnestness that signaled a waffle, "but I'm indeed honored to *run* as the vice presidential nominee." In her autobiography Mom wrote, "I wanted to throttle him."

Mom worried that Johnson had taken advantage of her. Did their close relationship and the access he'd given her make her soft and too believing? She worried that she'd missed something and he'd played her for the willing dupe.

Since everyone else was shocked by Johnson's move, Mom's bosses didn't criticize her for reporting his initial dismissal of the idea. In fact, they were thrilled that their reporter was so close to the man. And maybe because she didn't throttle him on camera, maybe because of her charm, he continued to give her the access he gave no one else. She scored a crucial interview at the end of the convention, talking to Johnson and his wife in their bedroom at the Biltmore, the only room big enough to accommodate the cameras. The interview went so well that when she finished, the CBS producers asked her to rush to the anchor booth to join Cronkite and

Murrow at the anchor's desk, the first time a woman had been allowed at the adult's table during a convention. As she walked in through the executives, colleagues and technicians to take her place, Murrow stood up, bowed off camera and said, "God-damn good news reporting, ma'am."

Chapter Fifteen

After the convention, CBS kept Mom on the Johnson campaign plane. She filed for the nightly news and CBS radio as she had during the primaries. The one new thing she brought with her for the general election was a flashy new brooch of emeralds, diamonds and sapphires. She had bought it for herself with the bonus they'd given her after the convention. She would wear it in nearly every broadcast for the rest of her life, not always to universal acclaim. The piece looks like a pricy peanut cluster, and a group of women from a Pennsylvania retirement community wrote in once to complain that it so irritated them that they taped a piece of scrap paper over the screen when she was on to obscure the jewels.

She traveled on the "LBJ Victory Special," as the vice presidential candidate's plane was called, and then on a whistle-stop train tour through eight Southern states. Kennedy had picked LBJ to hold the South. Traditionally a Democratic stronghold, it would be contested in the '60 election. Some members of the party hierarchy in states like Florida had already announced that they would not campaign with Kennedy. He was too liberal. Johnson was to go out and change their minds. He was also supposed to help build support with the Southern Protestants nervous about putting a Catholic in the White House.

These days, vice presidential candidates starve to be as relevant as Johnson on the campaign trail. They're dispatched to massage party functionaries in safe states until they're hauled out to play the attack dog against the top of the other ticket. They are asked to say the harshest things about the opposition in part because their popularity is expendable. Even if they go a little overboard, people won't penalize the ticket because they make their vote based on the top man, not his second.

Johnson had mixed views about his assignment. On the one hand, it was an honor. Kennedy was asking him to deliver a region crucial to his victory. Johnson had big dreams for Texas and the South. If he could keep them in the Democratic Party by stitching them together with Kennedy's Northern liberal and labor support, he would upgrade the region's political standing. The South would then be responsible for putting someone in the White House and would also have a patron in the vice president's office.

But Johnson, who was always uneasy about Kennedy and his family's motivations, saw prejudice in the assignment too. He considered himself a national force, but he thought they didn't. He knew that liberals and labor wondered why Kennedy had put a man on the ticket who had voted against everything they stood for. He thought the Kennedys didn't want him to stump in the North because they looked down on his accent and preacher's style. He knew Kennedy called him the "riverboat gambler." They had assigned the hayseed to pick up the hayseed vote.

After the nominating convention, Johnson figured out a way to show he could deliver politically. The Senators were in Washington for a special summer session of Congress, and it was driving Kennedy mad. His opponent, Vice President Nixon, was already much better known and was crossing the country shaking hands and attacking the young liberal Massachusetts senator while Kennedy was stuck in the Capitol answering roll call votes. To show that the time wasn't being wasted, Johnson arranged a lunch for him with old Democratic bulls. Kennedy had not been an inside player with the establishment leaders in the Senate and Johnson, the majority leader, was offering instant admission to their inner circle. If Kennedy could make the sale at lunch, thought Johnson, he might woo powerful forces in the Southern states the candidate needed so badly.

Kennedy wasn't thrilled about the lunch because he and his strategists saw the country differently than Johnson. Kennedy had been successful playing the outside game in the Senate and making a national name for himself. He and his campaign advisors didn't believe it was necessary to court people who might be powerful in Washington, but who lacked real power in their states. After all, the Washington Democrats had backed Johnson for the nomination and it hadn't worked.

Johnson invited Mom to the lunch to lower the tension. She was the only member of the press there, but she hadn't been invited for her professional talents. She was a warming influence meant to put everyone at ease. She knew Jack, and perhaps Johnson knew that his new partner liked to be in the company of pretty women as well, the way a thoughtful host might serve an honored guest his favorite wine.

The lunch was held in the hideaway of Senator Allen J. Ellender of Louisiana, where Mom had once handed out her mother's cookies. When she walked in, the room was warm and fragrant with the gumbo bubbling on the low stove. Georgia Senator Richard Russell, Harry Byrd of Virginia and John Stennis of Mississippi sat in deep Victorian sofas as if they'd been there since Appomattox.

As they waited for the nominee, the old men of the club grumbled. They were astonished that "the boy," as they called him, had won the nomination. They were pretty sure he was going to lose to Nixon. They were on the alert for signs of haughtiness from Kennedy. Since he had won the nomination without them, they imagined he already assumed that when he won the presidency, he would be their leader and have more to say about the nation's affairs than they would.

Kennedy arrived late, looking like he had barged into the wrong room. When the door closed behind him, he didn't settle down. He held on to the sheaf of papers under his arm as if he'd be leaving shortly or, worse yet, like he might review them while the others talked. He shook hands with each of them, all of them older, and addressed them formally with "Hello, Senator," to which each replied, "Hello, Jack."

As Mom described the scene in her notes, it was as if Kennedy was uncomfortable being chaperoned by Johnson. He didn't want admission to the club LBJ was trying to grant him.

The men talked a lot about the food. Ellender, who was known as "Chef Supreme," took considerable pride in his cooking. Everyone took several helpings of the okra, oyster and shrimp tail gumbo, a version of which is still served in the Senate. Kennedy just picked at his plate—not good enough for the Northerner, thought Ellender. The conversation never got rolling. Kennedy was vague about campaign strategy, and he kept calling them all "Senator." They all kept calling him "Jack."

To top it off, Kennedy left before anyone else, which gave them all a preview of the role he had in store for them during the campaign—which is to say no role at all.

The lunch was by any measure a failure, but Johnson kept trying even after his guest of honor had left. "See, I told you he really was a nice boy," he told his old friends. Mom wasn't sure what had happened and why Jack seemed so uncomfortable. This was perhaps because she was closer to Johnson than Kennedy and didn't understand the nominee's feeling about the men in the room. The Senate that Mom and Johnson loved was dramatic and compelling but it was also corrupt. Its largest personalities, whom Johnson had invited to lunch, cut deals and courted campaign contributions to ensure their political futures. Kennedy hated that. He would cut his own deals to win the presidency, but that didn't change his feelings about the low acts of the senatorial class.

After the special session ended on September 1, Mom was back on the road with Johnson. The campaign trail was as intimate as that lunch in Ellender's hideaway. The press packed into the little prop plane with Johnson and his aides. They had constant access to the candidate, which was great, but sometimes Johnson wouldn't stop talking. He'd argue with reporters for hours. He had a full dose of the politician's disease—he had to hunt down and convince the one person in the room who might disagree. They knew not to engage him too much before deadline, or they'd never file their stories.

In a CBS special prime-time program on the campaign in October, Mom sat with Walter Cronkite in the CBS newsroom. George Herman, who covered Nixon's running mate, United Nations ambassador Henry Cabot Lodge, describes the campaign as a leisurely, "gentlemanly" affair with an early knock-off time and a nap each day.

Mom's description of Johnson is just the opposite. "Senator Johnson doesn't know what a nap is," she says. "He's always been full of energy but on this campaign he's been going day after day hour after hour. He loves to campaign. If he's got a responsive audience he'll just keep on going until his wife puts a note in front of him and tells him he's spoken too long."

Johnson was fun and unpredictable. Early one Sunday morning, the candidate joked at a press conference in Pierre, South Dakota, that he hadn't gotten enough sleep. He bragged, with a wink, that there had been a vigorous interruption in the night. If the reporters didn't believe him, they could ask Lady Bird. The senator's wife looked over the crowd as if she hadn't heard him. Politicians campaigning in the post-Clinton era are not allowed to have had sex ever, let alone talk about it.

Johnson flew on a four-engine Electra which had been refitted with desks and extra-wide chairs to accommodate the campaign. Electras had crashed in the past due to weak struts under the wings and Johnson, knowing Mom's skittishness about flying, made a point of calling her to assure her that the plane had been reconditioned and was safe.

Campaign planes make members of the press nervous. Campaigns are always short on cash. The campaign managers who sign the charter contracts don't have to worry what that liquid is dripping onto the seats because they're sitting comfortably back at headquarters. The candidate, who is the only one who could demand a different plane, is too busy to worry too much about its safety. So particularly in primary season, reporters fly on dodgy planes operated by second-rate pilots who work out their anger issues by punishing the landing gear. Every time the plane lands it feels as if the wheels are going to spear through the fuselage.

None of the commercial airline safety rules really apply on the charters. People stand and walk around during takeoff and landing and leave their pagers and cell phones on at all times. Usually you can keep a phone conversation going anywhere below 8,000 feet. This makes the anxious half of the press corps very nervous. While the other half talks on their cell phones long after the repeated warnings to turn them off, they give their colleagues dirty looks, certain that the plane's instruments are spinning like slot machine dials. Once, during the Dole campaign, the impish CNN correspondent Gene Reynolds stood up during a particularly rocky approach and waved his open cell phone: "Let's all get on our cell phones and see where we land." I wasn't sure whether it was Gene's comment or the lightning, but half the plane looked green. The landing was so fast, unexpected and frightening I felt like a bomber pilot in one of those World War II movies: "Mayday. Mayday, we're going down. Tell Janie I love her."

Johnson ran his vice presidential campaign with the flair of an emperor. He jetted off whenever he wanted, sometimes changing his destination in midair. Often Mom's expense reports would include receipts for items of clothing she would have to buy to keep up with his changes in schedule, usually boots and a hat for unexpected ranch visits.

Johnson would invite his whole entourage, including the press corps, to the ranch on a whim. In Kansas City for the afternoon he informed everyone they were spending the weekend in the Texas hill country. Once from Austin, he called Lady Bird to warn her that he was arriving in an hour with nine reporters for a weekend. She learned to keep the beds made and the refrigerator stocked with steak and venison.

Mom was at the ranch for the famous Kennedy-Nixon debates. Lady Bird had cooked dinner for the assembled group and they planned to watch it on television. It would be voters' first real opportunity to see their candidates in competition. But Austin was an hour behind the East Coast networks and Johnson couldn't wait for the television delay. So they listened to the debate on the radio in the living room. Johnson wasn't shy scoring in front of the press. "One for Nixon," he would say after an exchange. "One for the boy," he would say when his running mate triumphed. In Mom's memory, the boy seemed to come out behind in Johnson's tally.

Johnson's aides had the predictable reaction to working for such an imperial force. When Mom asked Bill Moyers if he had a copy of the Bible to help her remember a passage LBJ mentioned on the stump, he pointed to LBJ and said, "Why would we when we have Himself?"

I also spent some time with a vice presidential candidate when I covered my first campaign in 1996, but I got Jack Kemp. Bob Dole had picked the former New York congressman to enliven his moribund campaign. Kemp had been a quarterback for the Buffalo Bills and was full of energy and ideas. At the front of the cabin was a black-and-white framed picture of him leaping and throwing a pass at the same time.

But Kemp was told to keep quiet and on message. To make sure that he made no news, the press was kept miles away from him. Even on his campaign plane he rarely wandered back to chat with us. Dole and his campaign strategists didn't trust Kemp. He was liable to say anything, particularly about supply-side economics, a quasi-religious economic theory that held, among other things, that budget deficits could be erased with enormous tax cuts. As a budget hawk, Dole had opposed this reasoning his whole career, but Kemp was evangelical about it. He could talk at length, swinging his arms as he proselytized about "dynamic scoring"—an accounting trick that magically turns a tax cut into a rapid increase in federal revenue.

But Kemp wasn't going to talk to us about these things. It got so bad that we taunted the candidate from the back of the plane with an orange, reviving an old bored reporter's campaign trick. We'd write messages on an orange and when the plane started to lift off we'd roll it to the front of the plane. The trick was to roll it in such a way that the momentum of the orange and the momentum of the plane would cancel each other out, causing the orange to stop for a second next to the candidate before rolling back down the aisle.

Usually Kemp would ignore the fruit, though sometimes he wouldn't. "Was last night a touchdown or a field goal?"—we wrote about the vice presidential debate in which Al Gore trounced him. Kemp scrawled his answer with a thick magic marker and rolled it back down to the waiting press corps. The reply read: "Touchdown—with a two-point conversion." The inevitable sports humor.

One day a camera guy found a watermelon. I wrote: "An orange after dynamic scoring." Kemp's reply? "We're all supply-siders now!" right next to a drawing of the notorious Laffer curve, which purports to show the relationship between taxation and revenue. This is what covering a vice presidential candidate reduces you to these days: fruit games.

Mom's first campaign seemed impossibly exciting. As powerful as

Johnson was as a politician, he continued to feel nervous about Kennedy. He felt shut out of the campaign strategy. And though Johnson thought he was the better man, he was in awe of the adulation Kennedy commanded. He liked seeing Mom on the plane when he was feeling mopey. "Nancy, you know the Kennedys," he said one day on the campaign trail, "will you tell them what a good job I'm doing? Or at least will you tell them how hard I'm trying?"

Candidates would never show a reporter such neediness these days. But then Johnson was doing more than just soothing his battered psyche. He was giving Mom the famous Johnson treatment. He worked the press in a number of ways. With men, he offered bargains. Do right by me, and I'll take care of you. He once bragged to one of Mom's colleagues that he knew CBS chairman Frank Stanton. The message was clear. If the reporter treated Johnson well, it would be good for his career. If he didn't, he would be cut off, and Johnson would have a talk with his boss.

With women, Johnson confided and pleaded. He "needed her," he told Mom, to get the message to the Kennedys. He also needed a tender and sympathetic ear. He wanted to be mothered. "He could make it sound as if he were incapable of running the world without your specific presence," she wrote.

Bonnie Angelo, who also covered Johnson, recognized another part of his personality in his public attention to Mom. "He would have seen it as a triumph over Kennedy to show that he had ownership over her," she says. Kennedy thought he knew reporters and he knew women. Johnson could show he knew about those things too.

The closer Mom got to LBJ, the more the rumors about a romance between them grew. One night in Chicago, the candidate tried to make them a reality. It had been a long, exhausting day on the campaign trail and Johnson had had a few drinks. They were staying at the airport motel and he wandered into her room in his pajamas. Mom had curlers in her hair. He made the pitch and she shot him down. She couldn't remember his exact words but many years later she would tell *Newsweek,* "there's no doubt in my mind he propositioned me. This was not an inference—this was a direct question. I do distinctly remember saying, no, that wasn't a very good idea."

Unable to hop into bed, Johnson paced around it. He talked about the campaign and Kennedy, waving his arms in the air. Soon press secretary Bill Moyers knocked on the door. Lady Bird had sent the former divinity student out to retrieve her husband. According to Mom, LBJ looked at Moyers and said, "What the hell is he doing here?" and then returned to his diatribe. Moyers watched and gently, and then more insistently, urged his boss back to his own room to get some sleep.

By the time the campaign ended, Mom was news. The *Austin Times Herald* wrote that " . . . an exciting breath of Yankeeland breezed through traditionally southern Austin . . . a pioneer in what is often thought of as man's work." Like so many of the yellowing clips she kept in her scrapbooks, this one carries that unmistakable lilt of amazement reserved for pieces about child prodigies. There's also a good dose of gee-whiz admiration and flirtation. "Nancy believes that home is where the heart is and home is any newsroom any place in the nation."

A day after the election, Kennedy flew down to Austin to visit the vice president–elect. At the airport, he walked right to her microphone. "After handshakes were exchanged the president-elect paused for photographers," wrote the *Bergstrom Jet Gazette*. "World famous CBS newswoman Nancy Haunchman [*sic*] then stopped him for an interview as photographers hustled for favorable positions." In the margin of that clipping Mom wrote to her parents, "not exactly the thing to endear me to my colleagues."

Chapter Sixteen

It was so cold the day Kennedy was inaugurated, the workmen finishing the viewing platform on Pennsylvania Avenue had to be treated for frostbite. The snow was so deep, thirty-five members of Eisenhower's staff had been marooned in the White House overnight. Mom walked from Georgetown to the Capitol, where she was to stand inside the rotunda relaying her impressions back to the anchors who were providing a running narration over the black-and-white footage of the ceremony. She told them Jack looked smashing in his white tie and carrying his gray felt top hat.

Maybe he would see her standing by the cameras and say hello, she thought. She straightened up and tried to catch his eye. During her ten years in Washington, she'd worked with him, seen him at parties, tried to squeeze a news scoop or two from him over the phone. They'd even been on a couple of dates before he was married. As she remembered all of this, she realized that she must not call him Jack if he came over to talk to her. "Mr. President-elect," she practiced to herself.

A heater under the lectern started a fire that delayed the ceremony an hour. Members of Congress and the diplomatic corps milled around inside the rotunda trading compliments on each other's hats and comparing horror stories about skidding in their cars on the drive in. They weren't going to take their frozen seats outside until the last possible moment.

The television commentators were doing their best to fill the airtime for their audience of 80 million. They identified once and future Cabinet members and took note of Kennedy's every cuff straightening. CBS commentator Howard K. Smith relayed the information Mom sent back. Kennedy was "bronze," "very healthy looking," and "already looking rather in command of the situation," Smith said. (Tan, rested and ready!)

Kennedy whistled to himself, rocked on his heels and then, with no eye contact to warn her, walked over to Mom. All the networks turned their cameras on the two of them. "Senator Kennedy is waiting and he's passing the time talking to CBS's Nancy Hanschman," boasted Howard K. Smith.

"When did you first imagine yourself becoming president?" she asked.

"Ever since I was a boy," he replied quickly, though he'd told her before that his political ambitions had started after his brother Joe died.

"When the hell do you think we'll start?" he said, in an aside not meant for the cameras but captured nevertheless.

Then it began. "Hail to the Chief" announced Eisenhower's arrival. Kennedy followed, walking through a file of Marine guards to the platform. Despite the cold, he shed his coat before speaking, a symbol of his fortitude and the result of his savvy planning: he was wearing long underwear.

Everyone at CBS was under pressure from their New York bosses. NBC had beaten CBS during the conventions and they couldn't let that happen again. Mom had even more direct competition. NBC had hired actress Dina Merrill to cover the inaugural ball. The Johnsons had promised they'd talk with her on air but arrangements sometimes had a way of coming undone after the show started. They might not be able to keep their commitment. As the prayers were read, Mom's mind wandered. She was hungry; she'd only had cookies for breakfast. Jack would be eating lobster for lunch even though the Catholics in the ceremony had been given special dispensation to eat meat that Friday. She'd gone all the way to New York to get her pink Dior gown, and it was too short. At least CBS had finally agreed to hire someone to do her hair. She'd been studying the biographies of the Cabinet officials and their lives were running together. Had

McNamara been to Harvard with Jack or was that Budget Director David Bell?

The thick sound of gloves applauding grew to a roar. She snapped out of her free association. Jack was standing to take the oath.

After his stirring speech, Kennedy headed back into the rotunda. He might speak to her again. She couldn't call him Jack. With the world watching she couldn't screw up. But he probably wouldn't come over anyway. He was president now.

He approached. "Hello, Nancy!"

"Hello, Senator!" she said.

Oh, well.

Any new administration is fun for Washington reporters. It's like the first day of school. You start a fresh notebook, make a list of new sources and bring an apple to the press secretary before breaking him in. There are so many possible stories and new figures with exciting plans. President Eisenhower had kept the press penned to a few rooms in the White House. The Kennedy administration immediately made life easier. James Deakin describes the Kennedy era in his book on the White House press corps as "a reporter's dream. All those bright, articulate people willing and anxious to talk. All those ideas tumbling over the dinner tables in Georgetown and Cleveland Park. All those new programs and policies to get America moving again. In the Eisenhower years, there had been no one to talk to but [press secretary James] Hagerty. Then the New Frontier came bursting in, and suddenly there was everyone to talk to."

Kennedy enjoyed journalists and enjoyed their company. He thought he knew more about journalism than they did. When he saw Mom in the hallway at the White House a few weeks after the inauguration, he waved her into the Oval Office. He didn't have much choice. "She just breezed right in," remembers photographer Marvin Lichtner, who was with her. "She really knew how to move, man. The president couldn't do anything but stand there and be photographed." That's when the picture on our piano was taken. That was Mom's first time in the Oval Office and she looks like she's showing Kennedy around. The room can do funny things to people. President Bush told me in an interview once that when his father occupied it he watched people stand outside the office planning to give the president a stern talking to but once they crossed the threshold they wound up saying, "Nice tie, Mr. President. You look lovely today, Mr. President." My first visit there with President Bush was just a couple of months after 9/11 as the war in Afghanistan was looking like a rout. My partner and I were there to observe a private meeting with congressional leaders and conduct one of several interviews we did with Bush for a *Time* story. I wasn't exactly relaxed. I stood up so straight I thought my spine could snap. You'd think after meeting all those famous people at the front door of Merrywood I would have had some portion of Mom's nonchalance. I had not one wee thimbleful.

Mom was one of Kennedy's favorite things: a woman. She was regularly mistaken for Jackie. They went to the same hairdresser and had the same taste in clothes. When the ladies of the press corps put on their annual skits about the men in power, there was no question that she would play the First Lady. Even Jackie Kennedy saw the resemblance. In a 1955 letter turning down an offer to model for a magazine spread, she suggested instead "the very pretty Nancy Hanchman [*sic*]." But there was more than sexual attraction between Kennedy and Mom. They loved their Irish roots. Mom told him stories—real or imagined—about her grandmother Mary Ellen Walsh who arrived by boat from Shannon, Ireland, at the turn of the century. They shared the same experiences with Latin Mass and incense and the other mysterious Catholic rituals. They even went to the same church in Georgetown.

Mom was not a member of Camelot by any stretch—but she was new and young and on the rise, which put her in the Kennedy orbit. If a rising tide lifts all boats, Mom's rose with Kennedy's even if she was not close to him the way other journalists like Ben Bradlee, Hugh Sidey and Charlie Bartlett were.

Kennedy loved television and it loved him back. He knew how to use the medium and he had an audience that adored him. Televisions were expensive, but 87 percent of Americans had one and placed it in the center of their living rooms like a shrine. In some Catholic homes Kennedy's picture rested on top of the flickering screen next to a picture of the Virgin Mary. By holding the first live televised press conferences in the nation's history, Kennedy used boldness and amiability to capture the country. Élan became as important as having your facts right. He turned government into a glamorous reality show and that made the press who covered him seem like celebrities too.

Almost immediately after the inauguration Mom wrote the new president a note to try to turn their on-camera chat into a formal radio or television interview. She explained, as if he needed it, that her broadcast would be seen and heard across the nation. He replied:

Dear Nancy,

Thank you for your note. I am glad our exchange was useful. You may be sure that I shall be glad to give testimony for your coast to coast on any occasion whenever it might be helpful. You can do the same for me.

Best, Jack.

She treasured that note. She put a picture of it in her autobiography. She also loved to point out that she'd dated Jack Kennedy when he was a bachelor. By the time I was old enough to hear her say it and read it in her autobiography, revealing you'd dated Jack Kennedy—even been in the same train compartment with Jack Kennedy—raised eyebrows. The conventional wisdom was that his libido was so gargantuan that if you'd dated Jack Kennedy it meant that you'd slept with Jack Kennedy.

Though she denied having an affair with Johnson, Mom seemed to delight in having people think she might have had one with Kennedy. In her autobiography she almost says it out loud. When she describes moving into Merrywood she notes offhandedly that she'd had dinner there many years earlier with Jack. Jackie and her parents were in Newport and he was in town for a summer Senate session. They ate out on the terrace with "bug-repellent lights . . . which electrocutes insects when they fly into them, making a hissing sound . . . After dinner we went swimming in the pool a hundred yards away. It was Olympic-sized . . . and full of leaves and bugs, and Jack said that sometimes there were snakes . . . There were a whole lot of mosquitoes because the pool was in a pocket above the river which didn't get a breeze."

That's all she wrote. She goes on about insects like it was a *National Geographic* field trip, but she says nothing more about her night alone with the famously amorous senator. Was she being discreet? She wasn't about Johnson. She talked about his clumsy advances. In 1976, when she wrote her memoir, there was no public need for discretion about Kennedy. His extramarital affairs were well known. To write an account of her quiet dinner with Jack and make no mention of whether passes were thrown or completed is malpractice. If he'd done *nothing,* that would have been news.

Mom's friends from that period don't think there was ever an affair, or even a one-night stand. Dad doesn't think so either and he believes she told him everything—the bad and the good, about her past. If she had had an assignation, Mom certainly would have seen the downside in trading on that information. She would have undone a lifetime of trying to be taken seriously and become another figure in the Kennedy menagerie—the newswoman next to the Mafia moll, the heiress and the Hollywood actress. But to be known as having had a quiet dinner with him was worth whatever new whispers she invited about what might have happened that night in the poolhouse.

In the end, Dad blew her cover by telling me the real story. She wasn't at Merrywood alone with Kennedy the way she makes it seem in her autobiography. She had dined there with a group that included Senator Scoop Jackson, whom she was dating at the time. It's not a huge lie, and she didn't make a career out of repeating it the way old Hollywood hangers-on do. But it's a low-rent Washington lie, an inflated tale told to impress your bar mates with your proximity to fame and power. She was better than that.

Children are supposed to be bothered by the idea of their parents having sex, not by stories of sex that didn't happen. But I'm uncomfortable because this little tale seems so grasping and not like the woman at the 1960 convention and the one talking to Kennedy in the rotunda who seems so genuine.

Writing this book, I carried Mom around in my head the way I would any subject of a profile. She wasn't my mother anymore; she was the person I was trying to figure out and put down on paper. Her life wasn't something I was related to. It was a series of bits I was trying to fit together. I spent so many months with the young Nancy Hanschman's letters and television performances, she became more real than the woman I actually knew. She shines on television not because she's a star, but because she's authentic: hungry and so eager she's a little nervous. For her, the news is a simple transaction: she goes where the action is and she comes back to tell us. She's just a conduit.

That's why her coy presentation of the Kennedy dinner is so disappointing. I've got an authentic Nancy Hanschman in my head and suddenly a very different person presents herself. I'm reminded of how Mom would lose her natural ease later in life and replace it with something less authentic. Her performances became stilted and she tarted up her past to remind people who she was. When you're defined by being around the powerful and famous you can lose any sense of who you are. You either have to keep going to parties, keep being seen in their glow, or you have to go out and keep telling the same old stories, each time adding a little more rouge.

In this light, Mom's later quote to a Jackie Onassis biographer saddens me. She told him that for Jack "sex was not much more than a cup of coffee." The quote is irresistible. It's racy, fun and clever. But she's trying to sound like she was an inside player who could speak knowingly about Kennedy's sexual appetites. She's intimating that she could make her coffee quip because she got that close.

She didn't have an affair. No one who actually had an affair with Kennedy or knew he was having them with other women would have written the credulous account Mom did for *McCall's*.

For a brief period in the early '60s, she wrote a regular column for the magazine. In July 1963 she covered the political happenings at Washington swimming parties and detailed the newly opened White House swimming pool which, as she explains to readers, the president doesn't use for socializing but instead for "relaxation and exercise."

Well, exercise of a kind. The swimming pool was a venue for some of Kennedy's most notorious escapades. Kennedy combined water therapy for his aching back with the therapy for the headaches he told his cabana pals he got if he didn't have regular sex. (A twist on the old dodge: I can't wait until tonight, I have a headache.)

Given what we now know about what went on in the pool, Mom's account becomes inadvertently comical. She details how the lights can be turned so low it's hard to see. Kennedy apparently "swims" before lunch and dinner, sometimes "even for just ten minutes."

"I never knew until the other day that Mr. Kennedy also swims frequently before he goes to bed," she wrote. "If there's a private party at the White House, he sometimes disappears briefly about 11:00 P.M. The word goes around that he's at the office; only insiders know that he's really relaxing in the pool."

I'd like to think that Mom really knew about JFK's activities and therefore her credulous account is just extremely clever. It's written with a knowing wink. She was clever but wasn't *that* clever. No one who had been one of Jack's momentary conquests or had known about them at the time would have written that way.

Chapter Seventeen

Mom's first year on air at CBS was a whirlwind. Her producer Don Hewitt had promised her she wouldn't cover women's stories, and she didn't. She interviewed generals about the Soviets, civil rights protestors outside lunchroom sit-ins and Mississippi Congressman Frank E. Smith about his break from his governor over the refusal to integrate the state university. The closest Mom came to covering a women's story was when she interviewed the head of the census department. "Mr. Burgess, the survey shows that one million more women say they are married than men do; what accounts for that?" she asked. "Well, men move away or travel and forget that they're married," he answered without emotion.

The interview has none of the razzle-dazzle and theatricality of today's television news. It's so primitive, it looks a little like a high school production. Now television producers would make Mr. Burgess walk down the hall or crunch numbers on his computer while they filmed him. He'd be coached by a team of government press officials to give smooth short answers with energy! and focus! and other buzzwords written on index cards for him to practice.

In Mom's interview, the fanciest thing the producer tried was shooting the exchange in front of a counter that showed in real time the pace of population growth. It clicked loudly, so that their conversation was regularly interrupted by what sounds like an angry child banging a tiny gavel.

A lot of Mom's early interviews took place on sofas, which made tense exchanges look like first dates. Jimmy Hoffa looked prune-faced, as if Mom had sat him down for a scolding. He faced forward and didn't look at her as he grumbled his answers.

I never would have guessed that she could be confident and plucky. Without ever having seen her interview anyone, I snickered later in life when she tried to give me lessons about getting in the face of reluctant sources; I thought she was just talking tough. But there she was blocking the hall as the secretary of the Air Force tried to sneak out of a Senate committee room after he had just testified.

In another piece, she interviewed the chairman of the Joint Chiefs of Staff. "Nancy, that's not a fair question," he says. "I wouldn't have asked it if I didn't think it was fair," she comes back quickly. The man with the medals answers her. I've since looked forward to using this trick.

In May of 1961, Vice President Johnson announced that he would travel for two weeks to Southeast Asia. CBS sent Mom. She was at the Kentucky Derby as a guest of the governor when the call came. The network hired a private plane and flew her back to Washington. She packed a second suitcase to complement the one she always left by her apartment door in case of breaking news.

The trip was a reprise of the 1960 campaign. Johnson told the press he would show the world his Texas hospitality, and he spread it around like warm butter.

When the entourage landed in Saigon, cheering crowds lined the streets. Johnson had expected a more subdued reception for a vice president and was pleasantly surprised. It was the kind of reception he thought he deserved every day. Mom's description in her autobiography is not politically correct, but it captures the magical atmosphere: "The Vietnamese are little people, and since both men and women wear knee-length pants and kimono tops, and since we landed at dusk, they looked like a nation of children in pajamas having a last fling before bedtime."

Traveling with a president or vice president can be intoxicating. That is, when it's not deadly boring. I traveled a lot with President Bush to foreign countries and it often meant hours in windowless ballrooms typing with 150 of my colleagues, eating at odd hours, and getting almost no sleep. There are so many people in the caravan surrounding an official visit, it's a huge disruption and burden for host countries: the traffic jams, demanding American officials and loss of revenue brought on by having to close down much of a city. But during the many times I traveled in the smaller press pool that shadows the president, I got a glimpse of the adulation showered on dignitaries.

When Air Force One lands, the host country puts on an elaborate welcoming ceremony: boot-clicking soldiers in South Korea, half-naked dancers and drummers in Senegal and singing children and marimba bands in Botswana. You ride through clear streets, lined with locals, as the entire city stops to wave and smile at you. In Uganda, I don't think there was a single gap in the three-mile line of people by the side of the road from the airport to the presidential residence. Locals can't distinguish the press vans from the official ones and so herald you like it's V-E day. In most countries, the locals are very eager to show the Americans their hospitality and effectiveness. If you ask someone for a ham sandwich, they might roll in a whole suckling pig for you.

Before an official press conference with Italian Prime Minister Silvio Berlusconi, we were treated like royalty. Instead of waiting in a cramped holding room for hours, sitting on folding chairs with only a bottle of water and the stale smoke of the local journalists to comfort us, we were served wine, fresh cheeses and fruits under flowing tents in the Borghese Gardens. We thought perhaps we'd been directed to the wrong holding area, but then remembered that Berlusconi also owned the country's largest media conglomerate. He believed that you had a better chance at favorable coverage if you had a well-fed press corps.

On the way to Asia with Johnson, Mom had time to send a postcard to her parents on Cedar Street. "Honolulu was beautiful and warm and we worked 24 hours straight—thanks to the time change and since LBJ goes at high full speed constantly this will be a *rough journey.*"

Johnson arrived in Vietnam as if he were trying to give himself a second heart attack. He pumped the hand of everyone in sight, trying to show President Diem the power of retail politicking. "He has to get off his ass," Johnson told the American press corps. "These people out here have to stop wearing white Bermuda shorts and sipping gins, and get to the people."

Johnson would stop his limousine on a whim, and rush out to shake hands. His security detail had to keep up with his damp white shirt as he waded into seas of locals. In one of Mom's pieces from the trip, she is yelling over the cheering crowd: "They may not understand what he's saying, but they sure do love it."

The trip continued on through the Philippines, where Mom sent another postcard to her parents—"We don't see quite so much as I'd like 'cause we move so fast and work 18 hours a day. I got sick in Manila, a real hell hole . . . keep track of any radio spots you hear from me—watch *Eyewitness* on Fri. p.m. Hong Kong beautiful but shopping not as good as I hoped."

In Thailand, the vice president was instructed in the proper way to greet people: He should put his hands together and bow. They would be offended if he tried any more generous bodily contact. Johnson performed the ritual once and then went back to shaking limbs as if he were trying to start a lawnmower.

Johnson was as much fun overseas as he was on the campaign trail. As the press corps followed him in the heat to the Taj Mahal, he explained that the temple symbolized a man's love for his wife, that it was the wedding anniversary of President Kennedy's sister Jean and her husband Steve Smith, who were along for the trip; that Steve Smith was a great lover; and that all the world loved Steve Smith. Johnson took Lady Bird by the waist and bent her over for a passionate kiss. Later, he compared his meeting with Indian prime minister Nehru to seducing a woman—"it was just like putting your hand up her leg."

In Pakistan, Johnson met Bashir, a camel cart driver, and invited him to the United States. Bashir ultimately took him up on his offer, to much fanfare.

The trip ended with stops in Athens, where the entire press corps drank champagne at midnight on the Acropolis, and then Bermuda. On one of the last evenings Jean Smith sat on Johnson's left while Mom sat on the right and asked him which of the two he found more sexy or glamorous. "I never would fool around with any of you

Catholic girls," he replied to the laughter of the drunken reporters.

Kennedy had sent Johnson to show Asian leaders that the United States was committed to that part of the world, and Johnson was doing it the only way he knew how, by politicking like he was running for sheriff. He thought the trip a wonderful success. He not only loved playing to the locals and press corps, but he loved being on a serious mission. Normally, Johnson complained that he was kept "like a fox on a leash."

I could see how Mom got intoxicated by Johnson. He put on a show. He was an excessive personality. There was always something to see even if there wasn't news to cover. His escapades remind me of covering John McCain. I rode with him for months in the back of his campaign bus, the "Straight Talk Express," during the 2000 Republican primaries. Every day he sat at the center of a semicircle of journalists and took questions. He told jokes, swore, debated policy and surprised us with his knowledge of obscure topics like the internal politics of the Syrian government. I also worked out an arrangement so that I was allowed behind the scenes into the hotel rooms at the end of the day, and backstage at debate preparation. McCain was so much more authentic and real than any other politician I had covered, I was drawn in.

By the time Mom landed back in the States she had made a little news herself. Johnson's invitation to the camel driver Bashir had made the papers along with the Pakistani's quip about Mom. "When you smile petals fall from flowers," he had said to her.

A month after the trip, Mom was the focus of one of Drew Pearson's influential "Washington Merry-Go-Round" columns. "Nancy Hanschman, the beautiful CBS news sleuth was regaling a dinner party at the home of Sen. Mike Monroney, on her trip around the world . . ." Calling her "as accurate as she is attractive," Pearson quotes her as saying "At the Taj Mahal the Vice President let out one of those bloodcurdling Texas war whoops . . . the interesting fact was that the Indians loved it. This was a real American. Through all the Texas frills they could see his sincerity and his democracy."

Mom had what she had always wanted. She was in the middle of the whirlwind, jetting across the world with one of the country's most powerful figures, regaling columnists at exclusive dinner parties who breathlessly reported her comments. Like many who get quick fame, Mom found it destabilizing. How would she keep it all together? How would she meet everyone's expectations? The frantic pace and insecurity made her think more seriously about stability and marriage.

Up until then, she had seen marriage as a trap. She told friends she would find the right man, but it wasn't her priority. "If pressed very hard, she will admit that if she had to make a choice between career and marriage, she'd take the latter," wrote one reporter in 1960 for *Good Housekeeping*. "For the moment, though, her idea of the best of all possible worlds is to be stationed with CBS in Washington and sent on assignment to Europe or Asia or wherever the big story is."

Mom figured that she would find her husband in the course of her life. Anyone not part of her world would require compromises she wasn't ready to make. If news broke, she was off and the coffee burned in the percolator. She had followed the advice of Doris Fleeson, the plain-talking columnist from Kansas who told her to "go anywhere, learn everything, meet everybody and it will make you a good journalist." This was a free pass: a respected professional giving her cover to follow her instinct and passion. It was like Sammy Hope telling her she could smoke in the streets of Paris. It would take a special kind of husband to support such an unpredictable routine.

Once she became a correspondent, though, the minor irritants of being a single woman were becoming more annoying. Maintaining a stronghold in a man's workplace was tiring enough, but she also had to defend against the social pressure: A girl really shouldn't be that old and unmarried. She was tired of having to make panicked calls to her father to find out what to do with the plumbing or if she had enough insurance. When she went home, everyone wanted to know if she had a special fella. "For our mother in Wauwatosa it was as much or more a matter of talk that Nancy was so old and not married than that she was on television," says Mary Ellen.

When Mom felt unlucky, she bought travel insurance at the airport and made the beneficiaries the orphans at St. Ann's in Washington. The independence that once made her feel exhilarated and superior started to feel lonely.

She was also struggling through her nighttime prayers and Sunday Mass. Intimate affairs outside of marriage were morally wrong and her guilt prompted her to end her last love affair with Cord Meyer, who was newly divorced, something the Catholic Church also did not condone.

She might sin in private, but in public she could not break with the church by marrying a divorced man. She would be abandoning part of her identity: the daily Masses as a little girl at St. Jude's, the nuns at Clarke College and the hours of confession at Holy Trinity. Plus, Kennedy had made it hip to be Catholic. Behind the scenes, private mores might have been loosening (Kennedy was seeing to that), but in public, even lapsed Catholics in Washington were going to Mass and eating fish on Fridays. Mom, who loved the Kennedy mystique, would no more break with the church than she would go back to wearing hoop skirts.

In 1960, the average American woman got married for the first time when she was twenty. By the time Mom, at age thirty-four, started looking at her dates acquisitively, the pool of eligible men was tiny. Most men of her age were already married. She couldn't marry the divorced ones. Any bachelor left in the bin was usually bruised fruit—they were unmarried for a reason. Some politicians were older and unmarried. But she didn't want that life—the plasticine wife who holds her husband's coat and her tongue while waving to the crowd with a face of stupified affection.

Widower was the only category left. Fortunately, her friends Patty and Ed Cavin had just the date for her. They invited Mom to their home for dinner with Wyatt Dickerson, a successful investor and real estate man whose first wife had died of breast cancer, leaving him with three young daughters.

Mom prepared for their first date by reading the business section. She was nervous but not hopeful. She had dated columnists, senators and even a spy, but never a businessman. She'd never met "Dick" Dickerson, but she was pretty sure she couldn't rely on an evening of intramural chatter about Kennedy's civil rights program or Johnson's trip to Asia.

Dad was described by one profiler at the time as a "blond Tarzan." He was attractive with bright eyes and close-cropped hair and he looked younger than thirty-seven. He had been in the Navy and after the war lived in Hollywood for three years. He had acted, lived with a matinee bombshell and worked out at Muscle Beach. Though he had returned east to marry his high school sweetheart and have a family, he still carried himself like a man onstage.

He had been born in Roanoke, Virginia, had just one sister and wanted to be in the middle of the action. But small towns, small families and ambition are where his similarities with Mom ended. She thought he talked too much about the film business. He mentioned actresses and actors Mom hadn't heard of. She wasn't interested. She talked about politics with her friend Patty, a radio and newspaper reporter, exchanging gossip about Kennedy administration officials Dad couldn't follow. If they had BlackBerrys back then, they both would have been checking their e-mail midway through the appetizer course.

Chapter Eighteen

The story of my parents' engagement in December 1961 always puzzled me. The same day that my father proposed, Mom's long-time friend, Paul Niven, tried first. He and Mom had had a boozy lunch with their colleagues and then gone back to her apartment for coffee. The heavyset Niven ended up down on one knee.

"Nancy, will you marry me?"

"Lose fifty pounds first," she replied.

"What will you do for five?" he shot back.

Mom loved to tell this story. She prized clever quick people. That's why I know the story at all: it was part of a set joke. But if Niven was serious, her response was brutal. And even if he was kidding, calling him fatty still seems a little harsh.

Dad arrived a few hours after Niven's pitch and made his own offer. He got a more serious answer: Mom said she would consider. A few days later, they went to the horse races. He bet heavily on TV Lark (clever Dick) and when the horse came around the bend a winner, they decided to get hitched. "We lived happily ever after," she wrote in her autobiography.

The story is too tidy. It's also devoid of emotion or feeling. You don't have to be a journalist to know there's got to be a backstory. There was, saved in a manila folder I found wedged between "Personnel" and "Merrywood furniture" in one of Mom's boxes. Inside were my parents' love letters, written in the fall of 1961. The tale of a courtship I never knew about is told on onionskin stationery from European hotels.

In the fall of 1961, a few months after their first date, Mom was traveling through Europe on a press club junket. Dad was there on business. In the early morning before flying to another city for meetings, he would slip a letter to "My Dearest Nancy" under her door. When he arrived in his next city, one from her would be waiting, starting simply: "Darling."

"I have the most beautiful thoughts and feelings about Nancy," Dad wrote from a café in Paris. She wrote: "I've discovered lots of little places that you would love. It is more cheerful by far when you are here."

Did I really want to read these letters? Did I really want to go back and tease out some meaning from their romance? Or adjudicate their breakup again? Who did what to whom? I know how this movie ends. I witnessed its messy final act. Aren't the children of parents who fight always trying to make peace? Why was I looking for an encore fight? Still, I was irrationally hopeful. Maybe this time our heroes would see the road sign and not pitch their convertible over the cliff. Nope. The brakes lock, the tires squeal and over they go. I have the divorce papers in triplicate to prove it.

I wonder how the marriage that produced me fell apart. But mostly I want to know what happened to Mom. Why is this person Dad fell in love with so different from the woman I knew? And was she really different? Was her more authentic self just hidden from me? It may not be the marriage that changed her, but by the time I got to these letters, I was hooked. I wanted to know how she turned out.

My Dad is still alive. At age eighty-one, he plays hide-and-seek with his grandchildren under a green comforter in our kitchen. He doesn't know I have spent the morning reading his letters. I feel like I'm ten and he's walked in on me hunched over some stolen candy. Maybe it's not fair for me to stare at his private past, though in the letters he seems remarkably consistent with the man I know: loving, clever and sometimes very harsh.

Dad didn't give up after that first dinner, and he knew how to impress. When he heard she was going to London he immediately started rearranging her itinerary.

"Nancy, you can't stay at that hotel," he told her.

"Oh?"

"It's like staying at the Harrington," he said, naming one of Washington's dreariest hotels.

"I see."

"I will arrange to have you stay at the Savoy."

Dad laid it on thick. When Mom landed at Heathrow, she was greeted by a chauffeur driving a gleaming black Bentley. When she was delivered to the hotel, she was giddy. The other guests were so much more chic than she expected in London. They all seemed to be moving in a choreographed dance of white gloves, smart neckties and knowing nods. Her room on the top floor was full of bowls of freshly cut flowers.

She wrote a letter to her parents on the hotel's light blue onionskin paper: "Dear Mother and Daddy, I have a top floor room at this hotel which is so swish I am thinking of opening a bar here. It overlooks the Thames and is the best view of London . . . There is a lovely band concert just down the river which I can hear way up here." She tucked a few blank pages in her case for her scrapbook.

Dad arrived a few days later. Dick Dickerson seemed to know everything as he escorted Mom around town. At the National Gallery he pointed out the difference between a Manet and Monet. She wondered how the son of a druggist from Roanoke, Virginia, knew that. He somehow acquired hard-to-get tickets to *Beyond the Fringe*, the hottest comedy show in town.

He was weightlessly charming the way the heroes are in old movies where everything seems to be prepared for them before they walk into a room. He kibitzed with waiters and joked with cabbies. At parties in Washington she had looked across the room to see him making men he'd just met laugh like they'd been friends since college.

While they flirted, Mom kept up her broadcasts during the trip, taking her daily variety show *One Woman's Washington* overseas. I discovered this when I had a friend at National Public Radio transfer an unlabeled spool of reel-to-reel tape to cassette. I had no idea what I would hear when I played the tape on my drive home. Mom's voice was bouncy and light as she reflected on a recent theft of Goya's *Duke of Wellington* at the National Gallery in London:

It intrigued me that such a theft could have occurred and I had a morbid fascination to see just where the picture used to hang. I asked an American businessman, Mr. C Wyatt Dickerson, to go with me. Since he's an art expert, he raised some objection to taking an excursion the purpose of which was to visit an art gallery to see where a picture no longer was. But reluctantly he agreed.

Oh boy. She's got a crush—a National Gallery–sized crush. That's the powdered sugar I heard in her voice when the piece started. She's flirting with Dad on the air. She's brought him into the piece, just as she had found any excuse to mention her new boyfriend at the dinner table as a young girl in Wauwatosa. "Please pass the potatoes; you know, Dick Dickerson likes potatoes!" As the piece continues, her flirting gets out of hand:

I thought it would be easy to spot just where the picture used to hang—you know the usual telltale marks on the wall when you take down the picture. Maybe even an empty nail. But no such luck. I walked around for 30 minutes trying to find the scene of the crime. This was no easy search. It became a game to find out where the duke used to hang. Sort of a treasure hunt in reverse. There was no sign that said: "The Duke of Wellington hung here." We did find a little room where there were no paintings at all. Just those dirty dusty outlines of where former picture frames had marked the wall, which prompted Mr. Dickerson to comment that this time maybe they had made off with an entire roomful. Well, thwarted at every attempt to find out where the Duke used to hang I looked for a guard so that I could ask him. That was a search too because it was almost as difficult to find a guard. Having finally found a guard I quickly looked around to make sure that I hadn't lost Mr. Dickerson. And just that quick the guard was gone, which caused Mr. Dickerson to comment, "Well, now they've stolen him too." . . . I finally got my answer from a guard who wouldn't even look at me. He did solve the mystery. The painting hadn't been hung anywhere. It had been placed on an easel . . . By this time Mr. Dickerson had completely disassociated himself from me. To be honest about it, he was pretending he never met me and I was somewhat subdued when I retrieved him from under a Rembrandt. On leaving the National Gallery I asked Mr. Dickerson if he had ever been tempted to steal any paintings, just to get away with it you understand. He rather disdainfully said, no, but he did feel tempted to straighten quite a few and I must say there was plenty of opportunity because several were crooked. Not dishonest, you understand, just not hung straight.

Her voice has in it a clear, bright-day lilt. Like so much of this detective hunt, hearing Mom flaunting her affection for Dad is more powerful than reading the more overt professions in her letters. It's so very different than the voice I associated with her intimate views about Dad, which, when I was hearing them as a teenager, were cold and mean.

She wrote Dad about the spot, which she taped while they were apart for a few days: "I wrote about you at the National Gallery—hope you don't mind—but I make you out to be clever and intelligent and me out to be an idiot—a thesis to which you most probably subscribe anyway!"

After London, the two traveled to Ireland alone. Mom turned into a child there. She talked about her heritage with every wool-wrapped local she met. She told Kennedy stories and insisted on performing every act of Irish tourism she could, including the tricky upside-down kiss of the Blarney Stone. Dad dutifully followed along, keeping quiet about his Scots-Irish heritage. Mom was so anxious to soak up every piece of local color that Dad joked she wouldn't go to the bathroom unless she could find a nostalgic toilet.

Mom and Dad were clearly in love and somewhere in the middle of this trip things got serious. Dad tried to move past the chauffeurs and rounds of cocktails to talk of a more enduring relationship. That posed immediate and difficult questions for Mom. She wondered if the fun they were having would survive if they got married. Could her career? Dick had three daughters. Would he really not ask her to change her life?

The tone of their letters started to change toward the end of September. They had one foot on the gas and one on the brake as they fishtailed across Europe: Passion in Ireland, anger in Cannes and reconciliation in Paris.

"Why do you love me?" she wanted to know. She worried he loved her too much. He wasn't critical enough of her, the way she was critical of him. Would that heedless love wither under the stresses of marriage?

She also didn't trust herself. Was she in love with him as she had been other men? What she admired was a man of sensibility and romance. Her last serious beau, Cord Meyer, had written her long and passionate letters quoting Shelley and Keats. This was love as she imagined it: full of passion *and* intellect, fountain-pen prose and op-ed articles. Dad may have known about Impressionism but he had an aversion to people who engaged in showy literary performance art.

Mom was now paying a price for those romances with Meyer and Ken Keating. Her faith or social custom had ended those relationships, keeping her from confronting the hard choices of commitment she was now forced to confront with Dad. She could have fun, but she always had an out and could retain a glorious illusion about what could be. Even if she didn't pine for those men specifically, she thought she would find all of their qualities in a replacement with none of the technicalities that had undone those relationships.

Dad got tired of being quizzed. She wasn't honestly testing the strength of the relationship, she was trying to find excuses for why it wouldn't survive. She wasn't taking it seriously. By the time he met her in Cannes, they were talked out. His letter to her there suggests that by then they were strangers.

"Hello," he says.

"Hello."

"I gather you would like to be alone."

"Yes."

"Goodbye."

Dad returned to his room and tried to say farewell for good. "It will be very lonely without you," he wrote. "It will be sad for me to know that a precious part of my life is gone. I will think of you often with love and tenderness and I will wonder why we were brought so close together."

As he wrote, the phone rang. "The incorrigible Mr. Niven and I are in the bar," she said as if everything were peaches again. "Would you like to join us for some wine?"

He dropped his goodbyes and stayed one more day. The next, he was gone before breakfast, angry all over again that she didn't seem to want to get serious. He added another farewell note to the one he left the day before. He pushed his pen hard enough to leave grooves in the paper forty years later: "My presence seems to create an unpleasantness for you."

I recognize his language. I'd never read these notes before, but I recognize the judgment in Dad's voice from childhood scoldings. "I believe that many of the things you consider important should really be limited to mental exercises or minor interests," he writes. She doesn't want lectures. "Your pious little farewell note was received," she writes after the night of wine drinking, "which I shall ignore."

In the middle of these exchanges, Dad returned to Washington. He kept proclaiming his love, and still trying to force a serious talk. Mom resisted. Still in Europe, she detailed the drinks she was having, the work she'd done and how boring it was to be alone now that Dad and her other traveling companions had gone. The roller coaster correspondence continued, but their sentiments weren't in sync, and the overseas mail schedules made communication even more difficult. Her letters of contrition arrived too late to soothe the bitterness he expressed in a letter she hadn't received. "Had I answered your letter the day I received it you would have got a full passionate love letter," she wrote. "Had I answered it the next day, we might not have communicated ever again."

Even their affection for each other was backhanded. "Nancy, with all of your silly tempers, disappointments and misplaced affections," he wrote, "I love you because of these quirks—not in spite of them . . . I'm trying to tell you to stop running." She replies: "I am puzzled by your reference to 'misplaced affections.' I have affection for you. Is that misplaced? Come now . . ."

Mom traveled to Vienna, seeing the sights and filing regular radio reports. One night she got a surprise phone call from Vice President Johnson, who was returning from the funeral of United Nations Secretary-General Dag Hammarskjold. He wanted Mom to meet him in Paris.

No one in my family had ever heard about this call. Mom had never even told Dad. Picking through a secondhand bookshop in the wilderness of Maine, I found it in a book called *The Flying White House*, co-authored by a former Air Force One captain. I found her name in the index but didn't get around to reading the account until I was almost finished writing this book. According to the Air Force One captain, Ralph Albertazzie, as Johnson boarded the plane in Sweden, he said to the radio operator: "Get Nancy Hanschman on the phone. She is in Paris and that's where we're going."

The operators on the plane and in Washington tried to find Mom but despite their reputation for being able to find anybody anywhere in the world, they could not track down the object of the vice president's affections in the French capital. "Well, by God," said Johnson, "then call CBS in Washington, or New York, and find out where she is. I want to talk to her."

Silly me, I thought Niven and Dad were the only ones competing for Mom's affection. There must have been something about her in Europe that made men cluster around her like this. I'm reminded of those snapshots of her first European tour: the men circling in a holding pattern.

Johnson grew impatient as the radio operators tried to find her. The Air Force pilot went ahead and changed course and notified Air Force Command Post in Washington of the vice president's changed itinerary. Finally they found Mom in Vienna and the vice president got on the phone.

"He started right in, pleading with her to leave Vienna and get to Paris," recalled Albertazzie, who could hear the conversation on his headset. "'I want to take you to dinner, I want to entertain you,' he kept telling her. And Nancy was saying, 'Oh, Mr. Vice President, that's sweet of you and I'd like to do it, but I'm here on vacation and I just can't leave Vienna now.'" LBJ leaned in. "'Honey,' he said. 'I've been waiting for this opportunity to take you to Paris, so you just come meet me now—please. We're going to have a good time.'"

I don't know whether I'm more surprised that Mom turned down the in-flight pleading or that she never told anyone the story. As much as she enjoyed being near power, I'm surprised she didn't say yes. She wasn't married yet, and it might only have been an invitation to dinner. Maybe she could have just had coffee and a croissant.

Even though her letters to Dad suggest she was just the kind of woman who would jet to Paris, she didn't go. In her autobiography she wrote more broadly about the Johnson Treatment: "He could give anyone, man or woman, a big build-up and if you weren't used to that sort of thing—and who is?—you could feel like a king or queen. . . . It was all just one more example of his overblown rhetoric, and anyone who didn't know how to cope with such attention was apt to take it for meaning more than it did."

Mom would later suffer for not maintaining a journalist's distance from President Johnson, but she obviously had enough perspective about him that she was able to turn down his invitation to join him in Paris.

When the music stopped, Dad won. He got Mom to sit still long enough to take him seriously. By December 1961, less than two months after their tour in Europe, they were engaged. Finally Nancy had something to tell all those nosy neighbors and childhood friends in Wauwatosa when the smiling couple arrived for Christmas dinner on Cedar Street. Dad was quiet and polite and modest. He joked with Fred and shared stories of playing football since Dad had gone to Duke on a football scholarship. They all liked him. (Forty years later, Mary Ellen was still irritated at how much Dad praised Nancy. "She could do nothing wrong in his eyes," she remembers. "It was thoroughly boring.") When Mom and Dad left, my grandfather said, "We struck gold with our first son-in-law, maybe we've struck gold with this next one."

As much as the Hanschmans liked Mr. Dickerson, my grandmother was nervous. Nancy was smoking too much and seemed jumpy. My grandmother told my grandfather that she had a bad premonition. He felt the same thing but maybe they just didn't know their daughter, who had now lived away from them for ten years. On each visit, her clothes seemed a little more foreign, her expressions a little less familiar. She was a smart girl, Fred reasoned. She knew what she was doing.

Her parents were right to be nervous. The wedding almost never happened.

In January 1962, a month before they were to walk down the aisle, Mom spent her days on astronaut John Glenn's frozen lawn. She was there to report the reactions of his wife, Annie, to her husband's space adventure. Because Mom was tied to the mission, so too was the rest of her life. Eight times the orbital mission was delayed and eight times Mom's wedding and honeymoon had to be postponed. The situation got so desperate the vice president got involved. At a party at Bobby Kennedy's after hearing about the delays, he called over JFK and said in front of Mom and Dad, "You've got to get this space shot worked out so that these kids can get married."

Dad suspected Mom was stalling for time and she was. How would she be able to cover a historic moment like this if she had three girls and a husband? Yes, marriage required sacrifice, but so much? "I will go from waking alone at nine to waking with five people at seven," she kept saying to him.

It all wore Dad out. "I must say goodbye," he wrote a month before their wedding day. "You insist upon being amused at all times and prefer pseudo intellectual conversations with no personal depth . . . When marriage, family, responsibility and personal decency become factors, you no longer have the overwhelming emotion you think of as the excitement of love."

His letter is brutal and thorough—three pages of single-spaced legal paper, both sides. He didn't want to call off the marriage, of course, but he couldn't get through to her. A widower who had watched his first wife's slow death, he knew what the stakes in a marriage could be. "I'm worn out from beating my head and heart against the wall," he wrote. "You want a jester who will delight you with intellectual noises . . . your intellectual insecurity (which is all in your imagination) requires superficial intellectual stimulation and frantic gaiety."

It seems harsh, but Dad wasn't alone. His letter is tucked inside an NBC envelope with four others from her mother, father, sister and Jesuit priest, who all wrote to her and told her in one way or another to get serious. Mom sealed and scored the flap from left to right to warn or detect anyone who might be snooping.

"Some of your doubts have more validity than others," wrote Father Fitz, who would ultimately perform the marriage ceremony. "Some are superficial and can be confused with fear of the future, even irrational fear. These we should disregard. Your life has been independent and 'rather gay' in the good sense. You seem to say that you have never been married before so 'how will I know I'm going to like it?' To be a bit humorous, that sounds like the Britisher (very conservative) who said: 'Nothing should ever be done for the first time.' Again, I do not think this is a good reason for serious doubts."

Her father wanted to fly to Washington to sit down with her. "You seem so far away and that makes me feel helpless," he wrote. Her mother wrote, "I have the feeling you weren't getting down to basic facts. I think your job will have to come second if you want to be happy and that's not easily done." She worried Mom wasn't taking her vitamins. "Don't let it get you down," she concluded aimlessly. "It's been fun having you for a daughter and I don't want it to change for any of us. You've had a good life and used your head and I know you will continue to do so. I hope you don't do anything that goes against your religion. I know that was so important to you when you were younger." They're firing advice into the air hoping something hits.

Mary Ellen's stationery matched her dainty blue ink, but she wrote with a fist. "The entire situation in which you find yourself is the result of never having had to think of anyone *but* yourself for 35 years," she started, echoing precisely the argument she made to pull Mom back from Europe in 1948. "In your particular job and life this is not too unnatural but it is unfortunate. You haven't learned that to sacrifice something precious to you is the surest way to reap twice as much happiness as you ever had before . . . I only hope if you choose to wait longer and continue to partake in the fascination and glamour of your job and life, you won't find you have waited too long. If the adjustment is difficult at 35 years, it may be beyond you at 40 . . . Just remember there will be another Nancy Hanschman coming over the horizon one of these days and you'll be forced into compromising."

Mom must have felt so alone. She could have told her sister off, but she must have known that she was right at some level—there was more to life than a plate full of formal invitations. That's why she'd been thinking more seriously about getting married in the first place. But if Mom knew this intellectually, that didn't mean she was convinced she'd come to the precise moment to jump.

The uncoordinated group effort of telling her to get serious must have been brutal. There was no more powerful blow than to accuse Mom of not being serious enough about work or about life—now she had a chorus of people telling her this.

But wait; she had made her career out of ignoring people's criticisms. Why did these voices bother her so much? Because they had a standing that the others didn't. She was hearing an echo of the paralyzing sentiment that had brought her back from Europe. She was being self-indulgent. Forget self-discovery, return to obligation. Work had provided her with the cover, the excuse to follow her own impulses. She wasn't being self-indulgent, she was doing her job, which just happened to match her own internal rhythms. But her work was being framed as self-indulgence and marriage the natural, expected, dutiful course she must embrace.

Mom had no one to turn to who might help her make the opposite case, to argue it was okay to wait to get married, that she was hesitating because she had genuine concerns or even to argue that she didn't need to marry at all.

Whom could she talk to at the office? The men who were encouraged to forget their children from the moment they picked up their fedora in the morning until they put it back on the hat stand for the night? Her female twenty-two-year-old assistant who had just gotten enthusiastically engaged?

Her friends were not much help. "I hated getting married," remembers Pat McCarrick. "I was out in Bethesda and I felt like I didn't know anything." When Mom saw her friend wrestling with two young children, she looked ashen. "She didn't like it at all," remembers McCarrick.

If she'd talked to Pauline Frederick, the NBC broadcaster probably would have only confirmed her fears. "Something would have to be sacrificed," Frederick said about trying to have a family and a news career in Judith Gelfman's *Women in Television News*. "When I have been busy . . . it has meant working day and night. You can't very well take care of a home when you do something like that, or children."

Mom made lists of pros and cons and shared them with no one. She wasn't just giving up cocktails and spontaneous convertible rides through the countryside. Marriage meant giving up her life's organizing principle. The beneficial side of the daily dash to a deadline was that it provided direction and meaning: A story broke and she went after it. She knew why she got up in the morning and what was expected of her. Now she was entering a world where achievement as a wife and mother was much harder to measure. She couldn't improve her skills by practicing in the bathroom mirror. How could a day be designed around anything but adrenaline? It must have horrified her when her sister wrote, "Dick has a right to and you an obligation to provide a normal, happy, homelife where he and his wants come first."

And yet Mom signed up. Was she boxed into a corner? Could the famous television girl really afford the public embarrassment of calling off an engagement? The group effort must have worked a little. She loved Dad enough and, she told herself, she would come to love him more. She even found a way to make her prayers easier: She started to think about taking on his three girls as an act of Christian charity. Her previous romances had been digressions; tending to the girls would be an act of repentance.

On February 22, 1962, Mom and Dad were married in a small Catholic ceremony. Mom wore a light peach silk satin dress and Dad a simple blue suit. His three daughters dressed identically in blue. There was a fancy reception at the F Street Club. Vice President Johnson sent a cable.

What held Mom and Dad together for twenty years? Passion? Religion? Fear of society columnists? Convention? Sacredness of contract? How did two such volatile particles cling together after starting under strain? I didn't witness a lot of cuddly scenes growing up at Merrywood, but the letters remind me that my memories overshadow all that I didn't see—the long walks and giggling that didn't get written down and put in sealed envelopes. I see knickknacks that I now own in the background of old pictures of the two of them, and I realize there are stories, hundreds of them, of sustaining love and shared history that only the two of them knew.

I find an echo of that love in Dad today. He doesn't like being reminded of his courtship hardball. "You're bringing back a lot of memories," he says looking over the dinner table. He doesn't mean pleasant memories. Suddenly I feel like I've trapped him. In a press interview, this is usually where you feel like you've gotten somewhere, but why am I doing this to my Dad?

He's now been divorced from Mom longer than the twenty years he was married to her. He's detached and unarmed. He's remarried and doesn't have any of that old rage. He can't even conjure it. When I lived with him, our late-night talks would eventually wind up being about Mom. Throughout my high school days there was plenty of tension for him to mine—the divorce took time to finalize and then they had to sell Merrywood and split the furniture. I would present some new grievance—she was being stingy with money or was insisting I attend some party—and off we'd go. We'd assess her inflexibility and obsession with status.

Now he defends her. He wants to protect her. "She was very religious. She made every effort to live by the book. There were a few times that real life made it difficult and a few times when she felt that she had erred and sought redemption. I don't know if you want to expose the very few events in her life that she considered religious blemishes." He's anxious to tell stories about how hard she worked and how she never wavered during their toughest times. "It was a wonderful marriage for a long time," he says, "until it fell apart. A lot of that was my fault. I put your mother through some very hard times. She was wonderful through all of it."

Chapter Nineteen

Mom attacked mothering as if it were a new beat. "We were by the pool," remembers Elizabeth, "and she brought out this big merlot-colored encyclopedia. She showed me the pictures of male and female reproductive organs and told me a thirty-five-year-old man would get excited if I touched his thigh and then 'it would kill your father if any of you girls got pregnant.'" From identification to procreation, she covered a lot of ground in that one short conversation. She was used to tight deadlines.

Mom was nervous about jumping on the running board of the Dickerson family. The girls' mother had died from breast cancer two years earlier after four years of surgery and relapses. How could she win their affection and run the household and not intrude on their memories of their mother?

Mom worked at the transition, tucking in the girls, talking to them about boys and clothes and dazzling them with unexpected surprises. One weekend she arrived with a large gray suitcase. When the girls ran to greet Mom and their father, Mom dropped the case and they opened it. Toys and clothes wrapped like Christmas presents tumbled onto the grass.

Jane, the youngest of the girls, was the most eager to embrace her new mother. Shortly after Mom's first visit, she ran into her arms and buried her face in Mom's mohair jacket. "She smelled like flowers," says Jane, remembering Mom's Femme by Rochas perfume. Not long after, Jane asked if she could call her "Mom."

"Of course," Mom said, swooping down to pick her up and twirl her. She was thrilled to have won that name of recognition.

Jane, age eight, lobbied her sisters. "You'd better be nice to Nancy Hanschman or she will die and she'll go up and tell Mom and then you'll really be in trouble."

Elizabeth, age twelve, and Ann, ten, were more skeptical. When Dad sat the girls down to ask if it was okay to marry Nancy Hanschman, Anne said no. She was notoriously difficult. Dad once had to carry her kicking and screaming into school and sit her down at her desk. She was still in her pajamas.

Louise, the housekeeper who had been their surrogate mother, lobbied Ann: "If you love your father you'll say yes."

Mom planned their meals, school outings and weekend fun. She was also concerned that they had gone for so long without a mother they might be missing some of the crucial lessons women teach each other.

When Ann, the middle daughter, got cramps during a trip into town, Mom took her to her Georgetown apartment. "She fed me Excedrin and a hot toddy," says Ann. "She put bourbon in the hot toddy. It accomplished the mission. She also explained that a lot of women make the mistake of putting a heating pad on their stomachs when it's really your back that needs it."

You didn't need to be a girl to get the toddy treatment. Mom applied it to paper cuts, I think. One of my first memories was Mom's attempt to drown my cold with a toddy. Hot, sugary and full of bourbon, it made me gag. She'd have to get me to like bourbon some other way.

While she learned how to manage the girls, house and home on the fly, work was her sanctuary. She continued covering Johnson for CBS, but as 1962 came to an end, she was looking elsewhere. NBC wanted to hire her. The network's *Huntley-Brinkley Report* was the top show in the business, and CBS had changed in the ten years she had worked there. Her mentors at the network were gone. Murrow was working for Kennedy as head of the U.S. Information Agency, and Sevareid was stationed in London.

Her restlessness seems pretty obvious in her public comments. She sounds cranky and not necessarily grateful to CBS for putting her on the air. "It only took six years as a producer of public affairs shows to make them sort of forget that I was a woman and put me on the air," she told one profiler that year. "Men make it so difficult for women to break into the field. The ones who do get in are really very good at their work. I suspect they are far better than most of the men. That's how it always is with persecuted minorities . . . You hear the voices of women newscasters all over Europe and in the new countries. In this country a woman is still associated with non-thinking. The profession is still riddled with prejudice. Do you realize that the National Press Club doesn't discriminate against lobbyists, against Negroes, but does discriminate against women?"

It's surprising to hear Mom speaking out that forcefully. It's obvious she believed this privately, but it seems impolitic to keep reminding CBS that they were too dumb to put her on air when they were in fact putting her on air.

It's bad office politics, and she was supposed to know politics. To cajole bullying and powerful politicians, you need to know what motivates them and what bothers them. Why didn't she know how to play the inside game with her bosses? Perhaps because her bosses only understood when they were brained with a stapler. Just because CBS had put her on air, that didn't mean that men who controlled the newsroom thought she was equal to the other correspondents. She thought she'd broken a barrier when all she'd done was move into a new pen where she was supposed to sit tight, smile gratefully and play her role. Even when she got scoops with real news value, Mom was having a hard time getting on air. She would report them on her radio program *One Woman's Washington,* but not on the more marquee programs. Even when she had discovered that Kennedy was going to rearrange the entire Joint Chiefs of Staff after the Bay of Pigs disaster (a leak from LBJ), it was worked into the TV anchorman's script as "CBS News has learned that. . . ."

In May 1961, ABC hired Lisa Howard, a former soap star and actress with no news background. It didn't help discourage men from thinking women on the air were merely there to look pretty. Howard had followed a model nearly identical to Mom's for getting on the air: She made her own scoop. She literally grabbed Nikita Khrushchev by the arm during his visit to the United Nations for his only American interview. But from the start, her tenure had been fraught with controversy. She was fired after the interview because it was seen as pure propaganda for Khrushchev. She was rehired but her reviews were dismal. The *New York Herald Tribune* dismissed her work as "all puff and no pith." A *Time* magazine profile portrayed her as an unenlightening barracuda: "lacking polish and a real reporter's knack for the trenchant question, she packs plenty of punch: a mixture of sass, brass and self-confidence wrapped in a package guaranteed to lure males."

Though Mom had come out of the news division and not show business, the discrimination was overt. Men didn't think she could handle the job. But it was less hostile than it would become in the late '60s and '70s as women took to the streets to protest for equal rights. What Mom faced was a soft bigotry that was perhaps more pernicious, because it came from some of the men she most admired.

While she was in Europe giggling in museums with Wyatt Dickerson, she filed two reports with famous CBS newsman David Schoenbrun. He was like Murrow—a stylish former war correspondent respected for his judgment and credentials. In a radio interview, Mom asked Schoenbrun about French culture and cuisine. He responded knowingly about the subtleties of the country in which he had lived for twenty years. He even made the French penchant for America-bashing sound artistic and inviting. He then turned to the French treatment of women: "They treat food and women the same way. They make you feel good and lovely and wonderful to eat."

"I may never leave this city or this country," said Mom with a laugh. "Say, now you brought up the question of women. That's one I'd like to talk a little bit about."

"Me too."

"I bet. We always hear about Paris being a risqué place. Is Paris so much more gay and the women so much more lovelier here than anywhere else?"

"Certainly not. I would say the most beautiful women I've ever seen in the world are from America. You're a perfect example of one, Nancy."

"Oh David, thank you. Were you like this when you lived in America?"

"Yes indeed, but although American women, and as in food, the original material is good, something happens to them; something goes wrong later on. They're beautiful women but they seem to lose their individuality. They start looking alike I think. In France the women are not just pretty women but they are exciting women. They walk as if they are beautiful, they act as if they are beautiful. They are above all happy to be women. They don't want to run things. They don't believe in equality of the sexes. They believe that the sexes are unequal as indeed they are. They would argue for equality of rights. That women have the same rights. But they're different and as we say in France: vive la différence."

In the course of his answer, the timbre in Schoenbrun's voice picked up considerably. This is a topic he liked: "They believe in expressing their own personality in being what they are themselves and that makes them exciting and different and changing all the time."

"Which is a good way to be. No doubt," said Mom before signing off. After the interview was over her last comment was captured on tape. "I was so fascinated by what you were saying, we ran over."

You can hear in Mom's voice how much she admires her older CBS colleague. And yet the message he's selling about French women—and by extension American women—is one that she's railed against in the States: Look pretty and distinctive and don't break out of your station.

By the end of 1962, Mom's stories for CBS television were slipping toward softer news. She interviewed entertainer Danny Kaye and reported on the arrival of the *Mona Lisa*. The closest she got to the White House was an interview with Mrs. Kennedy's social secretary on the First Lady's schedule. They had said she wouldn't do women's stories, but the reports she was filing for television were fluffy.

Her assignments changed because her CBS bosses weren't uniformly thrilled with her performances. She had a particularly difficult on-air moment during the John Glenn space flight early in 1962. Television reporters were not allowed inside the Glenn house because *Life* magazine had an exclusive contract with the astronauts and their families. But Mom had become friendly with Annie Glenn. She had talked to her about her marriage and what it would be like suddenly to be a mother to three new girls.

So, when Annie agreed to come out and talk to the cameras after the shot, it was natural for her to approach Mom. When she did, it upset a careful arrangement Mom had made with her colleagues from the other networks. They had decided that for the big moment after the successful orbit, they would question the astronaut's wife in turn. They had drawn straws. Martin Agronsky of NBC was to be first.

When Annie came out, NBC was in the middle of a commercial. Mom tried to honor the agreement, nudging Agronsky instead of talking with Mrs. Glenn. But he had no intention of going ahead, since NBC wasn't even on the air. He wanted everyone to wait. Don Hewitt, the CBS producer who had hired Mom, could hear on live television that Mrs. Glenn was talking to Mom. Why wasn't Nancy talking back? "For Christ's sake, talk to her, open your mouth," Hewitt shouted into Mom's ear.

Mom explained, on the air, that they had agreed to take turns and that she would begin as soon as her colleagues had asked their questions. Hewitt just yelled. She kicked Agronsky with her foot to get him to ask his question. His network, NBC, was still on commercial so he wasn't talking. Hewitt kept yelling: "I don't give a shit who promised what to whom. She's talking to *you*! Take off your ear phones and give them to her so that she can talk directly to Walter [Cronkite]." Mom tried to protest, but Hewitt shouted: "Take the goddamn phones off and give them to Annie Glenn."

NBC's Agronsky should have moved when he had the chance. By handing over the earphones, Mom hooked up Annie Glenn to the CBS party line. She and her children in Alexandria, Virginia, could talk to Cronkite in New York and John Glenn's parents in New Concord, Ohio. By the time the other two networks were on the air, all they could do was watch Annie talk to Walter and her children talk to their grandparents, but viewers of NBC and ABC couldn't hear Cronkite or the grandparents so when they'd had enough of the confusion they turned the dial on the television to CBS.

When it was all over, Agronsky told his colleagues in exasperation: "She kept kicking me all the time we were on the air." In her ear Hewitt complained, "She's really not very responsive to directions."

Mom started talking to NBC executives in Washington and did what she could to improve her chances of getting hired. On a trip to

New York she visited the office of David Sarnoff, the imposing chairman of NBC and a legendary broadcast pioneer who built the RCA network. He was named a brigadier general by Eisenhower for assisting in the 1952 presidential campaign. Mom told the secretary she had an appointment. The secretary said that General Sarnoff didn't have a Nancy Hanschman on his schedule.

"Well, never mind that," Mom said. "Mrs. Florence Lowe has told me to come see him."

"Oh," said the secretary, straightening up at the name of Mr. Sarnoff's close friend. "General Sarnoff is not here at the moment but I'll be certain to tell him you stopped in."

I heard this story from Mom's longtime friend Bonnie Angelo. Bonnie knew the story because Florence Lowe used to tell it for a laugh. She'd never had a conversation with Nancy Dickerson about David Sarnoff. She certainly hadn't told her to go see him. "Your mother was jaw-droppingly bold," laughed Bonnie.

As Mom started her third year with CBS, she also had a new problem: my brother. CBS didn't welcome the news that she was pregnant and as spring approached, she started showing. Would viewers really want to see a pregnant woman on television? Her approaching due date became new reason to limit her assignments. Meanwhile, NBC president Bill McAndrew had seemed delighted by the news.

"When's Labor Day?" he asked.

Mom, who had been so used to hiding the fact she was with child, or at least not talking about it around the newsroom, answered: "It's always the first Monday in September."

McAndrew hired her anyway. In May 1963 the move from CBS to NBC was announced and a wire arrived immediately from London:

THE WHOLE THING IS NOTHING BUT A LOUSY NBC PLOT TO DEPRIVE ME OF MY CHIEF SOURCE OF NEWS GOSSIP WISDOM GOOD COMPANIONSHIP AND THE COFFEE BREAK WHEN I GET TO WASHINGTON STOP I HAVE ASKED REASSIGNMENT. . . . GOOD LUCK ANYWAY. DAMMIT. ERIC SEVAREID.

Chapter Twenty

In July 1963, just a few months after Mom joined NBC, my brother Michael was born. The network celebrated with a press release: "NBC News has its first baby." (Mom's friend Paul Niven sent over a wire: "Let us hope that Michael takes after the network in which he was conceived rather than that into which he was born.")

When she got married, Mom hadn't really wanted children. It was one of the objections she had talked about with the priest before saying yes to Dad. But the girls changed her mind. She liked being a mother, but she also wanted to contribute something of her own to the Dickerson family. A new child would bring them all closer. That instinct may have contributed to her decision to take in a young boy from St. Ann's orphanage during the family's first Christmas together in 1962. When young Jimmy carried away his wooden suitcase after his four-day stay, she was overcome with grief. She was convinced she wanted a child.

So she had Michael, apparently without much effort. "On July 10 I left the office, went to a lovely dinner party for the Vice President and Lady Bird, got up early the next morning and produced Michael Wyatt Dickerson," she wrote in her autobiography. "By the time I came out of anesthesia, Dr. Walsh was already en route to Hyannisport to care for his most famous patient." (From hair stylist to obstetrician, Mom seemed to share everything she could with Jackie Kennedy.)

Thirty years later, when Michael discussed the birth of his first boy with her, she confirmed our suspicions that at our births she had not exactly been among those present. "She asked questions that raised serious doubts about whether she had ever had children at all," remembers Michael.

When she talked about sisterhood, Mom liked to quote from *A Tree Grows in Brooklyn*: "It was the only thing the women held in common—the sure knowledge of the pain of giving birth." Since women knew about childbirth, Mom thought, they didn't have to talk about it. So she didn't, not out loud, for profilers or in her book. For her, childbirth and family had to be no big production. She discussed her children in the same limited way her male colleagues did—the birthdays and big dances—but she didn't go on about the daily process. And she certainly didn't complain; that would have given the boys ammunition against her. Women who wanted to be just like her could have used a little guidance, but she wasn't there to give it to them. Even in her 1976 autobiography, published when the women's movement had introduced the biological realities of childbirth into the workplace, Mom wasn't going to write about what it was like to haul herself around the newsroom during nine months of pregnancy. In 1991, Meredith Vieira stepped down as a *60 Minutes* correspondent after network executives would not allow her to work part-time to accommodate the birth of her second child. In an article in *Mirabella* magazine on the heated debate about women and their tough balancing act between work and family, Mom weighed in with this:

"I was on the air Friday, Michael was born on Saturday, and two weeks later I was back on the air. The same thing happened with my second child and two weeks later I was in Miami at the Republican convention. Everyone was stunned to hear I'd had a baby; most people never knew I was pregnant."

She sounds like an army ranger talking about Nam. *I'd been shot but I charged the hill anyway and took out two of their gun nests. I had them stitch me back up and I was on the front again the next day.* If childbirth couldn't be a sign of femininity to her viewers or her male colleagues, it would be a sign of her endurance. The message to women coming after her seems clear: Hide your belly and power through, sister. Stoic, but not very helpful.

Accompanying the NBC press release about Michael were pictures of Mom in her nightgown smiling over the darling sleeping baby boy. He looks untroubled and tidy in all of the pictures. That's because he's just arrived from central processing. A baby nurse was hired and he was brought on- and offstage at the right moments already bathed, powdered, fed and burped. In a profile a month later Mom confirmed the parenting strategy. "Adjust the baby to your life, not the household life to him," she said. "I try to do that, and he seems pretty happy with the operation." (Whatever his name is.)

Now we smother our children, but the parenting ethic for women of Mom's generation and class was just the opposite. Dr. Spock might have been revolutionizing parenting elsewhere in America, but many of Mom's contemporaries, particularly in the upper classes of Washington, believed that if you coddled your children, they became soft. "People thought raising children was simple," says my father. "You didn't spoil them and you made them independent. You didn't spare the rod or you spoiled the child." It wasn't just convenient to farm out the child care; parents kept at a distance from their children because they thought it was healthy for the children.

Dad had been making a modest living when Elizabeth, Ann and Jane were born. He knew what it was like to change diapers and fuss with a helpless bawling infant as you tried to live your life. He schlepped his family around to various jobs and small rented apartments. At one point, Jane slept in a dresser drawer in her parents' room. For Dad, it was a great gift to be able to spare his second wife the sleepless hours and unpredictable disruptions of a new child. By the time Mom was in the maternity ward, Dad had made his first fortune. So Mom raised her babies like the aristocracy. Not only could she afford a private room in the hospital, there were soft-handed nurses in the wings to whom she could hand over the babies for maintenance the minute she arrived home. She was not the only one. The wives of many of the powerful men she covered may not have worked at the office, but they weren't spending the day at home either. They spent their afternoons at the club or shopping and their evenings at dinner parties with their husbands.

Mom wasn't gooey on the issue of babies, perhaps because unlike other women of her generation she never bonded with her mother over the subject. Her mother wasn't around. Mom wasn't cold—the right Irish ballad could make her weep—but the undifferentiated love of children wasn't in her nature. Some people rush to cradle and baby on the other side of the room. They invite stories from near strangers about laden diapers and teething pains. They serve an important societal function since new parents are prone to tell even the toll collector stories about their children. But this was not Mom's way.

There was no peer pressure about parenting at work. The men she competed with certainly didn't arrive Monday morning talking about their chapped nipples the way they did their golf scores. If they did, she might have taken up breastfeeding just to compete. If she were giving birth today, Mom undoubtedly would join the rest of us in the competitive parenting that is now a part of the professional life. David Gregory, the NBC White House correspondent, works his pediatrician almost as regularly as his most useful West Wing source. We have a wing in our house devoted to all of the books we read to make sure we are loving, feeding and massaging our newborn in the right way.

In the celebrity profiles, Mom didn't have to prove how she was home by six to bake orange and black Rice Krispie treats for her son's Halloween bake sale the way female correspondents do today. She talked, without guilt, about her staff. "The only way you can work is to have good people helping you at home. I have three—Louise Peterson, Helen Hammond and Lucille Jefferson—and I wouldn't know how to get along without them. As a broadcaster, I have various news assignments and never know where I'm going to be. I'm not in my office very much, and my work is at odd hours, so I have to feel that I can rely on the good judgment and responsibility of my help at home and know that they love the children. But I make sure they know that if they have a problem and need my help, they can reach me through the office, and I'll be right along."

With young Michael smoothly engaged with his minders, Mom could make it back on air three weeks after his birth for the March on Washington. NBC put her high on a shaky platform above the crowd. Maybe Mom had to rush back to work to look like she wasn't asking for special female favors. But there are also some stories you can't pass up. Even if she'd been given six months of maternity leave,

I can't imagine she would have stayed home to watch the march on television. I know I wouldn't have.

Some years before I started writing this book I put Mom's name into a Google alert. Every time her name appeared somewhere on the Internet I was notified. One day, Joyce Ladner, a scholar and former president of Howard University, arrived in that digital stream. She mentioned Mom in a *Washington Post* piece about her experience at the March on Washington. She was then a nineteen-year-old college student, and Lena Horne, whom she had met earlier that summer, took her by the hand and introduced her to Mom. "She told Nancy Dickerson to interview me instead of her," Ladner wrote. "She said, 'This young lady lives in Mississippi.' It was the first time I truly understood the power of the media, because my mother saw the interview on television. I reasoned that if Mother could see the support for the march . . . then surely she would feel that the commitment . . . I made to fight for justice was worth the price."

I e-mailed Ladner and she wrote back: "When Lena Horne had me follow her up the scaffold for the interview, your Mom was very kind, gracious, but spirited," she wrote. "She seemed pleased to interview a young person from the Deep South. After the interview she said something to the effect that she was pulling for us. My mother back in Mississippi and countless other family members and friends saw me interviewed. Forty-two years ago, that was quite something—to bring the local and national interests together and focus them on a young person from a little Mississippi hamlet called Palmers Crossing. I followed your Mom's career over the years until she retired and remarried. I always saw her as a woman who shattered a whole lot of barriers for us all. Oh yes, she was sharp too. Even in that heat, she didn't have a hair out of place and her makeup was perfect."

Mom helped Joyce's mother see what her daughter was doing and now Ladner has helped me see a little of Mom.

Chapter Twenty-one

The day Kennedy was shot, the networks stopped all programming and switched to news. Some 175 million viewers tuned in for the four days of coverage. For almost forty years, it was the most massive and concentrated broadcast in history until the attacks of September 11, 2001.

Viewers weren't just reacting to the news. They were reacting to images of a nature they'd never seen before: The First Lady in her bloodstained suit returning to Washington with her husband's casket; the president's alleged murderer Lee Harvey Oswald bustling through a crowd of police and reporters at the Dallas jail and then, with no warning, Jack Ruby stepping out and shooting him. It was the first live murder on television. It seemed like anything could happen on that box.

Immediately, television surpassed all other media as the source of national news. It became an emotional reservoir for the country as they expressed shock, anger and grief. The Kennedy presidency had made the men and women who covered him look glamorous. Now those correspondents would connect to people in a profound way. When Walter Cronkite removed his glasses and wiped his tears to announce Kennedy's death, he mirrored the nation's anguish.

Mom was in the NBC bureau when the news broke of the shooting. She was ordered to leave for Andrews Air Force Base. Robert Kennedy was planning to fly to Dallas, and she was to get on that plane with the family. Information was sketchy and wrong. She had no car, and there were no cabs. The only driver she could find was the janitor.

"Come on, let's go," she said, grabbing him by the shirtsleeve.

The two of them sped out of the parking lot for the long drive into Maryland.

"Where is the radio?" she said, looking at the blank dashboard.

"I don't have a radio."

"What?!" She screamed. She considered getting out of the moving car as it sped down Nebraska Avenue. Instead she suffered the forty-five minutes in agony. Had Kennedy died? Had Bobby already left?

When she got to Andrews, the Secret Service wouldn't let her in. She found an agent she knew and talked her way in. Mom hung the microphone on herself like a necklace and started filing radio reports. "We are here, members of Congress have arrived and leaders of both the House and Senate are here," she started. "Their wives are with them. Their wives are in tears." No one knew what was going on. Bobby wasn't leaving. A plane was coming back but they weren't even sure who would be on it. The networks had decided to share the video from the tarmac and it was NBC's job to deliver it. Bob Asman, Mom's producer, arrived after a motorcycle cop had allowed him to drive through the traffic on the median. He shouted to Mom inside the gate. "You have no idea what confusion reigned," remembers Asman, who was also barred by the jumpy Secret Service. "On her say-so, they let me in."

The phone companies had agreed to give NBC extra capacity to send back live pictures, but no picture was going through. At one point, the camera crew was told to cut the lights. The plane was coming in and they were blinding the pilot. A minute before the plane touched down, Asman finally got a picture up and captured the plane screaming down the runway.

The routine for a presidential arrival was very specific and is little changed today. The steps are rolled up to the front of Air Force One and the president is the first to come out. But that night, Bobby Kennedy raced up the steps. There was confusion and the cameras shot an open plane door with no one coming through it.

"We had no idea who would come out of that plane," remembers Asman.

Suddenly there was commotion at the back of Air Force One. A hydraulic lift was moved into position. Only then did they know what was happening.

"I thought, oh my God, that's the president's body," remembers Asman.

When Jackie Kennedy walked to the waiting ambulance, the door was locked and she had to run around to the other side. "I forgot that we were on the air and put my mike down thinking I could help," wrote Mom. "I saw the stains of the president's blood all over her dress, but didn't mention them on the air. Like everyone else I was trying to find a way to protect her."

At the end of the evening, NBC sent Mom out to Johnson's house, The Elms, to report on his return. The neighborhood was swarming with police. Television floodlights had been installed. Neighbors served the reporters coffee and snacks. Others offered insights about how well they knew the Johnsons, desperate to establish some link with the history of the moment.

When Johnson arrived around 10:00 P.M., the light inside his limousine was on so that he could read the papers. He looked up and waved at Mom standing with her microphone. But his car did not stop. There would be no interviews that night.

The engineers couldn't set up a television shot, so Mom commandeered the phone line of a neighbor and at 10:30 she filed a radio report from their living room: "President Johnson has arrived at his home. As he drove up, he acknowledged the greetings of people waiting for him . . . The Secret Service men who accompanied President Johnson carried their guns in the open. Mrs. Johnson said that the whole event is like a nightmare."

On Saturday, November 23, Mom started the day early in her hooded raincoat outside the White House. In the downpour, she tried to name the dignitaries and Kennedy friends as they arrived. She noticed the quiet and sad acts of transition, instructing the cameras to follow the president's rocking chair as it was carted away. It rained so hard messengers had to be sent to bring fresh raincoats for the marathon broadcast. Though she was wearing gloves, her hands shriveled like she'd been swimming all day.

That afternoon she joined other NBC reporters for a show called

Lyndon Johnson: What Kind of President? She said he had always considered himself ready for the presidency because he had worked in Washington for thirty-five years. He knew the Congress and he knew the bureaucracy. Martin Agronsky, who had been Mom's competitor when she covered John Glenn's orbit for CBS, noted that Sam Rayburn had always been upset that Johnson took the vice presidential spot on the ticket.

Mom gently corrected him. Rayburn initially opposed the move, but later reversed himself and endorsed Johnson's place on the ticket. Mom may have been right. According to historian Robert Dallek, the day before Kennedy's nomination in 1960, Sam Rayburn had already reversed his opposition to the notion. He told Massachusetts Congressmen and Kennedy loyalists John McCormack and Tip O'Neill that "if Kennedy wants Johnson for Vice President . . . then LBJ has nothing else he can do but to be on the ticket." He also told the two men that he would tell Johnson to take the offer if Kennedy made it. Of course in Mom's notes from that night, Rayburn told Johnson not to take the post.

Whatever the truth was, Mom's correcting Agronsky, however gentle it may have been, immediately rankled her colleagues. She was not only presenting herself as the world's expert on Johnson, but they thought she was in some way taking unseemly delight in the ascension of the man she knew so well. "There was a feeling in the air that she was kind of saying: 'Now my guy's president,' " says Ron Nessen, who covered the Kennedy and Johnson White House for NBC at the time. "Everyone was mourning Kennedy and they felt like she was boasting a little about Johnson."

After the show Mom got a phone call. It was Johnson. He immediately launched into a critique of the show. "You corrected Agronsky without making a fool of him," said the new president. "Rayburn changed. He did want me to take the nomination, and you set the record straight without making him eat crow in public. Only way to do it." He then invited Mom and Dad to dinner that night at The Elms.

One of the first things you notice when you visit the replica of Johnson's Oval Office at his library in Austin are the three television screens. He was obsessed with the coverage of his presidency and clearly from his phone call to Mom, that obsession started almost as soon as his tenure did.

Johnson had deep animosity for Kennedy, and yet after his assassination he had to be keeper of the Kennedy flame. He had to show continuity. That was the only way to make a smooth transition and heal the country. In the midst of their horror and shock, people had to know that Johnson was going to follow the path of the slain president's administration. That meant Johnson didn't want any discussion of how his mentor Rayburn might not have initially endorsed the Kennedy-Johnson alliance. All hints of tension and bitterness between the Kennedy and Johnson factions not only had to stop, but they had to be airbrushed out of the past. Though it wasn't necessarily her intention, Mom was helping in that cause and Johnson appreciated it.

Johnson was letting her know right away that he liked having her on his team, and he wanted her to stay there. He didn't know the White House reporters who had covered Kennedy, so she was a welcome and familiar face. She would spend the next five years benefiting from his careful attention.

When Mom and Dad arrived at The Elms the night after the assassination, the president was not yet back from the White House. The Secret Service frisked them down to their underwear as if trying to make up for their own failures in Dallas. Lady Bird was upstairs. She had attended a prayer service that day and visited with Jackie Kennedy. They were greeted by Luci Johnson, barefoot in a green Chinese robe.

Mom and Dad traded small talk with her. Luci was focused on the irritating restrictions that would come with being a presidential daughter. "How would you like it to have Secret Service men with you every minute of the day?" she asked. Even now she couldn't talk to a boy late at night without the phone light going on in her parents' bedroom. Her father, seeing it, would either monitor the call or interrupt to tell her that she ought to be asleep. She concluded that living in the White House would only be worthwhile if she could have her own private line.

When Johnson arrived, Lady Bird came downstairs on cue, with a drink and popcorn. After kissing her hello, the president returned to the subject of Mom's exchange with Agronsky.

In his early days in the House, he explained, he was trying to get funds for a public works project but an older, stronger congressman had opposed it. Johnson maneuvered the program into committee and then onto the House floor. He won the debate on the floor but in doing so publicly put down his older opponent. Afterward, Rayburn took him aside and said, "Lyndon, you feel pretty smart because you got what you wanted. But you also got yourself an enemy. A really clever fellow would have won without ridiculing a man on the way, and earning himself an enemy for life."

Everyone nodded. Johnson paced. He walked over to the television and started talking back to NBC's Huntley and Brinkley. He was determined that the country should be calm, and whenever the broadcasting duo said something he thought was inflammatory, Johnson would bark: "Keep talking like that and you'll bring on a revolution just as sure as I'm standing here."

His speechwriter Horace Busby and Judge Homer Thornberry arrived. The president explained that he'd ordered the Secret Service to protect House Speaker John McCormack because he was worried about a government-wide takeover attempt. That afternoon the Soviets had made a show of good faith by turning over a complete dossier on Lee Harvey Oswald's activities during his years in Moscow. Johnson was relieved but not settled.

"Maybe they're out to get us all," he said. He was going to keep the armed services on alert. He wasn't sure the assassination was the work of just one man.

He worried about conspiracy theories. He talked about how Lincoln's assassination still had unanswered questions " . . . Damn sure that kind of mystery doesn't happen here. I'm going to make sure there isn't one damn question or one damn mystery that isn't solved about this thing. You can be sure of that . . . not one damn unanswered question."

He interrupted himself, walking over to the phone and pushing one of its buttons. He picked up the receiver.

"Is this the White House?" Johnson said. "Oh, sorry." Then he punched another: "The White House? Sorry." He looked over at his wife. "Bird! Come over here and get me the White House. That's going to have to be changed! The whole damn world could go up in smoke and I wouldn't even be able to get Dean Rusk. Take me ten damn minutes to reach the secretary of state."

The White House secretaries who logged Johnson's activities every day as president recorded the moment with almost comical blandness. "[President Johnson] said that one of the first things he would like to do is revise the White House operator system. It was too slow for him . . . All other things would be left the same at the White House. Didn't want to change anything."

Finally the president got through to his National Security Adviser McGeorge Bundy. He reminded him to "get those wires out fast" to every country recognized by the United States to assure them of the continuity of our government. Then without irony after the phone debacle he told Bundy: "I don't want any of them thinking that we don't know what to do."

Next in the secretary's log is: "Told Nancy about Rufus bravery." Johnson's first letter as president had been to the Kennedy children. His second had been to the head of the Secret Service commending agent Rufus Youngblood. Immediately after the first shots in Dallas, Youngblood threw Johnson and his wife on the floor of the car.

"There we were hunkered down in the car and he had his body on us," said Johnson. "And Bird was hunkered down there with us too. We were hunkered. Rufus moved so fast. It was one of the greatest things I have ever seen, Nancy. I didn't know Rufus had that many reflexes."

At one point Judge Thornberry called his daughter to reassure her, just as millions of parents had called their children that night. LBJ took the phone from Thornberry and started talking. "Is he your boyfriend?" he asked. "What's his name? Buddy? Well, put Buddy on, I want to talk with him. . . . Buddy? This is Lyndon Johnson, your new president . . . just fine thank you . . . Thank you . . . need all the help we can get . . . Well, Buddy, take good care of that little girl who is with you . . ." Johnson was trying to comfort the country one person at a time.

Mom and Dad were watching Johnson come to life as a president. He'd been plenty animated as vice president, but now he had real power, power of the kind he had as majority leader.

Before they left, Lady Bird asked Mom what she should wear to the funeral. Black obviously, but the new First Lady didn't have any suitable black clothes in her wardrobe. The next day, Mom sent over her black coats and dresses and had a local shop send over some hats. The First Lady, who was both rich and frugal, was astonished that anyone would have so many black clothes. Mom was shocked that Lady Bird didn't have any.

When Mom got home after dinner, she immediately went to the typewriter and hammered out stream-of-consciousness recollections on flimsy brown Western Union paper the news services used to send bulletins. She didn't report on the specific details of the evening but she spent the next several days pretty sure she had a sense of the new president's mood. The notes she typed take some work to understand. One line reads: "Rayburn here." That would have been something. He had been dead for two years. The shorthand referred to Johnson's aside to her that he wished his old friend had been alive at the moment of crisis.

Of course she was in the tank for Johnson after that night. Reporters are always trying to piece together what goes on in the room. We usually have to rely on the faulty memories and agendas of one person who was in the room and will talk, or worse, a secondhand account of the action. Watching history unfold in front of you while you sit on the sofa is intoxicating and indelible. The world was mourning, searching and wondering what the new president would do, and there she was watching him. People were looking to him for answers and action. She watched him trying in ways big and small as he roamed the living room to calm everyone's fears, protect the country and give the government and the people some path to hope. She was a sucker for anyone who tried, even if they failed. Having seen how deter-mined and wrought he was that night made it hard for her to judge him too harshly later. She knew he had a good heart and she knew even if he was doing the wrong thing, he was doing his best.

The next day, while Mom was reporting for NBC, CBS was run-ning some of her old Johnson footage. Mom stood on the White House lawn as the cortege left for Capitol Hill. Half a million people were waiting to file past Kennedy's casket. Black Jack, a riderless horse with boots turned backward in the stirrups, bucked so badly he nearly trampled her. A few hours later, she stood on a platform outside St. Matthew's Cathedral, shivering as she identified the friends and family arriving for the service. That night there was another procession, this one less familiar as dignitaries lined up to pay their respects to the new president. Neither she nor her colleagues could identify many of them, particularly the men in robes and headdresses. There was no list. They mumbled a little, filling the dead air. When a familiar face like French Prime Minister Charles de Gaulle appeared, they all became reanimated, finally able to talk about someone they recognized.

NBC covered the death for seventy-two hours and thirty-six minutes. Mom worked that entire time filing reports to television and radio. A few weeks later she received a letter from an editor at Random House asking if she wanted to write a book about the new president. "In all the television all of us watched, yours was the fresh voice and the fresh point-of-view, both toward the tragedy and the new President." Then 443 radio and television critics named their radio and television people of the year. Judy Garland and Andy Williams took away the television prizes. Arthur Godfrey and Mom won the radio prizes. "Nancy Dickerson walked away with the 'Woman of the Year' in Radio," wrote the *Radio Television Daily*, "for her fine coverage of the news surrounding the John F. Kennedy funeral."

Thirty-six years later, I was awakened early one Saturday morning by *Time*'s Deputy Managing Editor Jim Kelly. John Kennedy Jr.'s plane had disappeared on the way to Martha's Vineyard. The magazine closed on Saturdays, so we were right up against our deadline. He wanted me to fly immediately to the Kennedy compound in Hyannisport, where one of Bobby's children was getting married that weekend. John Jr. was scheduled to attend the ceremony. I was covering Congress at the time but had parachuted into massive media swarms a few times, so I was sent from Washington though the New York bureau was closer.

I put in my contacts and grabbed a bottle of saline solution and my computer bag. I flew to Boston and then ruined a rental car by driving over the speed limit on the shoulder to get past the weekend beach traffic.

By the time I got there, the whole Kennedy compound had been cordoned off. Usually an opening can be found somewhere. If you've ever tried to keep squirrels off a bird feeder, you know what it's like for policemen trying to keep the press in their pen. But over forty years, the Kennedy family and local police had been perfecting their lockdown. And on Cape Cod, they had geography on their side. So I sat on a low stone wall with my colleagues peering at the white tent put up for the wedding that had been called off.

I spent a lot of time being offered coffee by the neighbors. I flagged down caterers driving home with their uneaten canapés and talked to waiters with their uniforms still on hangers. No one had much to say.

The television correspondents were helpless. Their networks kept cutting back to them and they had nothing to say. Correspondents who had been vacationing nearby jumped into action but wound up talking about what *they* had been doing that foggy night Kennedy's plane went down. NBC scored a minor coup because one of their medical correspondents was also a licensed pilot and was vacationing nearby. He could at least talk about plane navigation with the Kennedy compound in the background.

Editors kept calling my bureau chief in Washington wondering why I wasn't breaking through the press lines and running down the half mile to report on the family's grieving. They were on deadline and many of them had never been reporters so they didn't really understand the pickle I was in. "Can't he do something," they complained, "doesn't *his family have any friends?*"

If I'd been writing this book at the time, I might have had a little more to say, at least about the Kennedy family's familiarity with death. Mom's folder marked "Kennedy" contains identical prayer cards for Jack and Bobby's funerals. On one side is a black-and-white portrait, and on the other is a prayer and a quote from his political life. She kept the Western Union telegram inviting her and Dad to Bobby's funeral with its strict rules for entrance—"this telegram must be presented at the church. Please enter by the side door to the chapel." I also came across some notes she'd made after spending the weekend at that Hyannisport compound in 1965. She had talked to Bobby about his rocky relationship with LBJ, and his brother's legacy. Bobby showed that he could be as frank as JFK. "I always assumed that you and LBJ were off in the bedroom somewhere," he said offhandedly. In her notes Mom wrote: "Eunice has a normal reaction to the fact that her brother is no longer alive. The adaptability of the others does not seem so normal though."

I ended my evening searching for the hotel where the wedding guests were staying. It was approaching midnight when I found the main one. No other reporters were there. I tried to get some of the guests at one of the bars to tell me what they knew. One of the guests called me a vulture. Those who did talk were useless. I did run into an old family acquaintance. We'd shared the same housekeepers and our parents had been friends.

"How are you doing?" I was actually *just curious.*

"I'm not saying anything," she said, taking a few step backwards.

Before crashing at 3 A.M., I scraped together a few skinny quotes from some guests hanging outside smoking cigarettes and filed them to New York. It was a dismal and fruitless day for the second generation of Dickerson reporters.

Nancy Louise Hanschman, age seven, 1934.
(Author's collection)

Café life at the start of Mom's first trip to Europe, the summer of her senior year at the University of Wisconsin. Trocadero, Paris, 1948. *(Author's collection)*

Sharing a laugh with political rivals Lyndon Johnson and Hubert Humphrey at a women's press club dinner in 1960. *(Ed Clark)*

Planning 1961 inaugural coverage with her idol, Edward R. Murrow, left, and CBS News producer Don Hewitt. *(Marvin Lichtner)*

In the Oval Office, shortly after JFK became president. This was Mom's favorite of the photographs she displayed on the piano at Merrywood. *(Marvin Lichtner)*

Interviewing First Lady Jackie Kennedy, 1962. *(Jack Brown)*

Reporting with NBC's Bob Abernethy from Andrews Air Force Base, November 22, 1963, as President Kennedy's body is flown back to Washington. *(City News Bureau)*

Laughing with Lady Bird Johnson, 1961. *(Marvin Lichtner)*

The Dickersons, 1967. From left to right: Ann, Jane, Dad, Michael, Mom and Elizabeth. *(Elizabeth Kuhner)*

Dancing with LBJ in the East Room of the White House, 1967. *(Estate of Stanley Tretick)*

Conversation with the president, January 4, 1971. From left to right: President Nixon, John Chancellor (NBC), Mom, Eric Sevareid (back to camera; CBS) and Howard K. Smith (ABC). *(The White House)*

Mom and Dad at a party with Secretary of State Henry Kissinger, 1975. *(Author's collection)*

Merrywood, Mom, and me, 1975. *(Harry Naltchayan)*

To Nancy – With appreciation & Warm Regard
Ronald Reagan

With President-elect Ronald Reagan at the party in his honor at Merrywood, January 1981. *(The White House)*

Mom with John Whitehead at the State Department shortly before their marriage. *(Author's collection)*

Our last photograph together, at my wedding in September 1995. She was shocked that I knew how to dance. *(Author's collection)*

On the 2000 campaign trail before covering the Bush White House for *Time. (Brooks Kraft)*

Chapter Twenty-two

Mom's long relationship with Johnson paid off. She started 1964 at the center of NBC's coverage providing analysis of the new president and the challenges that faced him. She was the first to interview Lady Bird on television after spending a week shadowing her, including traveling to a "poverty pocket" coal mining town to build support for the president's war on poverty.

NBC was very happy that they had Johnson's favorite television reporter, but Mom was getting other scoops too. One clear day in May, a twin-engine prop plane mysteriously crashed just outside of San Francisco, killing forty-four people. It wasn't on Mom's beat, but Dad had done some business with pilots and got a tip that the answer to the puzzling crash was in a recording of the pilot's last words. Mom dialed around and that night reported that a deranged passenger had brought a revolver on board, opened the cockpit door and shot the pilot. The plane's recorder had captured it.

"My God I've been shot," screamed the pilot. "I've been shot."

The news was splashed across the front pages of the nation's newspapers the next day, crediting the scoop to an NBC Washington correspondent. It was a nice way to commemorate her first year at NBC. A telegram from Bill McAndrew, the president of the news division, arrived the next day. "Congratulations on a Great Job it was in the Best Tradition of the Best News Team in the Country. We are all proud of you."

Two weeks after Mom had made the front page of the *New York*

Times with her scoop, the paper's magazine ran a long piece called "Women Don't Like to Look at Women." In it, Lee Graham, a famous family psychologist who dished womanly advice on television, explained why women still had such a tough time getting jobs on the airwaves. The article is a bonanza of political incorrectness.

While Mom was being praised by one boss, another, Julian Goodman, the vice president of NBC News, seems to have missed the memo. "Finding a really competent radio or TV news reporter is difficult, and when we do find one, that person is rarely, if ever, a woman." NBC had hired the first television newswoman—Pauline Frederick—and now they were promoting their new hire Mrs. Dickerson, but Goodman lumbers right along. He explains that even the newspapers had little time for women. "How many women have their own bylines unless they're handling special features, human-interest stuff and women's page chatter?"

Goodman wasn't alone. His colleague Giraud Chester, another NBC vice president, said "a woman's manner is not suited to news and serious discussions. She may be all right as a panelist on a game show, or even on a public affairs program if she's provocative enough or has a 'hate' value. But she's ineffective as a moderator or an M.C. . . . She is not in the habit of asking probing questions or getting tough with unruly guests . . . she generally prefers to be the gracious, glamorous hostess. She'd rather have her hair in place than her brains. The audience won't buy it so we can't afford to do it."

NBC radio executives were just as charming. Robert Wogan, vice president of the radio network, said, "put them in front of a microphone—and a camera as well—and something happens to them. They become affected, overdramatic, high-pitched. Some turn sexy and sultry. Others get patronizing and pseudo-charming."

The piece runs through a few reasons women don't like to see other women on television. "You bet women don't like to watch other women," said one unnamed television producer. "It's jealousy: Women have all they can do to get through their daily routine of housework, kids, pin curlers and gossip. How do you think they like it when they turn on their TV set and there sits this goddess with the right hairdo, makeup and dress, plenty of poise and a brain besides?"

To work on television, a woman must be unthreatening like

Lucille Ball, Shirley Booth and Martha Raye. "Women don't usually have the authoritative personality that men do," Joseph Cook, program manager of WCBS, is quoted as saying, "And that's good. Who likes authoritative women anyhow? Any woman who could manage this would sound too much like a man. So why not hire a man in the first place?"

I had always assumed Mom faced a stronger form of chauvinism than I see today—tough women are bitches, pretty ones are gossiped about. Mom was both difficult and pretty so she would have gotten a double dose. I imagined that meant she dealt with a lot more whispers and a sprinkling of overt comments. But what is so striking about this article is that it's all out in the open.

Four years after she had first appeared on television the leaders of her profession and her network could still enumerate at length for the *New York Times* the reasons a woman did not belong on the air. Even the NBC promotions department hadn't updated their terminology. Before the 1964 Democratic Convention in Atlantic City, the seventeen NBC correspondents were gathered like a football team in front of an NBC flag for a photo. The caption read: "The Men Who Will Cover." Apparently the caption writer couldn't be bothered to work out the logic problem since seated along with the sixteen "men who would cover" was a woman in a skirt. Nor did they change their ad copy. "Follow These Men," read the full-page ad in the *New York Times* with a picture of Huntley and Brinkley and Mom and her new partner Ray Scherer.

Mom and Ray had been on the White House lawn in the days after the Kennedy assassination. They had worked so well together the network decided to make them a team.

Ray was a tender and gentle man from Indiana. I've watched old clips of him and he had an easy Midwestern feel. It was like he was about to hand you a lemonade on a hot day. White House correspondents are so stylized now it can be hard to get past the theatrics. Ray didn't contribute to that. He was just a reporter. "They called him the farmer and her the steel magnolia," remembers Mom's director at NBC, Max Schindler. Mom told one interviewer, "We think differently, Ray and I, which is good. Sum it up this way—Ray is salt, I'm pepper."

Their partnership must have been difficult. Working with a partner is not easy under any circumstances. I covered Congress and the White House with Jay Carney for five years at *Time* and it was wonderful, but we were the exception, somehow knowing how to feed our egos but not at the other's expense. Journalists want to be the first ones to break into the room and have every head turn to hear what we have to say. A partner gets in the way. In television, that tension is exacerbated. You can have a double byline in a magazine, but there's no room on the screen for two people. There's just too little airtime. If your piece gets on, the other guy's doesn't.

Mom had access to Johnson and she didn't share. That must have driven Ray mad, though he wasn't completely shut out. He went where Mom couldn't. He may have been the only reporter to interview Johnson in the nude. LBJ often invited male reporters into his private quarters. Once, while talking to Ray, he took a shower. That was just one of LBJ's tricks. Some reporters had to endure a conversation while the president sat on the toilet.

I didn't know who Ray was until after Mom died. A friend said she'd grown up in the country near an old colleague of Mom's. She offered to introduce me and so one drizzly Saturday my wife and I drove with her into the Virginia hill country to visit Ray and his wife at their weekend house. We sat on the narrow back porch eating cheese from a worn wooden plank and drinking tea out of chipped mugs. The dogs wove in and out, leaving red clay footprints.

"She was very competitive," said Ray.

"She had sharp elbows," said his wife, Maudie, quickly, pouring us tea. I got the sense Maudie might have piped up like that when Mom and Ray were working together, offering her opinion if she thought her husband was being too kind to his pushy partner. "Please tell me she couldn't cook too. We all had to hope that she didn't have some hidden domesticity too." I laughed, and said she must have hid it from us as well.

The Scherers weren't bitter or angry. They liked Mom, and they were just describing what she was like. Ray and his wife were almost as interested in learning about Mom as I was. They talked about her parties and her glamorous life. It's clear Mom and Ray weren't close. The Scherers described her with a little of the mystery and rumor journalists use when we talk about the famous and powerful we cover but don't really know. Mom's other NBC colleague Ron Nessen said much the same: "She was much richer and had a different life than the rest of us."

"She had parties that everyone attended," said Ray. "I think the president used to go to her house. [NBC president] Julian Goodman was worried about that. They said she was too close to the people she covered. She used to come in and tell us things and we'd say: 'Jesus, Nancy that's a story,' but she couldn't report it."

After a little while our conversation switched to the politics of the day. Ray and I talked over all parts of the Clinton presidency. We bantered. He'd retired in the '70s, but we used the shorthand Washington journalists use. All the stories usually come back to the question of power, who has it, how much, how they'll use it and what will happen when all those actors try to assert their power simultaneously. The conversation has a rhythm that's identical no matter what the time period.

My wife and I finally left after overstaying our welcome. We saw Ray and Maudie a few more times before Ray died. He and I would debrief each other about Clinton and the Gingrich Congress and whatever else was on the front page that day. It was as if he were my bureau chief asking me what I had learned out on the beat. The last time I saw the Scherers, I drove them home after a party. It was snowing so I walked them to the door of their little house tucked away in the city. They had an enviable life. Covering Washington politics warps people. Covering it for a network can warp you even further— it's heady stuff when a president regularly calls you by your first name and airport travelers stop you to ask you for your autograph. The money the networks now pay makes life easier but adds more stress and more warp. Ray and Maudie appeared to have escaped all of that.

Chapter Twenty-three

In the spring of 1964 Mom and Ray and everyone else in the political press were trying to figure out whom Johnson would pick as his running mate. The most tantalizing contender was Bobby Kennedy. But the attorney general and the president were back to hating each other. There had been a blip of fellow feeling after John Kennedy's assassination but soon they resumed their decade-long feud. Kennedy thought Johnson was squandering his brother's legacy and Johnson thought Bobby was undermining him with the party, his administration and the country. There was no way that Johnson would choose Kennedy, but the party could pressure the president into putting him on the ticket. In late July 1964, *Time* magazine reported on the "boomlet for Attorney General Robert Kennedy. Chicago's powerful Democratic Mayor Dick Daley, a longtime political pal of the Kennedy clan, has made it known that he favors Bobby. So have a clutch of Northern and Midwestern Governors and state and county party chairmen. From his sickbed in Boston, Ted Kennedy declared himself in on the boomlet. NBC Correspondent Nan Dickerson reported that Jackie Kennedy would return from cruising Yugoslav waters to attend the convention and 'help Bobby.' " No one called Mom "Nan" anymore, but the boys at *Time* liked to give the girls nicknames. Mom had reported on the two o'clock news that Jackie and Bobby had discussed the possibility of his joining the ticket during a weekend in Hyannisport. They weighed whether he might take advantage of the likely groundswell of affection for his family at the convention and accept a draft for the second spot.

Luther Hodges, Johnson's secretary of commerce, called shortly after Mom's broadcast. "Mr. President, have you heard about Nancy Dickerson's report?" he asked.

Johnson had heard about Mom's story and had his press secretary call over for the script. He would have to put a stop to the Bobby rumors by the end of the day. "It just means a war and I might as well lay it down," Johnson told Secretary of State Dean Rusk. "I'm not going to serve unless I can serve with whomever I want to."

A few weeks after Mom's report, he made an unprecedented announcement. No one from his administration would be on the ticket. That put an end to one set of rumors but sent Mom off on a new hunt for whom Johnson would pick. Would it be a Midwesterner like Eugene McCarthy or Hubert Humphrey, or would it be Mike Mansfield from Montana, or Iowa governor Harold Hughes?

When the Democrats gathered in Atlantic City that August, Johnson had still not made his announcement. He'd told the networks to save three minutes after his nomination on Wednesday for the news.

Mom had spent the days before the convention with Lady Bird and her daughters filming a half-hour special on the family. They looked over old scrapbooks and traded family stories. It was the kind of soft-focus tableau that candidates kill for because it shows their more human side. This is why *People* magazine gets full access to the candidates before conventions.

Mom's last act before leaving Washington was to attend Lady Bird's White House lunch for Senate wives. Muriel Humphrey sat next to the First Lady. It seemed deliberate. Was Johnson going to pick her husband, Hubert Humphrey, the Minnesota senator? After lunch, Mom dialed around to confirm her hunch. That same afternoon, an NBC cameraman at the White House walked by the Roosevelt room. LBJ called him in.

"Come here and have a drink with the next vice president of the United States," said Johnson, pouring three bourbons.

Standing next to the president was Hubert Humphrey, who had just flown down that morning from the convention in Atlantic City.

Mom had been working the scoop, so when the cameraman delivered the news, she convinced her bosses not to just pass it along through one of the anchors but to let her report the exclusive. Plus, she had picked up that Johnson was coming to the convention a night ahead of his schedule. If she found him, she could ask him about Humphrey on the air. The only problem was that no one knew when or where Johnson would arrive. By midafternoon, a Secret Service man tipped her off that Johnson would be landing at the helicopter pad not far from the convention hall. She called press secretary Bill Moyers, who didn't wave her away from the information.

She arrived at the helicopter pad just before Johnson did, dragging thick camera cable behind her in the August heat. She handed her purse with its microphones and research papers to a production assistant. The helicopter was whirring overhead. The assistant said that he couldn't take the purse because he couldn't get past security. As Mom told the story, he didn't lend a hand because he didn't like being ordered around. She snapped at him and put the purse over the crook of her arm and marched through the dirt. She looked like a very angry bag lady. The chopper approached and the floodlights were dimmed for the pilots. In her ear she could hear the director in the NBC control room screaming, "Switch to us, give it to us, she's got him, he's there and she's got him!"

Televisions across America on all networks cut from the dry delegate count to the stomping lady on the tarmac greeting the president.

The chopper landed and the lights were turned up. By this time the other reporters who had arrived were being kept back by the security men.

"I was the only mike in town," Mom remembered.

"Hello Nancy," said Johnson as he came off the helicopter with Humphrey, "I've been watching you all day and you're doing a wonderful job." She asked him about Humphrey and he confirmed it. She interviewed them both as they walked. It was the story of the convention. The next day the *New York Times* columnist Jack Gould wrote that her questions had been "right on the beam," a compliment she savored by hoarding 86 copies of the article. (Was she going to send them out with her Christmas cards?)

The other networks envied her for beating them to the punch. Her print colleagues were less envious. They were angry. Johnson had walked laps around the White House that afternoon and talked about Humphrey but their news wouldn't appear until the next morning's paper. Mom put it on air for 25 million viewers who would consider it old news when they saw it in their papers the next day. *Variety* mentioned the scoop when it chose her as one of the ten best television commentators of the year. They headlined their article "Nine Guys and a Doll." The *New York Times* ran a story on it: "Another First for Nancy." "Before the 1964 convention she was a well-known hard working reporter," says Dad. "But this put her in another world."

Career-making scoops like this feed the ego and drive your competition crazy. It's tempting to say that a big scoop is really only for the benefit of the gang of 4,000—the inside-the-Beltway/inside-the-media types who live in the political bubble. That's true, but there's more to it than that. If you get the scoop first, you've probably worked the story harder than the others and that means you can put the fresh news in context. In Mom's case she was also there to ask the questions, of Johnson and Humphrey, which added more context. Politicians want to frame issues their own way, and the more scoops we get, the better chance we have to frame issues in a more balanced way before their spin machines package it for delivery.

The young assistant at the helipad was Cal Thomas, a former official of the Moral Majority and now a syndicated conservative columnist.

Once she had a grudge, she kept it in her teeth like a seed. Twenty years after Atlantic City, when she and Thomas were commentators for Fox News, she made his refusal to help her the subject of a commentary. She told the story of the helicopter landing and then asked: How could Thomas act with such sanctimony when he had deserted her in her hour of need? Thomas didn't remember the altercation and wouldn't take the bait when I asked him about Mom's harder side, which he must have seen as a young assistant at NBC. "She was a wonderful and generous lady," he said. "She was not always perfect. None of us are."

Mom's scoop didn't make her life easier on the campaign trail. Everyone else in the press corps wants to think they're playing by the same rules, and she seemed to have an unfair advantage. They blamed her beauty and her relationship with Johnson. But the scoop also exacerbated the growing competition between print and television. The print guys thought television reporters were entertainers and not journalists. They resented the attention Mom and her colleagues were getting. *Time* could barely contain its contempt for the power shift toward television. "The appearances and disappearances of TV newscasters are logged by the press with a fan-club fidelity usually reserved for grease paint performers—which perhaps they are," said the magazine in August 1964. "Thus when NBC, eyeing San Francisco, decided to backstop its top news team of Chet Huntley and Dave Brinkley with another duo, the *New York Times* duly recorded their names: Ray Scherer and Nancy Dickerson. And when Westinghouse Broadcasting Co. signed novelist-playwright Gore Vidal to report both the Republican and Democratic national conventions, the *Times* gave Vidal's assignment headline prominence—meanwhile leaving unmentioned the names of several dozen experienced Timesmen who are likely to do a better job at San Francisco."

Campaign officials learned they could reach a bigger audience with less of a filter through television. This had practical implications on the campaign trail. Aides to the candidate started talking to the TV people first. The schedulers started accommodating television timetables as much as the newspaper deadlines.

Back then, filing a news piece for television was a circus stage event. Television correspondents had to get themselves and their film to a city where the piece could be put together by showtime. Sometimes that meant hiring a plane, flying ahead of the candidate to the next city on the itinerary, speeding into town with a police escort, getting the film developed and edited, and then appearing on the air just under deadline.

Once, as Mom covered the tail end of Lady Bird's whistle-stop campaign in 1964, she flew ahead to New Orleans to tape the final stop. Because Mom had been filing pieces all along the train tour she was cheered by viewers who had been watching the spectacle head for their town. President Johnson was there to greet his wife and gave Mom a big kiss in front of the waiting crowd. As the train pulled into New Orleans, her cameraman and director, who were still aboard, jumped off like hobos and scrambled down the tracks to set up to film the approaching train. They threw Mom a microphone, the cable spooling out across the gravel. She narrated and signed off the piece just as the train rolled in, the crowd roared and the camera ran out of tape.

Try doing that with just a pencil and pad.

By now those of us in the print media have lost; television networks, with their big audiences, have won. Television needs determine almost all campaigning and White House press travel. Networks also tend to spend a larger share on travel than print organizations. That gives them more influence over where and when the press plane flies. It leaves early to get to the next city so that the network correspondents can file their stories in time for the nightly news, or stays later than print would like, so that the television correspondents can file their pieces before leaving for the next city.

Arguing over timing and creature comforts may sound petty but life on the campaign trail is so exhausting that reporters tend to be cranky and protective of their prerogatives. What time you arrive at your final destination matters if it's a small town and you arrive late and the few restaurants are closed.

You rarely get a good night's sleep on the campaign trail. No matter what time you go to bed you're terrified you'll miss your wake-up call. I've set three travel alarm clocks and had all three miraculously fail me. Buses tend to leave on schedule because the candidate wants to be on time to the next event. Your colleagues have deadlines to meet so they're not going to hold the bus if you've overslept. Journalists are always dropping off the trail to write stories or go back and see their families. So if someone isn't on the bus, it might just mean they've already headed back to Washington.

Missing the bus in the morning means you're out of the bubble. Sometimes that's a minor nuisance. You catch a local cab, try not to stick to its seats, and when you make it to the event, hope you find the right security person. Local Secret Service agents are not the ones you want to find. The regulars who travel with the president or a candidate know the regular press members, but the locals don't. No matter how many pieces of press identification you show, it's going to be a long conversation. There might be a blood test.

If you get so out of the bubble that you miss the plane, you're sunk. You have to find a domestic flight. If you're in a small town, that means driving to a big airport hours away that has commercial flights. Sometimes you have to fly ahead two campaign stops to get back into the bubble. You must make your travel agent your best friend because on any given day you're going to call her in a panic and give her the kind of complicated word problem that made sixth-grade math so hard. *Katherine, I'm in Vegas and have to get to St. Louis by tomorrow morning. The flights through Chicago are knocked out by weather. Can you find me a flight through some Southern city that isn't having tornadoes? Oh and all the hotels in St. Louis are booked for a grocer's convention. Can you find me a place to stay anyway?*

The terror of being left behind causes all kinds of amusing early morning scenes. Once when covering John McCain, I woke up at 6:48 for a 6:45 departure. The bus was gone, and I had to bribe a deputy manager at the hotel to drive me to the airport. I arrived unshowered, unshaven and wearing the clothes from the long day before. I got on the plane but I looked like a homeless man. Fortunately, when we got to the University of California–Sacramento for the event, there was a cheap hair salon on campus. For four dollars I got my hair washed while McCain gave the same speech I'd heard him give a thousand times. I was so happy to have clean hair, I gave the woman a twenty.

Chapter Twenty-four

———

On election night in 1964, Mom was able to get into Johnson's suite at the Driskill hotel in Austin, but it was not an evening of high drama. Johnson pounded Republican Barry Goldwater into the topsoil, winning 44 states by 434 electoral votes.

Even so, Johnson couldn't completely enjoy the victory. He and Mom watched his nemesis Bobby Kennedy give his victory speech after winning a New York seat for U.S. Senate. He thanked every member of his family and previously unknown ward politicians. Johnson was irritated. "I wonder why he doesn't mention me," Mom overheard him say to himself. Kennedy might have mentioned the bus driver, but he never mentioned Johnson, the man at the top of the ticket who had won New York by a wide margin and presumably contributed to the senator's victory. "I wonder why he doesn't mention me?" Johnson said again after Kennedy stopped speaking.

Just a few days after Mom returned home from Texas, Dad took her for a drive. They crossed the Chain Bridge into McLean, Virginia. That part of the state was largely farmland then. Some early suburban tracts had been built but you could drive for miles along the Potomac River and see only forest.

Dad turned the car down a long steep gravel driveway surrounded by old oaks and tulip poplars. The road seemed to head to nowhere. Finally they came to an abandoned house, overgrown with ivy. The front windows were opaque with dirt. Leaves had collected on the front porch.

"I've been here," Mom said. She had dined there with Scoop Jackson and Jack Kennedy nearly ten years earlier. "This is Merrywood. Why are we here?"

"I've bought it."

"Are you out of your mind?" she shrieked.

The two exchanged looks. She looked at the house.

"Are you out of your mind?"

The drama did not end quickly. "It took quite a while for her to settle down," remembers Dad. "She came to live in Washington, not in northern Virginia."

In time, Mom came to see the possibilities of Merrywood. Its high dormers and ivy-covered brick were surrounded by enormous and ancient trees, the kind that would talk if they were in a picture book. Merrywood was not just a large house. It was an imposing property overlooking the brown Potomac. Inside the Georgian mansion, everything from the dental moldings to the heavy door handles had been handcrafted.

Jackie Kennedy's stepfather Hugh Auchincloss had owned the house, and legend has it that Jack Kennedy wrote *Profiles in Courage* in one of the third-floor bedrooms, when he was dating Jackie. After Jackie's family moved out in 1961 a syndicate planned to develop a massive high-rise apartment complex on the property. The neighbors started making protest signs immediately. The development would ruin the skyline and natural settings. They blamed Jackie Kennedy's mother and stepfather for selling to the syndicate and caused such an uproar that President Kennedy thought he might be asked about Merrywood at a press conference.

Attorney General Robert Kennedy, whose famous Hickory Hill estate was just down the road, stepped in. He found an old scenic easement and slapped it on the house. Construction was halted, and a legal battle ensued. Eventually Congress appropriated over $750,000 to buy the air rights to Merrywood in perpetuity, which meant that nothing over or around it could ever be built higher than forty feet— the height of the house.

The move ruined the syndicate's plans and soon they were looking to sell. Dad decided to buy the house with the idea that he might develop some of the land away from the river for homes within the forty-foot restriction.

Mom and Dad spent most of 1965 restoring the old house. They flew to New York and Paris to buy furniture, including the $35,000 Queen Anne chairs which would be mentioned in every profile afterward.

They made new money look like old money. Future owners of Merrywood with ready cash and even more handy bad taste did just the opposite. Since we left, they clamped on factory-fresh cupolas, balconies and additions in mismatched brick. When I saw the Sotheby's real estate catalog of the renovated house after one of the subsequent owners put it up for sale, it was like looking at my grandmother in fishnets.

The new house matched Mom's increasingly prominent role at NBC, which the network hoped to capitalize on in their coverage of Johnson's inauguration. Inaugurations, like conventions, have lost their luster, but when Johnson took his oath of office on the Capitol steps in January 1965, the networks were anxious to showcase the formal, traditional proceedings after the traumatic transition to power following Kennedy's murder.

Television was also still new enough that each big event offered new ways of presenting the news. ABC was still a relatively young network, so to compete with the other two established networks they tried gimmicks. As part of the network's "youth movement," to attract a younger audience, it assigned Marlene Sanders to cover the inaugural and they brought in an attractive Canadian broadcaster named Peter Jennings.

Five days before the inauguration, Mom was at the office when she started hemorrhaging. They rushed her to the hospital; she had suffered a miscarriage. While she recuperated, her assistant brought her research materials to her bedside. President Johnson and Lady Bird sent over an enormous bouquet from the White House florist.

She was back on her feet in time to make it to the inauguration. She stood in the Capitol as she had four years earlier. This time though, the Capitol Hill policemen had cut everyone out of the entrance passageway. But Mom knew them, so she snuck through.

When Johnson arrived with senators she'd worked for on the Foreign Relations Committee, he spoke to her just as Kennedy had at the last swearing in.

"Hello, Nancy," he said, asking her about her recuperation. It was another scoop covered on all three networks simultaneously.

"Naturally, competition among networks being what it is, I did not gain any new friends," Mom wrote later in notes that would never make it into her autobiography. "But I wasn't really aware of the animosity of my colleagues, which was genuine and intense. For a network which earns money based on an audience count, too much rides on the coverage of the great national event for them to take these matters with a sense of good sportsmanship. They are deadly serious. Outside of NBC, the attitude was, 'How the hell did she get out there again this year?' There were a good many dirty looks and while I have a zest for the competition and perhaps even for the kill, I resent it when people call me a 'bitch' for doing well what a man, having done the same, would be applauded for." (This makes a son smile.)

Two weeks later Mom hosted a party at the F Street Club for the president after the State of the Union address. This was extraordinary. No member of the White House press corps today would have sufficient social power to throw such a party. And their networks probably wouldn't let them. When I arrived as a reporter in Washington, Katharine Graham had that kind of social influence, but she was the publisher of the town's newspaper, a position of far greater stature and power than a mere political correspondent.

Mom was becoming famous enough for her father to send word from the hinterlands about her reputation.

> Our friends keep telling us about seeing you. It's funny—we hear from people now that you have become a celebrity—that really is funny but we like it. It is lots of fun. We are very proud of what you have accomplished. . . . you know Nancy quite a lot of people ask me a lot of questions about you—Ordinarily I'm not much to do a lot of talking and yes Dick they ask me about you too and you can imagine me when I go into my dance and tell everybody fondly about my family in Washington."

The more famous Mom became, though, the more she under-mined herself. She was becoming famous for just being there—for just being the dame with the microphone. She asked lawmakers probing and difficult questions on *Meet the Press,* but that's not why she was famous. Viewers knew her because Lyndon Johnson was drawn to her. As John Horn, media critic of the *New York Herald Tribune,* put it, "when watching the public appearances of President Johnson it's wise to keep an eye on the network that has Nancy Dickerson." NBC used that quote in a full-page ad after the inaugu-ration to boast about its coverage. Steven Roberts wrote a version of the same thing in the *New York Times:* "Reporters who have been lost too often in the crush that always surrounds the peripatetic president have finally found the answer: stand next to Nancy Dickerson."

It's not easy cultivating a relationship that puts you that close to a president. But all the skill, hustle and emotional intelligence Mom needed to get that access and keep it ultimately fed the view that her talents were limited to standing in Johnson's shadow. Once he left, her career would be over too.

Viewers also started to think about her the way people think about modern art. They look at a white canvas with a squiggle and think "I can do that." Or, they think the painting shouldn't cost as much as it does. This was the sentiment of one article, which led with: "Nancy Dickerson gets paid $75,000 for gabbing for five minutes." In one interview, Mom bristled at still having to prove herself and blurted out the names of her old CBS colleagues as character witnesses: "You can ask Howard K. Smith and Eric Sevareid if I'm not a good reporter!"

In *Parade* magazine, someone from Mom's hometown of Wauwatosa asked celebrity columnist Walter Scott, "Is it true that President Johnson has a crush on Nancy Dickerson, the NBC com-mentator, and gives her scoops?" (I imagine the questioner to be some former bobby-sock rival from high school). He took up Mom's defense: "A: Not true. Nancy Dickerson knew Lyndon Johnson when he was in the Senate and she, as Nancy Hanschman, worked for the Senate Foreign Relations Committee. The president told her on TV that he had chosen Hubert Humphrey as his running mate, but even though they are old friends, he is giving her no exclusives."

Constituents were writing the president too. In the LBJ Library is this handwritten letter from an angry fellow in Xenia, Ohio.

July 28, 1965

Dear President Johnson,

I have for a long time watched your favorite news reporter Nancy Dickerson snatch you away from the other news men. This burns me up because I feel it is unfair. I know everyone has the right to like one reporter more than another but it is unfair for you over nationwide TV to show your preference. I have seen several examples of this and since I know that for a fact CBS News is a lot better than NBC any day I am especially angered. By showing your preference you cause other networks to lose prestige unjustly. I would like to know why you scorn all other newsmen and always pick her. You can't deny that you did, because it has been witnessed by many millions of people.

Despite the complaints from some quarters, Mom continued to mine her relationship with the president. Her file in the LBJ Library contains stacks of letters and invitations she sent the president.

Telegram to White House, August, 1965:

HAPPY BIRTHDAY. YOU LOOK GREAT BUT HOW DOES IT FEEL TO BE 57? LOVE AND A GREAT BIG BIRTHDAY KISS FROM NANCY DICKERSON

After one press conference she sent a several-page critique: "I thought it might have been better during the conference if you had read less and extemporized more on questions . . . I think it was wrong to end the conference at 3:25, since it cut off some questions."

Mom's LBJ file contains numerous letters from the president, most of them personal.

Dear Nancy,

It's nice to start the day with a warm and generous letter like yours. It makes the rest of the daytime hours easier to face. Thank you, my dear.

The president had a particular affection for female reporters. "No president has lavished as much attention on Washington's women's press corps as Lyndon Johnson," wrote Vera Glaser in *Parade* in 1965, "and they love it." He felt particularly comfortable with Mom. As his daughter Lynda put it to me: "She was a friend but also she understood. If you sneezed she would say you had a cold. She wouldn't go running off and say you had some dread disease."

That sense of perspective did not go both ways. One day, Johnson showed Mom that his hand was bandaged. She asked him what was wrong. He looked down and said simply, "Cancer." "My God," she said, "I'm so sorry." They were interrupted before she could ask about it further. She prepared to go on air with it and called his office to get confirmation (by then she knew better than to trust his word alone). There was no cancer; he had simply had a wart removed.

If anyone at NBC was concerned that Mom was getting too close to Johnson, they never mentioned it at the time. They were in fact, delighted with her access. It meant anyone who wanted to know what the president was doing turned to NBC. And it was driving the other networks to distraction. CBS's White House reporter, the young Dan Rather, asked to be assigned to the London office.

Time magazine did its best to add the maximum amount of spin to the switch:

RATHER RATTLED

On the night of Johnson's election, the President's affectionate "Hello, Nancy" was heard so often that some viewers wondered why he didn't sing it. All this understandably rattled CBS White House Correspondent Dan Rather to whom the "Hello, Nancy" refrain in all likelihood began to sound like the awkward bounce of a head rolling over uneven ground. (His.) On Inauguration Day . . . Rather shadowed her like a spy who had been left out in the cold. "Hello Nancy," said Lyndon on his way to the platform. People who were close to Dan Rather say he winced. Now there he stood in the ten-gallon shade of a pretty girl from Wisconsin.

Chapter Twenty-five

In 1967 Gore Vidal published *Washington, D.C.*, a novel of ambition and double-dealing in the nation's capital during World War II. He made the geographical center of the story Laurel House, the fictional name of his childhood home, Merrywood. After Mom and Dad bought the house in 1964, they made it a central part of Washington society. Senators, Cabinet officials and movie stars attended formal parties and lounged on the back lawn with a cocktail at lunchtime. The scene unintentionally matched Vidal's fictional one down to his description of the piano in the garden room: "As in most Washington drawing rooms, the piano's essential function was to serve as an altar on which to display in silver frames the household gods: photographs of famous people known to the family." (The title of the Chinese translation edition captures the spirit of the book, the house and Mom's life: *A Fiery Desire to Be on the Political Stage.*)

An article on the front page of the Style section of the *Washington Post* in June 1967 proclaimed "Nancy is the No. 1 Great Society Hostess." The author, Maxine Cheshire, was a famous Washington troublemaker. If she wrote about you and didn't ruin your career, she was at least going to ruin your day, but the piece was glowing. "You seldom read about it when she entertains," Cheshire wrote. "But she has the kind of guest lists that political novelists are always weaving into books about the power structure of Washington. . . . Nancy Dickerson is a leading party giver within what is known as the 'Secret Society.' That's the elite inner circle within 'The Great Society' made up of the people closest to President and Mrs. Johnson . . . Night after night the $35,000 Queen Anne chairs around her dinner table are occupied by men who shape the country's destiny."

In *Parade*, Jack Anderson wrote an almost identical article, titled "TV's Nancy Dickerson is now mistress of Merrywood—and it's still the center of Washington's social swirl." Mom and Dad were also profiled in front of their famous home in *Cosmopolitan* and *Vogue*. In a cover story for *Ladies' Home Journal* on American entertaining, Mom and Dad pose by the front columns as the quintessential formal party hosts: Dad is wearing a double-breasted dinner jacket, and Mom wears a ball gown.

Merrywood was not the only social venue in town and Mom was not by any means the town's only famous hostess. Across the river in Georgetown lived a cluster of hostesses like Evangeline Bruce and Loraine Cooper, but Merrywood's scale and Mom's national fame made our house like nowhere else in Washington. Mom was a full-fledged celebrity. She was no longer the eager and nervous woman interviewing Teddy Kennedy at the 1960 convention. She had arrived and she was in command. *Vogue* led its report on the Washington "generation now at peak energy, peak ideas" with a picture of her. Behind her on the steps of her new mansion sat the four darling Dickerson children and their father.

She was the center of every party, even the ones she didn't give. Helen Bartlett remembers watching her change the social order at her house. "The women used to go upstairs after dinner parties and the men would go in the library and I would cut their cigars. Your mother changed that. She went in with the men because that's where the news was, and after that my mother said, 'I'm going in there too.' That was a revolution in our house."

Airlines held the plane for her. Men wanted to sleep with her. Women glared at her, but they wanted to know her trick. Her trick was that she glowed on television. She was radiant and charismatic in an age where television reporters were still trying to look at the camera without squinting. Today, projecting beauty and intelligence over the airwaves is something the local anchor in Duluth can do. Back then it made her a star.

Like movie stars, Mom drew in her viewers, particularly young women. Her folders are filled with their carefully typed letters from little towns like Minot, North Dakota, and Plano, Texas. Her fans wanted to know everything about her, how she did her hair, what dessert she preferred and how she stayed thin. Young girls wanted to know how they could train for a career like hers. Her assistant, Francine Proulx, remembers meeting Mom for the first time in an elevator five years before she would work for her. "It was 1965 and I was working my first day at NBC, and I was wearing a Lord & Taylor A-line dress, and she said 'what a lovely dress.' I was on cloud nine for the rest of the day. I thought: 'Nancy Dickerson thinks this dress is pretty.'"

After Mom died, women I didn't know wrote me to say that she had been their inspiration. One of my bureau chiefs at *Time* told me that Mom made her feel that as a young African-American woman growing up in Harlem, she could do anything. Almost a decade after Mom's death, women were still citing her as their inspiration. One day while I was writing this book, another Google alert arrived in my inbox. In a story about Judith Shellenberger, a teacher honored at the White House, Shellenberger mentioned that Mom was her early inspiration.

I wrote to her and she responded:

> *I was a young girl who had dreams beyond my financial means. Nancy Dickerson—a beautiful, classy young woman—came into my living room every night and told me what was happening in Washington, D.C. and around the world. I was captivated by everything about her. She had a job where she met the most powerful people in the world—presidents, heads of state, diplomats. She was always impeccably dressed and was a huge role model for young women—particularly for me.*
>
> *She allowed me to dream of life outside my small town, and "what you believe can be achieved." . . . I can honestly say Nancy Dickerson changed my whole life by inspiring me to pursue my dreams . . . My whole career has centered on the motivation your mother gave me. The fact that I too could be a strong career woman. And as you know, I have met a sitting First Lady, many Senators and Congressmen, and the distinguished scientists my foundation honors. But none of my positive life experiences would have happened, if I had not had your mother as a role model.*

To women who found all the work and meaning they needed in their family and children, Mom seemed to be pushing beyond her station. To those in between who ironed the laundry and made the beds but longed to add to the collection of stories they'd written in college or the stack of oil paintings they kept in the broken suitcase, she was both an inspiration and a source of melancholy. I wonder how many mothers felt from their daughters the sentiment I hear now in letters about Mom. "Though I loved my mother very much," wrote one woman, "I considered your mother the perfect woman and wish my mother had a little more of your mother's drive in her."

The minute Mom came to Washington, she knew that she had to create a second public identity. She turned Nan from Wauwatosa into Nancy Hanschman who knew about Europe and American attitudes about Russia and who was tough enough to overcome the obstacles men put in front of her. Maintaining those two identities was hard enough, but becoming truly famous introduced a third character: Nancy Dickerson. Her image was no longer her own. People described her in fantastical ways, and she became as much a product of their imaginations as of anything she actually did.

In an oral history preserved in the Johnson Library, Joe Frantz, an aide to Lyndon Johnson, describes a trip to the Grand Canyon he took with her and Lady Bird Johnson.

"Nancy Dickerson retreated from the group and went further up on the flat. . . . NBC TV cameramen went up there, and they taped her giving her telecast. She was all in white, and she was in something rather filmy. It was really like a gown. I don't know what it was, I'd almost swear it was organdy. She was up there with that wind whipping, and there in that dark night, which is absolutely dark, of course, since you have no artificial light . . . Here's this bright spotlight and this almost apparition and good looking person standing up there talking about 'what a day it has been and how we have come to the end of the earth.'"

The nutcases started writing in too: "Dear Mrs. Dickerson, I am an English millionaire. I could use you, or rather God could use you, as a woman evangelist." The proposals of marriage and profound love were so numerous, Mom kept a thick file just for crazy people.

In 1967 Eleanor Lambert put Mom at the top of her inexplicably influential best-dressed list, headlining one of her syndicated columns: "Nancy Dickerson: My idea of a 1967 fashion symbol."

Dad's old friends from Hollywood, such as Jack Benny and Kirk Douglas, started dropping by the house. She mugged for the camera with Truman Capote and Frank Sinatra, who dedicated his song "Nancy" to her when she attended one of his performances. She danced with Gene Kelly and lunched with Gore Vidal. Bob Hope invited Mom and Dad to his daughter's wedding. When Sammy Davis Jr. came to town, they hastily arranged a cocktail party for him on the back lawn. Even substantive events had a Hollywood factor. Johnny Carson presented her the Albert Einstein College Award, given to the most influential woman of the year, putting Mom in the company of previous recipients Pearl Buck, Eleanor Roosevelt and Margaret Mead.

The writers of a popular '60s sitcom *Slattery's People* used her as a model for a leggy television correspondent who falls in love with the mayor of Boston. Broadway producer David Merrick announced that he wanted to put Mom in a show. She was included in a popular LBJ parody album and her name was the answer to quiz show questions and crossword puzzle clues. *Laugh-In* made regular fun of her as did Art Buchwald, the top political humorist at the time.

After Mom covered Luci Johnson's wedding, Buchwald imagined how she would sound reporting on the championship boxing match between Brian London and Cassius Clay: "They both look radiant. Cassius looks happy, thrilled, and delighted and very beautiful. . . . I believe this fight has a nobility and dignity about it that far surpasses anything we'll see in our time. It's done in such good taste. For one thing, both Mr. Clay and Mr. London agreed that they wanted to have a small bout with only their dearest friends present." Later, when there's a knockout, Buchwald writes in her voice: "Brian looked very beautiful all stretched out with hardly a muscle moving, very serene."

Buchwald was right to make fun of the wedding coverage. It was excessive. It was the first televised White House wedding and the networks covered it like a space launch. Mom hosted an hourlong special in which she interviewed the bridesmaids, the bakers, and the calligraphers, and followed Miss Johnson as she selected the silver and china. She sat down with the happy couple, who were clearly going to have a very traditional marriage. The nineteen-year-old Luci deferred to her husband Pat Nugent in all things and explained that he kept her from saying things she shouldn't. She couldn't imagine, she told Mom, trying to have her job and be a wife too. The groom explained his view of their relationship: "A wife should be subject to her husband and if she doesn't obey me she's not only breaking my law, she's breaking the laws of the church."

If a Democratic president's son-in-law said that today, pundits would denounce it as a pander to social conservatives and women's groups would march until the groom issued a clarifying statement.

From 1964 through 1967 Mom and Dad captured the last years of a golden age. The elites conspired to relaunch the social swirl and recapture Kennedy's vigorous energy. "Every party had at least a few senators or cabinet officials and a few big-time press people," remembers Fred Harris, who came to the Senate as a Democrat from Oklahoma in 1965. "It was all off the record and a lot of business got done." The salons of Georgetown and Cleveland Park were in full roar and Republicans and Democrats had no problem mixing after hours. "We were really doing things," said Harris. "The war on poverty and federal aid to education and civil rights, we hadn't had yet the urban riots, and the war in Vietnam was no bigger than a man's hand. There were new and exciting programs and new and exciting people. It was a brief shining moment."

At Merrywood Mom followed the Laura Gross model. If you were invited to the house you had to perform. She asked senators to explain their policy decisions, cabinet officials to illuminate the president's thinking and ambassadors to give the view from outside America.

Merrywood became so famous that tourists drove back and forth on the road trying to find its hidden driveway. Almost every day an unexpected car would come down the hill, circle the driveway and head out again. When Senator Harris drove a constituent by the house after picking him up from the airport, Mom noticed the car, stopped them and insisted they come inside for breakfast. Harris sheepishly agreed, stepping out of the car in his pajamas. His wife had planned to pick up their friend and the senator had made a last-minute decision to come along for the ride, assuming his friend wouldn't mind his informal attire and not expecting him to insist on seeing Merrywood when he heard the Harrises knew Nancy Dickerson.

Merrywood also attracted nutcases. After Mom and four-year-old Michael appeared in *Parade,* a middle-aged man came to the house to find them. Only my sister Jane, then fifteen, and the housekeeper Carolina were home. "Carolina came to me and asked me if I knew the man who was downstairs," remembered Jane. "I came down to find a very large white man looking in the refrigerator. I asked him what he was doing and after not much of a reply I told him he was trespassing and to leave immediately. I ran to the phone to try to reach Mom and Dad. Neither were around and of course left no information where they could be reached. The man had gone out the front door and I could see him from the library window and I called the police. The operator couldn't hear me because I was keeping my voice low. It was like right out of a movie. I finally got the story out and thought how the hell am I going to tell them where we live? Nobody could find the driveway. It's not like we had a cross street. Somehow I managed and very shortly after an unmarked car and a squad car arrived. They arrested the man and took him away. They later told Mom that he had been living out of his car on that access road near the house watching the family for a week."

Mom's fame also brought fickle viewers. If she didn't perform the way they thought she should, they were quick to turn on her. She lost the cushion she had when she came across as a gutsy Midwestern gal. Her pricey clothes, friends and beautiful family struck readers as awfully fancy living. They were on the lookout for any haughty behavior and Mom served it up for them in a silver chafing dish. "There are times," she told one reporter, "when I think I'm doing too much. But I don't want a dull life. When I'm old and nobody wants me anymore, I can always go back to teaching school."

Teachers of America unite! Educators from across the land wrote her letters in perfect Palmer's method script, telling her to get stuffed. Teaching was not a refuge for the old and unwanted.

Mom was hurt. That's not what she meant. She was trying to be humble. Some day she would be old and unwanted. She was showing that she recognized her fame would be fleeting. Readers thought she was looking down her pretty little nose at them.

Becoming famous also changed the way the public evaluated her work. Nancy Hanschman worked like the devil. Nancy Dickerson still worked that hard, but the whole point of the Nancy Dickerson image was that she made everything look effortless. People wondered why she was such a big deal if what she did was so easy. Only Mom's colleagues saw her manic discipline. "We were driving around Mexico City in a taxi cab somewhere," said Bonnie Angelo, "and all around us there were cars honking and people nearly being run over and Nancy was over in her corner of the car working on her script, just practicing, practicing like there was nothing going on around her. She was so determined."

Mom's producer at NBC, Bob Asman, tells a dozen such stories. Once when taping a piece at the new Russian embassy they had to shoot part of it in the rain. "She did one take and it was fine and I was ready to go," remembers Asman. "I said, 'Come on Nancy, it's fine' and she said, 'No, let's do it again.' She kept doing it again and again until it was exactly right and all the time it's raining but she wouldn't stop. By the end the script was just pulp in her hands."

Between reporting and her social schedule, Mom also ran the house. She wrote out the menus, clipped recipes from magazines and left them for the cook with detailed instructions on index cards. Keeping track of the household was like doing her taxes or expenses. She didn't find fulfillment in her daily obligations, nor did she race home because she couldn't stand to be away from the four kids, but she was determined to do what was expected of her.

She knew what had to be done to keep the house running and keep the kids clothed and fed and in school. "Without a lot of lists, I wouldn't be at all organized," she told one profiler. "With those, a fully manned staff at the house and a secretary at NBC, I'm able to leave unexpectedly, maybe for a week at a time. Otherwise I couldn't possibly go traipsing around the world like I do." She didn't button our overcoats in the morning or wash us behind the ears, but she wrote letters to our doctors, talked to our teachers and arranged our pickup and drop-off schedules through each busy day. When she could, she tried to integrate the kids into her life at work. She took my sisters to the 1964 convention, to tapings at NBC and to the White House for press conferences, Easter-egg rolls and picnics.

We never saw or understood the hours of parenting Mom put in in the back office. "Whenever she asked about you she was far more interested than any of the other parents," remembers Helen Bartlett, who ran a tiny summer camp my brother and I both attended. "There were other women who didn't work, but who you could tell didn't want to be mothers. She really cared about who you were as people." Her assistants probably saw more of this than we did. "She was such a good mother," remembers Linda Lamb, Mom's assistant during her early years at NBC and herself a mother of four. "She was always worried about something for the girls. When Ann and Jane called her up one day to say that they were bored she stopped what she was doing and typed up a list for them: twenty things to do in Washington when you're bored."

Parenting through to-do lists and a household staff was not a universally approved method. In 1964, *Mary Poppins* won five Academy Awards for a story that concludes that children should not be brought up by servants but by their mothers. Poppins succeeds in the narrative not because she is there for the children but because she helps to bring the mother home. Poppins would have delighted in sabotaging Mom's typewriter. *Your children wouldn't need a list of items to keep them from being bored, Nancy, if you were at home with them.*

I own all of Mom's household folders with endless names of staff that came and went, each time upsetting the careful balance that allowed her to go to work every day. One letter to a housekeeper who has run off starts: "Ernestine! What happened to you? Please come back."

Sometimes she just had to improvise. When one fill-in maid flaked out while two of my cousins were visiting, Mom took both of them along with Jane to the White House for a press conference. Afterward, the four of them took a cab driven by "a big, fat, happy man," as Mom described him. He seemed to know everything about everyone so she asked him if he knew a good cook. "It just so happens I cook myself," he answered. "I cooked for the Norfolk & Western Railroad." He turned around and introduced himself. "My name is Winston M. Jones; I eats no meat, I just lick the bones." He was hired on the spot.

Chapter Twenty-six

In the summer of 1967, Mom was thrilled to hear that *Look* magazine had commissioned a profile of her. She was even more excited when she learned that Stanley Tretick would be taking the photographs to accompany the piece. Tretick had immortalized Jack Kennedy by humanizing him. Tretick took the picture of John John peeking out from underneath his father's desk in the Oval Office and captured Kennedy on his sailboat and playing touch football in Hyannisport. In one Tretick portrait Kennedy drove a golf cart with every kid in the family compound piled on the seats, running boards and hood. (No image consultant would allow a politician to be photographed like that today. A candidate cannot be seen putting children in peril. Today the kids would be wearing so much padding and helmets they'd look like a hockey team.) He showed Kennedy had élan even in his unguarded moments.

Mom thought Tretick could round out her image in a similar way. She didn't need him to capture behind-the-scenes moments of her private life; she needed to remind people (particularly her bosses) that behind all the pearls and perfect hair, she was still a hard-working journalist. She had a radio spot and the morning news show every day, plus she filed stories for the evening news and the *Today* show. She was not just the beautiful, glamorous woman in the society pages.

Television news stars are familiar animals to us now. Their gargantuan salaries place them in the company of movie stars and platinum recording artists. In 2006, when CBS announced that Katie

Couric would be the first solo female anchor of a network nightly newscast, her annual salary was $15 million. But back then the glamorous news anchor was a new phenomenon. There were big stars of course—Murrow, Cronkite, Brinkley—but they were paid modestly and their stardom derived only from their solid performances every night. Mom was also paid modestly, but she could achieve the Hollywood lifestyle because of her husband's wealth and connections.

As people focused more on her fame, Mom was confronted by that same worry that had haunted her since her early days at the Foreign Relations Committee: Were her colleagues and the public taking her seriously? Tretick would show her doing everything well—chasing a story, throwing a dinner party for her powerful chums and stooping at the low table to help her four-year-old son blow out his birthday candles.

I didn't know who Stanley Tretick was when I first came across the *Look* magazine clip. I just liked the photographs. They were different from the hundreds of other ones I'd seen. They were deep and warm and looked as if when you touched the dark parts they would feel like velvet. Mom looks like a starlet playing Mom in a movie.

I searched for his pictures online and the first one I found I'd been looking at for ten years at *Time*. The picture of John Kennedy Jr. under his father's desk was prominently displayed in my office in Washington.

The pictures from Tretick's photo shoot with Mom are stored at the Library of Congress and I arranged to have them hauled out of cold storage to take a look. While I waited for the contact sheets, I looked through some slides Tretick took of Merrywood. While he was working on the piece, Mom and Dad let him wander the grounds in the afternoon sunlight. I spread the slides out on the light table and bent down to look through the plastic eyepiece.

It was the first time I'd really seen Merrywood since I was fourteen. When I jog on the C&O Canal near the house I live in today, I look across the Potomac River to see if I can pick Merrywood out through the trees. Even after twenty-five years, I can remember the feel of the lockworks on each of the doors and the sound of the wooden floors creaking long after everyone had gone to bed.

The first batch of slides are of the trees in the deep summer green they took on when it was hot in August. And the brick walkway looked just like that—chianti-colored and slick with moss. I can remember how it smelled to be near the rotting old poolhouse at the time of day Tretick was there. He photographed the canopy of maples and oaks in front of the house behind the line of boxwoods. I had promised myself I would climb up into that world when I was old enough. Tretick also took a photograph of the front door knocker that I used to raise and drop to hear it echo through the house when my parents were gone.

As I waited for the pictures of Mom I thought, *I am having a Rosebud moment in the Library of Congress.* Fortunately, the pictures of Mom soon arrived and I put on the disposable white cotton gloves and flipped through the contact sheets. Tretick followed her around for days. She must have loved having a famous photographer clicking all around her. It undoubtedly made her colleagues grumble. Toward the end of the Johnson administration, her career was in trouble. She was a Johnson girl and as his fortunes faded so did hers.

All presidents have difficult relationships with the press but by the end of his term, Johnson and the press were in open warfare. The public had begun to turn against the war and the president had lost his credibility. The press corps had adopted a rule: the more adamantly he denied something, the greater the chance it was true. Johnson "wanted the world to behave in a simple and straightforward way—his way," said his press secretary Bill Moyers. "He thought if he said something wasn't so, it wasn't so. He lived in the world's largest fishbowl but he didn't want anyone to know what he was doing until he was good and ready to tell them. And even when they [the reporters] caught him in the act [of lying]. . . . he denied it."

When Johnson couldn't cajole the press he resorted to extravagant acts of bullying and manipulation. He checked up on who was meeting with members of his administration, not only to hunt for leaks but also to manage access and give it only to those reporters he liked. He succeeded in planting questions during his press conferences and he bullied and badgered reporters who asked questions he didn't like. "You're going to ask a chickenshit question like that of the president of the United States," he once bellowed. By the end of his term, he and Mom were no longer chummy. She continued to request interviews and invite him to parties, but her folder in the Johnson Library is full of memos from White House aides finding polite ways to turn her down during those later years. The softer stories she might have done in the past weren't going to do anything to improve Johnson's poll numbers. He lumped her in with the rest of the press corps that had turned on him. Her daily newscast reported the grim developments from Vietnam and gave Bobby Kennedy more coverage than Johnson thought he was due.

She had been on the air for seven years, but in 1967 she had to prove that she had some underlying talent beyond maintaining her access to the president and his family. "The minor brains that sometimes take over the news operation of a network sometimes forgot all the rather credible reporting I had done in the past," Mom wrote in her unpublished autobiography notes. "I was dismissed as merely a 'friend of the Johnsons.'"

If Mom wanted to move past her image as Johnson's reporter, she had to develop new relationships. She worked to get close to Bobby Kennedy, the star of Democratic politics whom she had known since the '50s. She succeeded to some degree, spending a weekend with the family at Hyannisport, but she had to do more than show a little friendship with Kennedy to help her at NBC. She had to overcome the fact that people didn't like her. "They resented her because she was a woman but that was just the start," remembers Max Schindler, her director. "They resented her money and her wealthy husband and that she knew famous people so well."

Producers and directors found ways to undermine her. One let her keep reporting a story long after it had been cancelled for broadcast, so she'd be wasting her time on a piece that was never going to run. Another let her go on the air to report a fact he knew had been outpaced by last-minute news.

Several colleagues kept an outtake from the publicity photos in which Mom is bending over, her backside to the camera, legs splayed, her underwear showing. At the appropriate moment in the water cooler chatter, someone would bring out the picture for a good laugh with the boys.

"You don't want to see that photo," said Ron Nessen, who covered the Johnson White House for NBC.

My female colleagues in the press corps still battle against the crude jokes and the stereotypes. Men sometimes exorcise their career angst by acting like fraternity boys. They assume any female network reporter who acts tough hasn't been laid recently or enough. Or, if a woman has been successful its because she's been sleeping around. A woman who snaps at a cameraman must be having her period. At least the women today can commiserate in the press room with their female colleagues. Mom was alone. She didn't complain. She couldn't. She didn't want to be accused of being a fragile girl. When she was upset, she did what her friend Ed Williams, the famous lawyer, taught her: "You go into the bathroom alone and cry." To cope, she drew her allies closer. She treasured the secretaries, producers and directors who were on her team. "If she knew you were on her side she would do anything for you," says Asman.

Mom fought back in all the wrong ways. She was arrogant and abrupt with those she thought were against her, only deepening their antipathy. Because she thought the system was stacked against her, she lost perspective. She mistook judgment for oppression. Sometimes her stories weren't newsworthy enough to make the nightly news. Sometimes other reporters had been on the story ahead of her. But she saw these as made-up excuses to thwart her because she was a woman. She said so. Her colleagues thought she was a bitchy know-it-all.

Mom only hints at this in her autobiography: "I was raising five children, working a full day and often at night and on Sundays, and simply did not have time to waste. As a result I could be excessively abrupt, even arrogant, which naturally prompted retribution."

Another challenge for Mom was that by the end of the '60s, she was competing with other women at her own network. By 1968, Barbara Walters, Aline Saarinen and Pauline Frederick were all reporting for NBC. They didn't compete with Mom's Washington news beat, but they were interchangeable in the minds of many NBC executives. It was important to have a female on the show, but not necessarily important to have a woman doing one kind of story. Once Barbara Walters started co-hosting the *Today* show in 1964 it became less crucial for Mom to do pieces on the show: Viewers were getting their dose of femininity from Walters. Executives who preferred having male reporters do news and analysis from Washington could now freely embrace their instincts.

Mom didn't take Barbara Walters seriously. Walters came from soft news. After all, the host referred to Walters as "the new *Today* girl." Mom had been trained by Edward R. Murrow. She did serious news. It was outrageous if anyone thought she and Walters were the same kind of reporter.

The distinctions Mom made were lost on others because the distinctions between news and entertainment didn't exist even in Murrow's day. He was one of the pioneers of the celebrity profiles for which Walters would later become so famous. Mom was dismissing Walters in the same way newsmen did to the young Nancy Hanschman when they tried to keep her off the air.

With her career in flux, Mom needed to remind everyone of her proper place in the news world and thought the *Look* profile and Tretick's photographs would accomplish that. He snapped her reading wire copy as it spooled down her legs into the trash can in her tiny NBC office; he showed her leaning over a producer to discuss a script and filming a stand-up in the White House driveway. As she prepared to anchor her daily newscast, Tretick photographed her from every angle, capturing himself in one shot in the reflection of the monitor that read: "NBC News with Nancy Dickerson."

When *Look* magazine arrived in the mail, Mom was horrified. There wasn't a single picture of her doing her job. The piece made her look as substantive as a meringue. It did not recalibrate her image as a reporter who also threw parties. It made her out to be a party girl. "Washington's Most Serious Butterfly," read the headline.

At least they said she was a *serious* butterfly, but that was like being called the smartest dunce. In a profile four years later she was still angry about the story: "To her horror, the story ignored Nancy Dickerson, the reporter . . . Nancy fires with anger whenever she thinks of it."

The pictures are gorgeous but you can see how off message they were for Mom. In the first one, she's having her hair and makeup done. In the next, the largest of the spread, she's reclining in the backseat of a Cadillac. She's wearing bug-eye sunglasses and she's nearly prone. I know why. She's carsick. Even if the car were in park, she might have had to lie down. But if you didn't know this, you'd think she was waiting for an office boy to feed her mango in syrup. The caption reads: "With [a] Day Ahead for shopping in a rented limousine. Besides her other accomplishments, Nancy recently made it on the board of directors of Bonwit Teller."

The closest the piece gets to showing Mom at work is a picture of her dancing with Lyndon Johnson. Her smile peeks out just above his right shoulder. She's happy to be there. He's happy she's there too. No one is working. That's what the caption writer concludes too. "With LBJ at the White House Dinner. The President is a frequent booster of Nancy's abilities." (*Geddit, booster!* You can hear the rim shot.)

Up to this point, the profiles of Mom had been glowing. They included the odd quip or dig from a colleague, but only as evidence of the obstacles she had to overcome or the animosity her competence engendered. The *Look* article dismantles her piece by piece. It is a masterpiece of the form. It's not heavy-handed, it just quietly snips each major artery until no doctor can save the subject from the blood loss. It was written by Betty Rollin, a *Look* editor who would go on to write several books including the moving and groundbreaking *First, You Cry,* about her battle with breast cancer.

Here's the lead: "Building a social career in Washington is like baking a soufflé: It takes just the right ingredients, just the right timing and (to quote *Look*'s food editor) 'just the right amount of hot air to poof it up.' "

An anonymous source weighs in. "She's no Walter Lippmann but she always worked hard at relationships. She made it her business to know everyone." So she's a lightweight and conniving. To be fair, the writer does mention her talents and energy: Mom is praised for getting to Saks before it opens to have her hair done.

If Rollin had sat with Mom's psychiatrist to target her vulnerable spots she couldn't have hit them more accurately. Mom may have given her the coordinates herself. She let Rollin get close enough to show her how vulnerable she was on the topic of intellectual competency. "There wasn't much praise around our house," Mom says. "Once I got a '100' on an exam and my father said: 'Oh.' " This is the only profile that points back to Mom's lifelong need to be praised for her brains and hard work. To round out the unflattering portrait,

Mom hangs herself with her quotes: "I've got the job, the family and the clothes, I live in a historic house, I have a successful husband. It's a unique combination," she says. Oh and Mom, don't forget the limo and the gobs of ready cash.

This is the problem with being a first. Mom had no one to sit her down and teach her how to be famous. All those stars she drank vintage wine with didn't whisper to her that no one wants to hear about how well she was doing. Even if you're trying to make the point that you're just lucky, don't. People will misunderstand. Since no one taught her that lesson, she helped readers confirm their suspicions that she was self-important and boastful.

Rollin would later write that she didn't mind tricking subjects if she could get at their true essence by doing so. She might have done that here. (Later Mom would have tepid revenge on Rollin, writing a mildly astringent *Washington Post* book review of her book *Am I Getting Paid for This?*. However, the harshest line was edited out: "Having been the subject of her work, I found her both 'tricky' and 'sneaky,' to use her definitions.")

I don't know if Rollin sucker-punched Mom or if she merely captured the essence of what Mom had become. I suspect it was a bit of both. Mom was increasingly occupied with maintaining, and enjoying, the image of Nancy Dickerson. Going to parties, tending guest lists and buying all the right clothes is nearly a full-time job. Digging out scoops that don't come from access to those in power is lonely and sometimes boring work done largely out of camera range. Rollin might have purposefully blown off the serious reporter to paint a cartoon, but Mom also gave her the material to work with.

Chapter Twenty-seven

In July 1968, I was born. When Michael had arrived five years earlier, he was brought to Mom after he had already been to hair and makeup. I was presented in my plum-colored natural state. She nearly gave birth again. She'd never seen such a messy wriggling monster. She didn't want anything to do with me until I was cleaned up (and had graduated from college).

There were no NBC press releases. Robert Goralski just filled in on *NBC News with Nancy Dickerson* and let viewers know she'd be back in two weeks. That Mom had been pregnant at all had only been mentioned in one story about her at the time. "Nancy Dickerson is planning to go through her present pregnancy mostly wearing Courreges," said one *Washington Star* story about her fashions. "His architectural lines are proving just great for her at this time. There will be no maternity fashions as such for her." Mom didn't need special fashions because I hadn't made much of a mark. The airline stewardesses let her fly to Bobby Kennedy's funeral just a month before I was born because they couldn't tell she was pregnant. She had only gained ten pounds. No wonder I had to go to all those doctors in adolescence. She starved me.

I was not immediately welcomed by my brother Michael. While Mom was pregnant, every time he wanted to go swimming with her she told him she could only after the "new baby" had arrived. He became exasperated enough to yell down her throat, "New baby hurry up." When New Baby arrived, Mike wasn't prepared. He figured I'd be fun to poke at. Maybe he would stick butter in my ear. But otherwise his life would go back to normal. When it didn't and no one let him put me in the bread drawer, he suggested that since they'd gotten me from the hospital perhaps they should send me back.

Part of the problem was the baby nurse. She wouldn't let Mike touch me because toddlers are full of snot and spittle and germs newborns can't handle. Mom didn't care. She wanted family harmony. So she fired the nurse and found one who would hand me over. "Luckily Alma soon arrived to take care of John," wrote Mom in her autobiography. "She had a gentle, placid disposition and thanks to her John is a happy, relaxed little creature who smiled at an earlier age than anyone who has ever lived."

My first superlative! When you are the son of a woman who has accomplished firsts you start getting them at an early age.

Two weeks after I was born, Mom was at the Republican Convention hiding in the back of an NBC car trailing Maryland Governor Spiro Agnew. She was sick and exhausted but conventions had always been her thing. But the 1968 convention was different from her two previous ones. She wasn't promoted as one of the network stars as she had been in 1960 and '64. She was just one of the swarm covering the show. "I was sort of out of the action—NBC had given better campaign assignments to others—all men," she wrote in her journal. Agnew was a second-tier story at the time, a moderate governor who hadn't declared who he was backing in the convention balloting. There wasn't much doubt that Nixon would get the nomination, but the media was fixated on the "neutral bloc," those governors and party leaders who hadn't thrown their support behind him. Mom was tailing Agnew just in case he and Ohio governor James A. Rhodes, his golfing partner, decided to throw their votes behind Rockefeller.

She hid in the wheel well all the way to the Ft. Landerdale golf club. The idea was that she would surprise Agnew and get him on camera. Alas, it didn't work. The governor learned of the ambush and snuck out a back door. She stood alone with her camera crew miles away from the convention feeling silly and out of place.

But then her luck got a little better. The next day, during the nightly news, she learned from Agnew that he was going to be

Nixon's pick for VP. It was like a gift from the sky. She immediately phoned the producer and screamed that they had to break into the newscast. Whoever took the call thought she was being imperious, overheated and rude and hung up on her. The news was announced by the Nixon campaign and everyone reported it at the same time. NBC missed their scoop.

At the raucous and violent convention in Chicago, the Democratic party, in which Mom had so many friends, was coming apart. Standing in Senator Fred Harris' office at the stockyards near the International Amphitheater, she watched as he held the hands of two of his children and wept openly as policemen clubbed the McCarthy protestors they accused of hurling ashtrays at them from the fifteenth floor of the hotel. A few weeks later, Minnesota senator Walter Mondale, the future presidential candidate who, like Harris, had been a key supporter of Humphrey's presidential campaign, stood to speak after a Merrywood dinner party. He was disillusioned with his longtime friend and mentor Humphrey, who had not separated himself from Lyndon Johnson and the war. He was leaving the campaign. He sat down and the room was silent.

Nixon squeaked through in November and Mom was quickly working on forming new ties to the Republican administration. Every reporter was, but Mom had a particular sense of urgency to prove herself with the new crowd. While preparing for the inauguration she ran into Herb Klein, Nixon's communications director.

Klein reminded Mom that she'd introduced him to Jack Kennedy eight years earlier. He remembered that Kennedy had talked to her on his inauguration day and suggested it would be neat if Nixon did the same. Mom agreed.

When Nixon arrived at the Capitol, Mike Wallace of CBS and Sam Donaldson of ABC crowded with Mom, but as Klein had promised, Nixon led with her: "There's Nancy," he said as he and Johnson walked over to her. He told her that they'd just talked about his dog on the drive over. Wallace and Donaldson joined the conversation, too. It's extraordinary that the three of them were allowed to walk right up to Nixon and Johnson. Today no reporter gets within fifty yards.

In the afternoon, Mom followed Johnson out to Andrews for his departure from Washington. Everyone drank a little scotch, including the reporters and the president's staff. Mom wept as Johnson got to the top of the airplane stairs and waved. "I had separated from him completely on Vietnam," she wrote, "and he never forgave me. But I knew him so well and knew how hard he tried, and even if he was wrong, he tried so hard to be right."

That night Mom sat next to Henry Kissinger at Nixon's inaugural dinner (the show must go on) and the next day she wrote the new president. She planned to bury him in little notes the way she had Johnson, reminding him of their past acquaintance. It had been more than twenty years since Congressman Keating had introduced her to him and his dog Checkers. The message wasn't so subtle: Among the press corps, which he so openly despised, he could trust her. Nixon wrote back: "Pat and I particularly appreciated your gracious welcome to Washington. You may be sure we are glad to be back. We look forward to seeing you."

Mom hadn't dropped a stitch. NBC issued a press release boasting that she had been the first reporter to talk to the president the day of the inauguration. Mom knew what all Washington hostesses know: A new administration is an opportunity to throw parties, and the new crowd is as anxious to be welcomed into power as the permanent Washington dwellers are to ingratiate themselves with the newcomers. She threw a grand one at Merrywood for Secretary of Defense Melvin Laird not long after he was confirmed. She had known him since he had been a young congressman in the '50s. The papers noticed how adroitly she'd switched to the new beat: "The Dickersons, whose parties were attended by leading Democrats during the Johnson Administration, did not have a single professional Democrat on the guest list last night," wrote the *Washington Post* on the front page of the Style section. The *Oakland Tribune* wrote, "Just when everyone thought her Lyndon Johnson friendship was her real strength she upped and captured most of the top Republicans in town."

Mom continued to mix with nonpolitical celebrities as well. She and Dad spent several weekends in the summer with Frank Sinatra at Random House publisher Bennett Cerf's house. When Burt Reynolds and Jim Brown were in town filming a movie, Mom had a party in their honor at Merrywood. *Cracked* magazine started featuring a regular cartoon of a buxom female newscaster called Nanny Dickering on its back page. After Johnny Carson stayed at Mom and Dad's apartment in Florida in 1969, the comedian sent her the following telegram:

Dear Nancy:

Thanks so much for letting me use your lovely apartment during Super Bowl weekend. I'm sorry about the over-flowing bathtub, but fortunately it put out the fire. Luckily, it didn't damage the furniture which had been stolen the night before. Thanks again, Johnny.

In March of that year, Dad wrote to Mom from the Savoy Hotel in London, remembering their time together there nine years before. "I think about our first trip to England together and am so thankful that we didn't miss the boat . . . It would have been so logical and yet I really don't think either of us could have found anyone else during the last eight years that would have been a candidate. We have complemented each other, and I hope that I can age wisely to make your life better and happier. You have made me happy and proud—I thank you. I also thank you for understanding me and my strange ways of displaying anxiety and frustration. You have been a remarkable wife and an understanding mother. I just want you to know how much I am thinking of you."

Chapter Twenty-eight

———

In 1969, Mom and Dad owned apartments in Florida and New York, flew on private jets and drove a Rolls-Royce. Dad was doing very well. His company, Liberty Equities, was a thriving conglomerate, covered in the *New York Times* and *Wall Street Journal* as the quintessential '60s corporate animal designed on the idea that good management could be applied across any company. In 1968 the company added a $20 million purchase of Smithfield Foods to its various other holdings, which included a pipe manufacturer, real estate, a spray paint maker and a manufacturer of floor and table lamps. Dad's success not only sustained the family, it helped the marriage. "Since he's successful in his own sphere, there's no rivalry," Mom told one profiler in May 1969.

But a month later, Liberty Equities was $1 million in the red. The Securities and Exchange Commission halted trading on the company's stock and charged that Dad and several other officers had overstated the company's earnings. Dad resigned as president but stayed on as chairman to fight the charges, taking no salary.

For two years, the family lived on Mom's income alone. They sold the Florida apartment and the Rolls. They talked about selling Merrywood but they were worried that if they did, the proceeds would be frozen or eaten by court costs or disappear in a settlement.

At first, Mom and Dad's problems remained largely private. Then, in August, Maxine Cheshire dropped the bomb in the *Washington Post*. The gossip columnist had treated Mom remarkably well while she was a darling of the Johnson administration. But Mom treated her not as a member of the working sisterhood, but as a mere gossip columnist. With Johnson out, Cheshire appeared to make up for lost time. Titled "The Dickersons of Merrywood," her piece ran on the front page of the Style section and was syndicated across the country, including in the *Milwaukee Sentinel.*

The Style section was once the first part of the paper everyone turned to in Washington. Jack Kennedy reportedly said that he already knew the news, but he read the society pages to get the juicy stuff he didn't know about, which was just as important to the business of the city.

The Cheshire story was a clever hit piece: There were inaccuracies but that wasn't what made it so powerful. It was designed to use the most benign facts as evidence of a greater corruption. It described the Liberty Equities legal troubles, and then, after a few paragraphs, pivoted: "That was the financial page story. But it was Dickerson's spectacular success story that fascinated Washingtonians as a conversational topic." The rest of the very long story listed the facts of Mom and Dad's life, the parties they attended, the famous people they knew and the history of Dad's rise in the company. The gist was that he had made his money by trading on her fame. There was nothing particularly sinful in any of the particulars Cheshire laid out, but by covering them at such great length, the piece left the overall impression that each fact somehow supported the darkest assertions of the legal case.

Mom was devastated. She marked the inaccuracies with x's in the margin—dates confused, people mixed up and some acts of pure fiction—she found dozens. She then started to write a rebuttal under a heading: "Inaccuracies as a possible basis for libel suit in article by Mrs. Cheshire." She didn't know what she would say publicly. How would this affect her contract negotiations with NBC?

The next year and a half would be the hardest of their marriage and the hardest of Mom's life before she got sick. They tried to keep their stern exchanges out of our earshot but my sisters remember hearing them fight. Mom and Dad heard people whisper about them at parties. The Green Book, the Washington social register, took them off the list because of the actions against Dad.

And yet they never pouted. Mom and Dad had the identical reaction to adversity: They put their heads down and soldiered on. "She was amazing throughout all of it," remembers Dad. "She got out this little gray book and said, 'okay now we're going to figure out how much we have and how much we can spend.'" Their united front seems particularly amazing when I remember how cruel they were to each other when the marriage broke apart.

But the financial troubles changed the balance of their marriage. In an article about the psychological tensions that face couples with a famous wife, the *New York Times* had exempted Mom and Dad because they were each highly accomplished. That's why their marriage could survive the normal problems. Dad explained their tidy arrangement: "A businessman's life has limited dimensions, so it's more important that I understand her business and share her friends than she mine. Between 8 and 6 each of us goes his own way. After 6, what she brings home is a very exciting life. What I bring home is money."

After the summer of 1969 he wasn't bringing home money. Dad says Mom never held that over him at the time (she would during the divorce), but the fracture set up a new competitive dynamic that over the next ten years would eat away at their marriage.

They pushed on together. My father fought the charges and Mom dove back into her work. The unpredictable demands of the news business can wear on you but when everything else is deteriorating the deadlines and assignments can provide an order you can follow.

Mom and Dad kept up their stoic act at home, agreeing to bear their burden silently to protect the kids. There were some alterations. They took Mike out of private school and put him in public school. The staff was cut, but there was never a family meeting about the tough days ahead. "We thought we could protect everyone," says Dad. That was his way. When his first wife died he took the three young girls to Disneyland for the week to bury the pain.

In the summer of 1970, a year after the Cheshire profile, an article for *Cosmopolitan* makes Mom and Dad appear completely normal:

They work and play together. He: "The children are very blasé about Nancy being on the air. They much prefer cartoons." She: "Dick and I often have dates for lunch . . . We have a very nicely organized house here—I knock on wood, because last Sunday night the cook called and couldn't quite come back for a week or two." He: "When I get home Nancy's very well dressed—she's worked a hard day, but she's refreshed. Whether she's been here all day or not is unimportant—the children aren't here all day either. I guess if she were working at home all day she'd have a smock on." Her: "I would not have a smock on."

I don't know if stay-at-home moms wrote in to protest, but they should have. It's pretty clear the Dickersons didn't think much of women who stay home. I can only find one profile of Mom from the period where she discusses the Liberty Equities problems. "Dick has been completely honest, open and above board," she says. "He has supplied all the papers and records anyone has asked for. He is brilliant and therefore controversial. You know, if you're good at something, you're observed and if you're observed, criticism follows."

I can't help but think she's talking about herself when she says, "if you're good at something, you're observed and if you're observed, criticism follows." This was a coping mechanism she applied to help herself get through the day too. If people didn't like her it was because she was good.

Mom regretted putting on such a brave face at home. My sister Elizabeth remembers her telling her years later: "The mistake I made was in not talking to you girls. I was raised to keep a stiff upper lip and not to let these things show." At the time, Mom did consider telling the family. She wrote Dad about their financial difficulties: "We all have problems and perhaps you and I would be smarter to tell the entire family how tough it is for us, but my pride prohibits it. We've done it this far and I don't intend to knuckle under now."

The problem with burying everything was that Mom wasn't very good at not letting things show. She might not have sulked or broken down about the core issue, but the strain showed itself in other ways, making her seem arbitrary and heartless. "I remember being in the bathroom you could do a cartwheel in and talking to her about buying some new underwear and bras," says Elizabeth. "She had all of this beautiful lingerie and she said: 'No, that costs $24 and that's just too expensive.'" Mom told her she could sew her old bras if they tore. "I turned into Imelda Marcos later in life because I could never buy shoes."

Because they didn't know what was going on, the girls didn't understand it. "She had this huge house and all these clothes and she would give us the third degree every time we wanted to buy socks," remembers Jane. "It just didn't make sense."

In July, Mom traveled to South Asia with Mrs. Nixon for a special half-hour show on the new First Lady. They flew to Pakistan, Vietnam and India, stopping first in Hawaii to watch the American astronauts splash down after the first landing on the moon. Mom accompanied Mrs. Nixon to orphanages outside of Saigon, a center for the mentally retarded in Guam and a string of hospitals in Indonesia. When the special aired, Nixon kept saying to his wife, "Yes, Pat, that's the way you are. That's the way you really are."

The president liked the show so much he called Mom to pitch her on his idea for how she might interview him. As Nixon envisioned the show, it would take advantage of an upcoming ceremony at Redwoods National Park in California honoring Lady Bird Johnson. Mom would follow Mrs. Johnson and Pat Nixon through the forest then join Nixon and former President Johnson under a redwood tree and interview the whole gang.

Nixon pointed out to Mom that it would be the first dual interview with a president and his predecessor. When Mom pitched it, her NBC bosses didn't know whether she was overstating her access to the president or whether he was using her. Either way they weren't interested. They were wary of interviews arranged by the White House. The trip with Mrs. Nixon had been an exclusive arrangement and two such interviews was a bit much. They didn't want NBC to be Nixon's pet network.

Mom took her request up to Vice President Julian Goodman. He balked. "He was incredulous at the production envisioned by Nixon," Mom wrote, "and reacted as if he'd thought I'd had hallucinations." Goodman thought she was being played and she questioned Goodman's news judgment. The conflict ended in sour feelings and harsh mumbled accusations on both sides.

After NBC turned down the Nixon-Johnson dual interview, Mom pitched another idea to press secretary Ron Ziegler. She would interview Nixon as he gave her a tour of Camp David, the presidential retreat.

Her colleagues in the White House press corps were furious at Mom for making side deals. I know how they felt. When you cover an administration as the designated correspondent you have to stay on top of every press release and every development. Producers or editors call wanting to know *right away* what the president's position is on stem cell research, the conflict in Nagorno-Karabakh and if his plan for repealing the estate tax will help or hurt farmers.

You feel like a short-order cook but you do all that fetching because it's balanced by proximity—you get to ask the questions at press conferences. You get to interview the president's top aides regularly. You get exclusive interviews with him. So when someone swoops in and steals an interview with the man you cover every day, she's not just moving in on your territory, she's taking your reward. It's called being bigfooted and in addition to everything else, it suggests that your bosses don't think you can do your job. When the papers referred to Mom as NBC's White House correspondent, NBC's actual White House correspondent John Chancellor threw a fit and demanded that it be made clear that he was the network's man on the White House.

But Mom knew Nixon better than the beat reporters did and she also knew that presidents like to be with marquee names. They'll walk down the West Wing with Brian Williams and let him put his arm on their back like they're old chums because William brings in a bigger audience as an anchor than he did when he was a White House correspondent ten years earlier.

In May 1970, while Mom was negotiating her exclusive interview, Nixon held a press conference in the East Room. It was only a year and a half into his term, but the White House was already in crisis. Nixon had won the election promising an end to the Vietnam War but on the last day of April, he announced the invasion of Cambodia. College students erupted in protest. Antiwar fever, which Nixon had skillfully reduced to a tolerable level the previous fall, surged to a point unequaled since Lyndon Johnson's last months. Not only had Nixon expanded the war, cried his critics, he had usurped Congress's constitutional powers when he unilaterally ordered troops into Cambodia. Four days after the announcement, National Guard soldiers shot and killed four students at Kent State University in

Ohio. In Washington, troops were called to confront the thousands of antiwar protesters on the Mall.

The day before the press conference, the *Washington Star* printed a letter the secretary of the interior, Walter Hickel, had written the president pleading with him to pay more attention to his Cabinet members, communicate with the young protesters and muzzle Vice President Agnew, who had been attacking administration opponents.

Nixon looked like hell as he walked into the East Room. He stood in front of a microphone with no podium, which revealed his nervous body tics. His hair was slicked back and he moved his hands like a nervous entertainer. He looked a little like Ed Sullivan before a parole board. He hadn't slept much the previous two days. His upper lip had a shelf of sweat and he laughed nervously at jokes only he seemed to be hearing.

Nixon reiterated the need for the Cambodian operation and explained that he valued Secretary Hickel's candor. Mom asked one of the last questions. Why, she wondered, with his promise to tone down his criticism of those who disagreed with him, was Vice President Agnew going to give a speech that very night in which his advance text quoted him as saying that "every debate has its cadre of Jeremiahs, embittered older intellectuals, and choleric young people"?

Nixon responded testily. "Mrs. Dickerson, I have studied the history of this country over the past 190 years. And, of course, the classic and the most interesting game is to try to drive a wedge between the president and the vice president. Believe me, I had eight years of that, and I am experienced on that point. Now, as far as the vice president is concerned, he will answer for anything that he has said. As far as my attempting to tone him down or my attempting to censor the secretary of the interior because he happens to take a different point of view, I shall not do that. I would hope that all the members of this administration would have in mind the fact, a rule that I have always had, and it is a very simple one: When the action is hot, keep the rhetoric cool."

Despite his peppery answer, at the end of the press conference Nixon smiled and waved at Mom on his way out of the room.

Later that night at about a quarter past one, the phone rang at

Merrywood. One of the girls picked up and rang Mom and Dad on the intercom.

Dad handed Mom the phone. "She says it's the president." He figured it was a prank and went back to sleep.

"Who is calling Mrs. Dickerson?" Mom said, irritated.

"This is Nancy Hanschman, isn't it?" Mom woke up.

"This is Dick." It was the president. "That was the toughest question asked at the press conference and I appreciate it—gives me a chance to answer it and put it on the record. . . . I always like the tough questions, really makes me look better . . ."

Mom got out of bed. She was still waking up as Nixon rambled.

"I don't know what's the matter with the goddamn press. I'm the best thing they've got—I'm the only president they have."

Mom wrote in her autobiography that she tried to talk but Nixon kept going.

"I really love those marchers," he said. "I really love those kids, I really do."

"It didn't come through in the press conference," she said.

"But I do! I love those kids, and I understand what bothers them and what they're trying to say." Nixon fluctuated between flare-ups of imperious anger and unctuous solicitude.

"They didn't get that idea from your news conference," said Mom. "The best thing you did was suggest you were going out to see them."

"Oh sure, I told Haldeman and Ehrlichman to bring them all in here . . . 'Bring them all in here,' I said. I told them both I'd love to see the kids."

"That's not the way you put it in your news conference. You said you were going to go out and see them, not bring them in." Why not? she suggested. Why not go out and see the protesters?

The conversation rambled on for a while longer and at the end Nixon insisted that Mom bring the family to the White House for church that Sunday. He said she should bring everyone. "Now don't forget," Nixon said before hanging up.

Mom sat at the edge of the bed. "He hasn't been drinking," she said to Dad. "But I'd feel better if he had been."

In his diary from that Friday evening, Nixon's Chief of Staff H. R. Haldeman wrote, "He stayed up until after 1:00 on the calls . . . He was very tired and rambled on a lot." The next morning's May 9 entry begins: "The weirdest day so far. Started with E. [John Ehrlichman] call at about 5:00 saying P [Nixon] was at the Lincoln Memorial talking to students. . . . P completely beat and just rambling on, but obviously too tired to go to sleep."

Nixon took Mom's advice and went to see the long-haired boys and girls with their signs. The visit was a disaster. His discussion rambled over his travels—Mexico City, the Moscow ballet, the cities of India. When the conversation turned to the war, Nixon told them: "I know you think we are a bunch of so and so's." He told them that when he was young he thought Chamberlain was the greatest man living and that Winston Churchill was a madman. It was not until years later that he realized that Churchill was right. He confessed afterward: "I doubt if that got over."

Before he left, Nixon said: "I know you want to get the war over. Sure you came here to demonstrate and shout your slogans on the Ellipse. That's all right. Just keep it peaceful. Have a good time in Washington, and don't go away bitter." The students were baffled. They had no idea why he had awakened them to go on like that. "I know he was deeply agitated," Mom wrote. "If he talked to the students the way he talked to me, they had reason to be taken aback, and even a little scared." It was a very early sign of the loony and isolated behavior that would consume Nixon's presidency.

Saturday night Mom reported on the president's attempt to connect with the protesters. She didn't refer to her late-night conversation with him explicitly, but she was able to say that no matter how awkward the exchange had looked, Nixon did seem to care about the kids. She only gave an inkling of how unhinged he had been on the phone. She related the story to her bureau chief, but he thought she was exaggerating, perhaps overplaying her analytical skills. Mom had been pushing so hard to do analysis and cover Nixon more directly, he probably thought this was another attempt to go around the regular White House correspondents. "He gave me a little patronizing smile and suggested I needed more rest," Mom wrote.

Privately, Haldeman shared Mom's worries about Nixon. "I was concerned about his condition," he wrote that Saturday afternoon. "The decision, the speech, the aftermath, killings, riots, press etc.;

the press conference, the student confrontation have all taken their toll, and he has had very little sleep for a long time and his judgment, temper, and mood suffer badly as a result."

Nixon's horrible showing on the mall contributed to the institutional view, now accepted by all White House officials, that presidents don't benefit from doing anything serendipitously. Now, when a president wants to do something unexpected, the White House staff plans for it meticulously. It even gets a spot on the official internal calendar under the designation OTR, for Off the Record.

I learned this not long after coming to Washington as a reporter in 1995. I traveled to California with Bill Clinton to survey the damage after the Northridge earthquake. I was in the small pool of reporters that flies on Air Force One and follows in the small van behind his limousine. After an event, our van pulled to the side of the road. The president was stopping to get an ice-cream cone. Wow, I thought. It wasn't on the press schedule. I ran down the shoulder toward the gathering crowd. I strained to get a look at Clinton in the crush.

"They told us he'd be here an hour ago," complained a man next to me on tiptoe trying to get the same peek.

I looked around. Local Secret Service agents were pre-positioned. Local cops had been waiting there for this impulsive moment for hours. The owners of the diner had prepared several of their house specialties in expectation. It was as impromptu as a moon landing.

After Nixon's late-night phone call, White House aides called Merrywood. The president was very eager for the Dickerson family to attend the Sunday services. I wasn't yet two, so I was left behind, but the rest of the family drove through the White House gates. It was like entering an armed compound. Troop trucks and buses were lined around the White House and the Third Army patrolled the perimeter.

Things got weirder in the East Room. The Dickersons took their places in the semicircle of seats arranged around the makeshift pulpit. The preacher was a native of Czechoslovakia who had fought bravely for religious freedom behind the Iron Curtain, had been tortured and had escaped.

Since it was so close to Mother's Day, his sermon was titled "With Gratitude," with a nod to "Mudder's Day," as he called it. The girls giggled. Mom did too. Then the reverend made mudders the leitmotif of his sermon. And these weren't just any kind of mudders either. He told the story of one mudder, whose son was in jail, and when she went to visit him he bit her ear off to punish her for not having raised him better. For some reason the mudder didn't mind. Then there was another mudder whose son was getting married and whose fiancée asked for only one gift: the heart of his mudder presented to her on a silver platter. These were gruesome mudder fuggers.

My brother Michael loved it. He hadn't been expecting an adventure show when they'd dressed him up in the snaps and buckles of his Sunday best. Mom wrote on her program: "A mudder runs well on a rainy track," and passed it to Dad. After coffee in the state dining room the Dickersons muttered "mudder" to each other until they were in the White House driveway, laughing all the way home.

It was amusing and exciting for Mom, and a reminder that she still had enough status to receive a special invitation to the White House. But it didn't help improve the view inside NBC that she was an access reporter in an age where having close ties to the president was becoming less and less acceptable. But Mom continued to argue that the parties were a part of her work. Two weeks after the bombing of Cambodia started, Mom and Dad hosted a black-tie dinner for New York Mayor John Lindsay, who was contemplating a run for the presidency but couldn't decide whether to run as a Republican or Democrat. Dad teased him in his toast: "We are delighted to have our friends here from New York—Jeanne Vanderbilt, Mollie Parnis, Phyllis and Bennett Cerf; but especially Mary and John Lindsay. Everyone knows what difficulty John has about making his mind up about a party."

The evening was supposed to be about domestic presidential politics but it led to an unexpected foreign policy breakthrough. "One of those electric political confrontations which Middle Americans erroneously believe are happening all the time at Washington parties really occurred Wednesday night," wrote Clare Crawford in the *Washington Daily News* of the dinner. The accounts contained only the faintest hint about their financial troubles. "I can't wait to get out to embattled Merrywood," one anonymous party guest told the *Washington Post*.

At the time, the Nixon White House was in turmoil. Aides were engaged in open warfare with Congress over the president's invasion of Cambodia. Nixon's cabinet officials were also speaking out. Labor Secretary George Shultz had suggested that the president muzzle his vice president. Housing and Urban Affairs Secretary George Romney was clashing publicly with Nixon over the administration's economic policies. After dinner, national security adviser Henry Kissinger stood to address the current turmoil.

One president had been murdered, he said, another criticized out of office and now the Democrats were chipping away at Nixon. "We must have compassion, an act of love," he argued.

Hugh Scott, the Senate minority leader, stood next. A moderate Republican, Scott explained gently that he had been trying to show that compassion working on a compromise with the White House on legislation (introduced by senators Church and Cooper, who were also at the dinner) that would bring U.S. troops out of Cambodia by July first. Church, a Democrat, stood and fired back that it was Nixon who needed to understand the limits of his own power. He explained to Kissinger that perhaps what the president needed wasn't love so much as an act of Congress.

Mom was gobsmacked. She wanted lively debate, but the evening was getting out of hand. To ease the tension she called on her old friend Eric Sevareid, who cooled things with a speech on the difficulty of the times.

After dinner, the guests retreated to the living room as coffee was served. Kissinger and Scott huddled by the fireplace while the rest of the guests traded whispers over what had just happened. The next day Scott held a press conference and announced that he had reached a compromise with the White House on the Cambodia legislation after a long chat the night before with Dr. Kissinger.

Chapter Twenty-nine

In July 1970, almost exactly a year after Dad resigned from Liberty Equities, the *Washington Post* announced: "Nancy Dickerson to Resign." That was the public spin. She was fired. No one marched into her office to announce it. It's never done that way. Instead they shoved her to the margin. They did everything but move her office to the parking lot. She got the hint.

She was high maintenance, too close to her sources and she was expensive, the second-highest-paid correspondent behind Brinkley. Network executives had decided to replace her daily news show with Dinah Shore's entertainment program, which brought in more advertising revenue than the news. Once they'd done that they didn't work too hard to reassign her. When they think you're a star your bosses make room for you. They'll break into prime-time dramas just to show you clipping your nails. When you're not a star, producers can't find anything for you. They didn't assign her to do news analysis and limited her reports to appearing only on the *Today* show, where Barbara Walters had been hosting the show for six years. Even there, she had to give way to a White House or diplomatic correspondent if they wanted to cover the same topic. By that time Mom's only sanctuary was the occasional appearance on *Meet the Press,* which operated independently of the news executives. "We didn't pick NBC people because we had to," remembers the show's longtime producer, Betty Dukert. "We picked Nancy because she seemed to me to work extremely hard on *Meet the Press*. Not all reporters did that. Some would come on and go by the seat of their pants. She always studied and worked on it and thought about it."

NBC vice president Julian Goodman explained to Dad what was happening since Dad had been involved in Mom's salary negotiations. Goodman told him that Mom had become too much of a social figure. She was no longer a reporter. It might have been okay for columnists like Joe Alsop and Walter Lippmann to cultivate social relationships with people in power but Nancy was an objective reporter representing the network. A news network could not have its objectivity and uprightness threatened by her social status.

"She didn't believe me at first," my father remembers of telling Mom. "She had done so much. It was a blow to her. She didn't understand how anyone could get along without her." It was devastating because Mom had tried so hard. She didn't know what else she could have done. Throw fewer parties? It was the relationships she'd built socially that gave her the access, and the scoops and exclusives all derived from those personal relationships. She was working the same formula she had used when she booked guests on *Capitol Cloakroom*.

Years later when I explained my careful plans to sweet-talk, cajole and trick *Time* into promoting me out of my secretarial job, she regularly said, "You understand office politics better than I ever did. I thought if I did my job right, that was enough. I never understood office politics." I always thought she was being a little self-pitying. But now I realize that for all of the emotional intelligence she had to have to win over sources and charm them into talking to her, she had none of it at the office. Perhaps it was because she had to shut down her emotions so early in her career to handle the steady flow of fanny pats, put downs and jokes about "two shots." If you care what people think about you, there's no way to break the glass ceiling. Having a thick hide meant she didn't pick up on the signals and see herself as others saw her. "She walked with a little swish down the hallways," remembered Cal Thomas when I asked him about her uglier side. Another intern from those years told my sister Elizabeth the phrase that most clearly described her was "prima donna."

Mom's contract was up for renewal in October 1970. The network offered her no guaranteed slot and because she had no marquee program, they told her they were going to cut her salary. She was insulted. She told them she was leaving.

A letter from NBC vice president Dick Wald outlining the terms of her departure shows just how much they had whittled down the opportunities for her before she announced her resignation. "At the present time I do not foresee any assignments for you on the TODAY show . . . or one of the Radio Network EMPHASIS spots. These are all assigned. Also, although all of the planning has not been finished, there is not presently an Election assignment for you." The letter was written in July, four months before the election. Mom still wanted to work. They could have found her a slot if they'd wanted to.

On a scrap of paper Mom listed for herself the possible jobs she might want and the obstacles to each.

1. Limited opportunities.
2. Effect of Barbara Walters
3. My standing at networks: ABC (ok); CBS Richard Salant; [Don] Hewitt. NBC [Dick] Wald; [Reuven] Frank. PBS (ok). [These names represented producers who had mixed views about her talents.]
4. News jobs I would like:
    1. co-anchor—Chancellor or Cronkite
    2. replace Bruce Morton—CBS morning news
    3. CBS reports
    4. NBC news segment on Today program
    5. Summer replacement for Tom Snyder, Shana Alexander, Tonight Show

That's a pretty impressive list of the plum jobs with the industry. Her view of herself was leagues away from her NBC bosses' assessment of her abilities.

After her departure was announced, Mom was in limbo. She could have loafed, but she was constitutionally incapable of that. Her work had always sustained her and she was going to work her way through her own firing as well.

So a week after her retirement was announced, she was on the phone convincing Henry Kissinger to give her an interview for the *Today* show. The secretary of state had just returned from the elite, all-male retreat at Bohemian Grove outside San Francisco. There were rumors circulating that he might be leaving the administration. One of Kissinger's secretaries kept notes of the conversation:

Dickerson: How was Bohemian Grove?

Kissinger: It was magnificent.

Dickerson: I'd love to go there.

Kissinger: You can't—it's for boys.

Dickerson: I like to be with boys, etc. etc. Are you going to leave in January?

Kissinger: That's a story I put out to keep up the morale of my staff. Where does everybody get that story. . . . They have a new belly dancer at the hotel there and I want to get to know her.

Dickerson: Maybe we could help you get to know her.

Kissinger: I haven't focused on that problem. All these stories have no basis.

Dickerson: I just wondered off the record whether you were going.

Kissinger: I have to keep my staff together.

Dickerson: [She wanted to get together with Dr. Kissinger in the future.]

Kissinger: I have been trying for a long time.

Dickerson: It has been a long time.

Kissinger: There is all the ingredients for a mutual bargain. Let's hope no one is tapping this phone . . .

(Yes, or you'll have to explain this to her son someday.)

She never got the formal Kissinger interview. NBC's White House correspondent Herb Kaplow had been working on an interview as well and her bosses told her to back off. Kaplow had gotten to Kissinger first.

In an odd twist, despite the efforts of some executives, Mom's work picked up as she prepared to leave. In August and September of 1970 she hosted *Today* from Washington. Her ratings were very strong. Viewers wrote in and the network tallied the results. She received fifty-six favorable letters to Barbara Walters' two during the same period. "We hope that Nancy Dickerson is a permanent fixture on the *Today* show," wrote one viewer. Mom kept the reports hoping she might be able to use them to make the case to other networks that she was a popular commodity.

In a final messy quarrel with NBC, Mom had to fight to get paid for the three weeks she took off to have me. In her NBC termination folder I found the letter where the network must have backed down. " . . . We have decided that Mr. Klaric's deduction of three weeks pay in 1968 when you took maternity leave should be recompensed now and you should be kept on the books an additional three weeks." The SEC had just formally charged Dad in connection with Liberty Equities and another shareholder lawsuit had been filed. She had to fight for every nickel.

A week after she carried the last box out of her NBC office, Mom typed a letter to all of her children:

October 16, 1970

Dear Liz, Ann, Jane, Michael, and John Frederick:

Today I made out a will. If I die anytime soon, you all may wonder why I did what I did.

Times have been very difficult for the past year. Daddy has worked very hard to save what we have and not lose it all, but he has not been able to earn any money for over a year. We are deeply in debt and today the sheriff came with what is the 6th lawsuit, so far as I can count, against Daddy. I am making a lot of speeches and flying all over to earn some money. Each time I get in a plane, and as you may suspect, I am a terrible coward about flying, I worry about what will happen to all of you if there is a crash.

I found this letter seven years after she died in a folder marked "NBC Termination" that had fallen behind her fax machine in her New York office.

I was cleaning out the last remnants of her things. Mostly I was there to pack away her favorite books, with the inscriptions from Alistair Cooke, Eric Sevareid and Gore Vidal. It was quiet. I was the only one home. Reading it, I felt like I was twelve again, sneaking into her drawers to read her journals. I imagined I'd look up and see her in the doorway.

She'd made five copies of the letter and put the flimsy blue carbon paper in individual sealed NBC News envelopes addressed to each of us. "I leave each of you all my love and the fervent hope that you will always try to do your very best—better than anyone might rightfully expect—and the hope that you will never stop trying. I also leave my sincerest thanks for being so dear and so nice to me."

"Trying." It's the word she used to rehabilitate LBJ despite his failures. "Try, try, try," she'd written in the notes of her autobiography. That was the word that bound together all the people she'd admired over her life in Washington.

She was writing to herself when she said "better than anyone might rightfully expect." That's why her firing from NBC had hurt her so badly and why she was so confused about office politics. She had tried hard and worked hard and she'd still been fired. She had no idea why.

She was completely and totally alone. She had no money and no job. It's no mystery why she talked of death and her will in her NBC termination folder. It was the end of her career and the removal of the structure that had defined her for the previous twenty years. Perhaps a plane crash seemed the only natural next step in the downward progression.

She never told anyone that she was that worried. She couldn't complain to Dad. His burdens were already big enough. She didn't dare admit problems to her sister, with whom she'd competed so openly. Mom never even confided in her friends. "She might have said something about money but she didn't dwell on those kinds of things," said Pat McCarrick. "Nancy didn't tell you everything." It wasn't Mom's way. It was only later in life, after she'd seen a therapist and learned to talk even to herself about her feelings that she would refer to what she called in a 1993 journal "my well-known ability to hide, suppress, eradicate unhappiness." So she just typed those letters and sealed them away.

My brother and sisters and I wish we'd known. Elizabeth remembers how hard it was to reconcile Mom's life with the life she expected her kids to lead: "She had all these fancy clothes and trips and I couldn't understand why we were the potted plants. I never got it. That's where if she had been able to sit me down and say this is what's happened and even though we live in this mega mansion, we have to do this, it would have been better."

An explanation would have made life seem less arbitrary. Mom didn't let the girls see that she was vulnerable, though a journal entry from the time suggests she knew why they were so upset: "all of the three girls look at Merrywood and have no conception how difficult life has been for us and think we are richer by far than we are."

At the bottom of each letter to the children, Mom scrawled a little handwritten addendum. In the margin of my brother Michael's she bequeathed her letters from the presidents in the hopes that he might "try for President himself one day." At the bottom of mine she wrote, "always keep smiling and making people happy." My cousin Tom, who went to college in Washington in those tough years, says, "I remember your father watching you play and laugh. More than once he said, 'I hope he never loses that happiness.'"

I wonder if my parents both made such an issue of my happiness because my first two years were the hardest of their marriage. I now have a two-year-old son, the age I was when Mom wrote that letter, and he has the same kind of goofy, giddy attitude. After months of writing this book, carrying my parents in my pockets like little stones, I look at his small blond head among his stuffed animals and he is me—that happy little boy you want to protect. If I've had a tough day, I want to protect him even more, knowing the challenges he'll face soon enough. If I had been Mom and Dad, I'd have put my head down, kept quiet, worked harder and not told the kids, either.

Chapter Thirty

By the end of 1970 Mom and Dad could suddenly breathe again. The SEC closed the case with a slap on Dad's wrist and the cluster of civil suits were dismissed or dropped. He settled the largest action with the former company by returning most of his remaining shares of company stock.

As Christmas approached, Herb Klein, Nixon's communications director, called Mom. The long-promised interview suddenly came through. The White House, ever anxious to find a way to improve Nixon's press image, had decided to host a "Conversation with the President." It would show Nixon in a low-key relaxed way chatting with one representative of each network, including PBS.

The White House wanted Mom to represent PBS and called network executives to insist on it. The president of PBS, John Macy, was shocked. It wasn't the request that surprised him. Nixon officials had been on the phone before, demanding in a variety of ways that PBS provide the conservative viewpoint. But Mom wasn't a known conservative. Just the opposite; she was a Johnson girl.

So why was the White House asking for her? Nixon thought she would be sympathetic and improving his image in the press had become an executive order. Reporters had been invited in for cocktails to get to know him. Aides had been tapped as stenographers to attend all dinners and meetings to collect anecdotal material and feed colorful bits to reporters writing general interest stories. Haldeman recounted a scene in early December 1970 where the president and his aides plotted how they might use Mom in this effort. "In discussing ways to screw NBC, the P., thinking Nancy Dickerson is on CBS, asked me to explore the possibility of his doing a half-hour or hour nighttime special with her. It would be just a warm conversation about his personal views of the presidency after two years in office. It would make a darn good show."

Not surprisingly, the Nixon gang had their screwing wrong. Mom wasn't at either NBC or CBS and when they figured that out, they revived their plot. They would give Mom the exclusive and then ask the other networks to simulcast it. This represents a deranged misunderstanding of news competition. The other networks naturally balked. They wanted their own representatives, so an arrangement was made.

Still, it was a huge coup for Mom and PBS. She would be on the air with the top three men in the business and the public network would be considered, at least for that night, a co-equal of NBC, CBS and ABC. She had been sidelined and now she was back on center stage.

Working for PBS was emotional for Mom. Her old friend Paul Niven had moved from CBS to PBS a few years earlier. In January of 1970 he had died a gruesome death. He had fallen asleep in bed with a lit cigarette, woke up on fire, and leapt out of his town house window.

Mom decided to do the show in Paul's honor. She dove into the material as he would have, sequestering herself with her producer and researcher for weeks. They read newspapers clips, speeches and White House position papers. They drew up lists of questions and reordered them. They worked through New Year's Eve, pausing long enough only to celebrate with champagne in paper cups.

The final product of all the work was a single reporter's pad with seventy-one questions, including one from my nanny Veronica about why no one seemed to like Nixon. That number of questions seems like overkill since she'd only be able to ask eight questions. But interviewing a president requires that kind of excessiveness. You have to prepare for every possible mood, topic and shift in conversation. I interviewed President Bush five times and each time was brutal. You have to guess which questions are going to make a president angry and unresponsive, which are going to invite a mere recitation of his stump speech and which are just going to confuse him. Any news you want to make or insight you hope to glean you've got to thread through all those other obstacles.

All your preparation can fall apart in the room. Once you are on his turf, the clock starts and aides are jumping to usher you out. You have your list of questions and suddenly a tug-of-war begins. He wants to give you his talking points. If he can filibuster, his aides will call time and it'll be over. Your job is to get past all of that without interrupting him so frequently that he gets irritated and starts giving you one-word answers. One thing no president wants is a nutty news-magazine question. If you've made your question too baroque, you'll spend precious time trying to explain what you were trying to get at.

Mom had to balance all of that and still stay nimble enough to re-order her questions based on what the other three journalists were asking. On the day of the interview in early January '71, she camped out across from the White House at the Hay-Adams Hotel. While she sat having her hair and makeup done, her producer turned on the television. They wanted to get the latest news in case any late bulletins might shape one of Mom's questions. It was two hours until showtime. A "commentary on the media" followed the newscast and the commentator suggested that for the momentous presidential interview, Public Broadcasting should not have chosen Nancy Dickerson because she lacked "authority." Her makeup and hair stylists tried to distract her. Her producer just stared at the screen. The commentary continued for two minutes before she switched it off. Mom took her producer by the arm and said, "let's go."

When she got to the White House, her colleagues were just as nervous as she was. Howard K. Smith of ABC was muttering to himself over his notes. Eric Sevareid of CBS, Mom's idol and mentor, was pacing back and forth telling jokes. When Mom told him she was impressed that he wasn't nervous, he snapped back, "Good God! You ought to know I never tell jokes." She walked into the bathroom to compose herself and there was NBC's John Chancellor smoothing down his tie and going through his questions in the mirror.

It was freezing in the presidential library. Nixon sweated, so the White House had lowered the temperature to battle the effect of the lights. Mom fortunately had thought about this beforehand and wore thick white tights. When the president sat down, they were the first thing he commented on.

"Stand by, quiet in the room," said the director.

Sevareid leaned across the other two correspondents and whispered, "Nancy, you look absolutely ravishing tonight." And they were off.

From the economy to Vietnam to health care they bounced around the issues. Toward the end, Mom reminded Nixon of his campaign pledge to offer the country the "lift of a driving dream": "Well, as yet, many people have failed to perceive the lift of a driving dream. I wondered if you could articulate that dream for us briefly and tell us how you plan to specifically get it across to the people in the next two years."

Nixon hesitated. He looked a little lost before lowering his head and speaking: "Miss Dickerson, before we can really get a lift of a driving dream, we have to get rid of some of the nightmares we inherited. One of these nightmares is a war without end. We are ending that war. . . . But it takes some time to get rid of the nightmares. You can't be having a driving dream when you are in the midst of a nightmare." (On succeeding Nixon into office, Gerald Ford noted, "Our long national nightmare is over.")

The next day, the *New York Times* lead editorial picked up on Mom's question: "In short, there has nowhere in these first two years of the Nixon Presidency been the 'lift of a driving dream' of which he spoke in 1968 and about which one of his interviewers pertinently reminded him."

She had made news, which was a thrill, but the *New York Post* was even more generous to her personally. "It was this viewer's impression the other night . . . that Nancy Dickerson asked the most pointed questions as the representative of public TV. It was surprising to us that some Washington correspondents questioned her qualifications for duty alongside Eric Sevareid of CBS, Howard K. Smith of ABC and John Chancellor of NBC, who were all somewhat less than effectively aggressive with their questions."

The next day in his Cabinet meeting Nixon asked his secretary of state, "Do you think we freezed Nancy's ass off last night?"

The national exposure arrived at the right moment. Mom had

decided to strike out on her own, selling herself to local affiliates across the country. She would produce three commentaries a week and they would stitch them into their local newscasts. No one had tried such a thing before. She was convinced that she was enough of a star that people would gravitate to her. There was the data to prove it. She had the positive ratings from her *Today* show appearances and quoted a Lever Brothers poll on television personalities. Seventy-five percent of people knew Nancy Dickerson and knew her favorably. Her lowest rating was in the South: 65 percent. Her highest rating was in the Midwest: 85 percent. On her copy of the report Mom wrote at the bottom: "(Higher than Barbara Walters)."

While Mom handled the editorial side, Dad did the selling, signing up sixty stations across the country, including the top ten markets. It was the first time they'd been in business together. Both of them had lost their jobs and had their faith shaken. Given how hard things were, it's astonishing that they stuck with it and with each other. Later I saw the evidence of blame-shifting and finger-pointing, but at the time they both had the same response to getting knocked back: They just started walking up the hill again.

Mom not only did her weekly shows but a series of specials, including an interview with Treasury Secretary John Connally and a special on the women's movement. The latter was a hard one for her. She still wasn't comfortable with the movement, which by 1972, when the show aired, was in an all-out war with the men. In a piercing but accurate review of the show, Sally Quinn wrote: "Dickerson is uncomfortable with the subject and the language. She hesitates at questions, apologizes ("this may sound silly") and equivocates ("sisterhood, if you will") somewhat the way a white person might if hosting a show on the black movement with all white panelists."

Since the '50s Mom had regularly spoken out about the lack of women in the newsroom, but she didn't like the feminists. "I've never gone in for the bra burning," Mom would regularly tell her speech audiences. "Every movement has to have its silly fringe." Male executives were forced to hire women quickly to avoid public accusations of discrimination. She thought promotions became an act of putting points on the board. "And if they could hire a black and a woman they could take care of their tokenism in one swoop," Mom said. She thought the hiring lowered standards and cheapened her achievement. Men had made the same case about standards when she was promoted. Mom was being selfish, she liked being the Queen Bee but the women who came after her understood why the pace was quickening too. They didn't like being promoted just because they were female any more than Mom did. After women at television station WRC in Washington, D.C., took the station to court and the FCC threatened fines unless management diversified the newsroom, executives promoted Cassie Mackin. "I'm being used," Mackin said at the time.

Mom also thought the movement made her job harder. Before, men considered successful women like Mom isolated problems and a nuisance. In the '70s each woman in the newsroom became a political statement, a daily reminder of an argument that left everyone with bruised feelings and nursing grudges.

In her new life as a syndicated reporter, Mom was busier than she had been during her final days at NBC. She had to come up with three different ideas, report them and then construct the commentaries so they would still be relevant several days later after the film was mailed to the stations.

Her pieces were not objective. She was offering analysis, the kind of reporting her NBC bosses preferred to have the men do. This increased her enemies in the Nixon administration. White House fixer Chuck Colson wrote a nasty letter to Senator Bob Dole, who was then also head of the Republican National Committee, after Mom had reported that Republicans in Congress were upset with the president.

January 15, 1972

Dear Bob:

I thought you might be interested in the attached. This is what these liberal bastards (in this case, the correct word is bitch) love to seize upon—any kind of rift between Republicans.

I note here that Nancy says she talked with you. She didn't talk to me and I frankly can't believe that you said to her what she's used here. But, as I say, these kinds of reporters will pick at anything.

That was a delightful letter to find in a secondhand bookstore. Colson, who would later devote his life to helping prisoners, was at that time the kind of enemy a son would like his mother to have. He went to jail for his role in the Watergate cover-up and the book of his memos in which his little rage against Mom is included is a breathtaking compendium of how the small-minded can abuse the privilege of working in the White House.

While Mom was stirring up some in the White House, she was still working to keep her access. She wrote Nixon's secretary Rose Mary Woods, congratulating her on a promotion. Woods, who would later erase eighteen minutes of the most damaging conversations Nixon taped, wrote back. "Along with thousands of others who have known this man and his wonderful family over the years, I have no doubt whatsoever of the outcome of this disgraceful 'Watergate' affair," she writes. "Consequently your generous comments mean even more at this time than I can tell you!"

Mom's sweet-talking didn't work on everyone. She tried pitching the Nixon administration stories in ways she hoped would get them to open up, but they were on to her. An internal letter from the FBI is included in their files archived at the agency.

"Nancy Dickerson dropped by my office," wrote Cartha DeLoach, FBI liaison to the White House. "She desires to have a 7 or 8-minute program pointing out that the New Left is made up of a number of hard-core militants who are revolutionary in nature, and that these militants and red Chinese-oriented personalities are destroying many young men and women who ordinarily would not be involved in such matters. She asked for material for use in preparing such a program."

According to the letter, DeLoach gives her the brushoff. He offers her some public testimony on the matter. Recognizing the diversion, Mom lays it on thick. "While discussing other matters, Miss Dickerson told me that the President had called her at 1:30 a.m., on Saturday May 9th and had talked with her approximately 30 minutes."

The author of the memo then goes on to recount how Mom explained that she was responsible for encouraging Nixon's trip to visit the students. It's clear what "Miss Dickerson" is doing. In every way possible she is trying to show DeLoach that she is a friend of the president. She fails. He concludes his memo by showing his bosses he's no fool. "Miss Dickerson will only be furnished public source material." His boss scrawls at the bottom, "She is to be given only appropriations testimony. She is hostile towards FBI."

I'm delighted to see Mom playing the angles. I wonder if she would have sold out those young leftists as quickly as she promised in her letter to the FBI. I don't think so. I think she was telling the FBI officer what he wanted to hear.

Mom hustled to produce her three weekly pieces, but the weak economy of the early 1970s did not make it a good time for television experimentation. After three years local stations didn't renew their contracts. It was easier to tape pieces about crime than buy ones from Mom about inflation policy. To keep up with the bills, Mom and Dad sold two of the cars and some of Mom's jewelry. By the fall of 1974, they were both out of a job again and Mom wrote to Dad: "What plans do we have now that my earning power is no longer so great?" The answer was that she would finally write her autobiography, which she sold to Random House in 1975 for $50,000.

I asked her to dedicate the book to me. I don't know how I would have known about such a thing at age seven. When *Among Those Present* came out in 1976 it was the first time my name and face were published in a book. Late in the summer of 1975 I remember being hurried into my dress outfit like they'd scheduled emergency church. I was photographed with Mom in our driveway. It had something to do with the book but I didn't understand why until I saw the picture in the finished copy several months later.

In Mom's files I found the list of captions for the pictures in the book. They describe various shots with Dad, the presidents, Henry Kissinger, Murrow and my brother and sisters. But in the number six spot, where I wound up, the caption reads: "façade of Merrywood." I didn't make the first cut! It wasn't until just before the book went to print that Mom or her editor realized that there were pictures with her other children but none of her younger son. With nothing suitable in her collection, she had to get one taken and figure out where to put me. All the other slots were filled with famous people. She wasn't going to slot me into the space reserved for a letter from JFK. In the end, they went for a twofer. They didn't replace the picture of Merrywood, they just had me stand in front of the house.

The published book is a disappointment. Mom wasn't self-analytical. When she did discover something messy or vulnerable about her life she closed the door quickly rather than examine it.

But the unpublished book is a wonder. Her attractive authentic self—the Nancy Hanschman voice—was alive, but it never got a chance to speak in print. Her notes from her autobiography are far better than the book itself: She's complex, and interesting and sassy. "I have had a marvelous life," she writes in the unpublished introduction, "full of love and sadness, and earnest concern, and care, and worry and try, try, try, try—the one thing that attracted me to anyone or anything was those that cared and tried." She ends her introduction this way: "With apologies to none of my teachers—none of them taught me a damn thing . . . with apologies to all my colleagues who taught me everything I know . . . here goes . . . and to the critics beforehand, if any deign to review . . . I dare you to have lunch with me and find it boring!"

This voice does not exist in the book. Did she edit the good stuff out or was it her editor? I think it was probably a joint effort. He wanted a string of career highlights, not the messy truth or theories developed by looking back. She didn't fight back. She was anxious to play whichever role was called for. She was so anxious that she was willing to play on the rumors about her possible relations with Johnson and Kennedy. In a note to her editor about the title, she writes: "I am not above teasing a bit and recognize the value of ambiguity and suggest *An Affair with Power.*"

The book sold well and put her name back in the papers, but it also marked a passing. Mom was, at forty-eight, a veteran. Television newswomen had moved on in the six years since she'd left NBC. The networks and local affiliates now had several female correspondents. Ann Compton of ABC became the first full-time female White House correspondent. Cassie Mackin anchored the NBC Sunday evening news. In 1976, ABC paid Barbara Walters $1 million to host the ABC nightly news with Harry Reasoner, making her the first woman to permanently fill that marquee spot. The arrangement collapsed after two years. Reasoner was so upset at being paired with a woman that he could barely disguise his disdain.

Mom crossed the country pitching her book and herself at bookstores, rotary clubs and ladies' luncheons. The role of women in society had become a central cultural issue after *Roe v. Wade* legalized abortion and Congress ratified the Equal Rights Amendment in 1972. But Mom wanted to talk about herself, not the movement. She boasted about every landmark of her career, but she didn't want to talk about women in journalism because that took the conversation away from her achievements. She wanted to be asked about her life or her opinions about the Cold War and Carter's energy policy.

Owen Johnson learned just how tricky Mom could be when he tried to interview her for the University of Michigan public radio station. "The topic of the interview was women in journalism," he remembers. "I kept asking questions relating to the challenges for women journalists. She'd briefly answer the question, then talk about some part of her book. I felt like the whole interview was a tug of war." Later, Johnson became a professor of journalism and used the taped interview to illustrate how difficult it can be to keep control of a subject.

A week before Christmas 1976 Mom appeared on the Johnny Carson show. I screened the episode at the Museum of Television and Radio in New York in the same marathon viewing afternoon that I saw the footage of Mom at the 1960 Democratic Convention. She appears at the end of the show after a comedian whose trousers were too tight in the crotch and too loose in the ankles and one of those couples that always seem to sing on the telethons. I fast-forwarded and stopped as Mom walked onstage.

There was the stiff woman I remember from adolescence. The exhausted show biz couple that preceded her were as natural as Hepburn and Tracy compared to Mom. She sashayed from behind that multicolored curtain like she was on a fashion runway. She held her arms self-consciously as if she were doing tai chi. Maybe it was just her nerves. I hunched over as if someone in the museum was going to look over my shoulder and know I was related to her. Minutes before, I was inclined to stop people to show her reporting with Walter Cronkite in 1960.

She looks entitled, that's what's bugging me. She's behaving like it's her show and the people on the couches and the giggling white-haired man behind the desk are her guests. Her voice is throaty and theatrical as she dishes out pedantries about the Carter administration. I want to shake her. She's like a dinner theater actress playing Nancy Dickerson.

The interview is dull. Carson decides to fix that. He starts showing pictures from the book. He turns to the one of her dancing with Lyndon Johnson, her arm draped over his back.

"There was a rumor at one time," he says, measuring his words carefully. "I don't mean to be rude." He puts his hand on her arm. "I've known you for a few years, but there was a rumor at one time. Just a rumor. That . . . you know . . . Lyndon Johnson . . . *well*."

Mom laughs.

Does she get what he's talking about? I think she does. She's making him stew. I smile. Clever girl. I'm back on her side. She knows what he's getting at, but she's letting him twist out there. She's making him say it out loud.

"But you know what I'm talking about," Carson continues. He jiggles the picture. The audience is laughing. He hopes she'll save him.

"What are you talking about?" she says, batting her eyes.

The audience erupts in applause. They love that she's got him.

"The old reporter's trick," says Carson. "Where someone hands you a hot potato you hand it right back. No, what I mean was, it was not a romantic relationship [he's backing down now] but he looked at you with [pause] kind eyes."

"He talked about politics all the time," Mom says. "He once wanted me to be on the FCC, but who would want to be an FCC commissioner?"

FCC? What's she doing? Is she just not answering or did she not get it?

Mom talks about dancing with Johnson and how he liked to dance with all female reporters. "He was a darn good dancer." Oh no. She's clueless.

Bewildered, Carson goes to commercial break. When they return, they talk about Nixon briefly and then there's another break. The show is wrapping up.

Carson comes back on the screen for the last sixty seconds of the show. "Do you really want to clear that up?" he asks her.

"Yes."

"During the break Nancy asked: 'Did I leave the impression with viewers that I'd had an affair with President Johnson?' "

"Yes!" says Ed McMahon a little too loudly and quickly.

"Let me clear it up," says Mom. "No!"

"Darn!" says Carson slamming his hand on the table. That's the end of the show. Mom stands and does a little dance to the orchestra's tune. I want to hide under the desk.

Chapter Thirty-one

My first memories begin around 1975 when I was six. They are memories of abundance. I was in private school, the result of Dad's latest good fortune. In that year he had put together a deal that had won him a million-dollar commission in a single check. Dad also started an exclusive private club called Pisces in December of 1975, which became very successful. The parties picked up again and soon enough I was at the door with my older brother in blue blazer and gray flannel trousers.

My sisters were no longer at home. Elizabeth lived in town with her new husband, Greg, but her relationship with Mom had strained during the tough years of the early '70s. When she and her husband visited Merrywood, it often ended in a scene. Mom stormed out of rooms or refused to play tennis with them. When Elizabeth asked if she could have a silver dish that belonged to her mother, Mom hid it from her. "I just can't handle Liz and Greg here at any moment it suits them," Mom wrote Dad after a bad episode. "I have had a very disappointing career and a large pride that I have to massage and Privacy is what we all crave. I need it more than most because I normally spend a week meeting and talking with dozens of people and I want some time off. That is why I love to be alone." As the money returned, Mom relaxed a little but she could still deliver a dig. Once when standing next to Elizabeth before a mirror she exclaimed, "You have more wrinkles than I do."

I was aware of none of this sourness. I was experiencing the golden age of my childhood. This was before the divorce, before my brother and I learned to play my parents off each other. They were still a team. They took walks together in the spring and fall through the property with their favorite walking sticks and I would follow along or run ahead throwing rocks.

I remember them coming to check on me late one night and finding me still awake. "How do I know there is a God?" I asked. I was terrified. I was imagining what it was like when you die. That's it. It's over. Dirt. Dark. Done.

Mom's answer was something from her Catholic school teaching. I remember it was vaguely comforting, but unfulfilling. "Isn't it great to be John Dickerson?" said Mom, confusing me.

My father launched into a description of the blue crab of Maryland, telling me about its migration patterns and how it laid eggs and how its complex physiology was perfectly designed to achieve its goals in life. "None of that happened by chance," he said. "God designed it that way."

Dad's answer may not have been proof of a benevolent creator but it calmed me down and I was soon asleep.

Every Christmas Eve Mom and Dad hosted a party. It was the highlight of the year. A fifteen-foot-high tree that we spent an entire evening decorating dominated the front hall. Dad would string the garish colored lights and we would unwrap the ornaments Mom had collected over the years. Some were the size of grapefruits and weighed nearly as much. Mom strung garlands over the front hall banister, tying bright red bows every few feet. If she could have hired elves she would have—I mean other than us.

On Christmas Eve, Dad would wear his green velvet blazer and put on the Nat King Cole Christmas album. The Valentis, the Mondales and the Bartletts would arrive along with a few other families. My brother and I would hang their coats and stack the presents they'd brought for us. They were all magical, theatrical people to me, Washington figures who filled up the room by the sheer force of their personalities. I didn't know that Charlie Bartlett was a Kennedy intimate or that Valenti had played the same role with Johnson. I just liked to be around them to hear their wild accents.

Everyone got silly before dinner, which I would recognize later in life as the effect of ready martinis. We'd have an enormous meal and then everyone would perform. Jack Valenti, the head of the Motion Picture Association, would show a home movie, Senator Mondale and his family would act out a scene from Shakespeare. The Bartlett family would sing. My brother Michael would read from the Bible and Mom would make the family sing traditional songs with topically revised verses, like this one from 1976 during the energy crisis:

You better Be Good
You'd better not frown
You better keep speeds and thermostats down
Santa Claus is coming to town.

The party would also provide Mom with an opportunity to remind everyone of the time when I, seeing Senator Mondale in the robes he had brought for a Shakespeare scene, decided that I would dress up too. With all the families gathered in the garden room, I arrived in my Batman costume, hopping around karate-chopping and brandishing my utility belt.

"They were physical with each other," Helen Bartlett recalls of my parents, "and warm, and they wanted to share that warmth with other people." The Bartletts as their final act would sing out "three cheers for the Dickersons" as we smiled out from the doorway. "Yours was a family that was this beautiful entity," she remembers, "very intact."

Those parties were our one family routine. We didn't go to a regular houseboat on the weekend or make an annual spring trip. The Christmas Eve party and the days surrounding it were predictable.

The other regular gaiety of my childhood surrounded the Redskins games. Mom and Dad were close to the team's owner, Edward Bennett Williams. He was my godfather and for my baptism he rushed to the church with a freshly drawn Redskins contract awarding me the same salary as Johnny Unitas, the highest-paid player in the league at the time, should I decide to take up the game in twenty years.

We went to every home game. Mom and Dad sat in the owner's box and my brother and I sat just a few rows away. Afterward, the party would sometimes come back to Merrywood with the Williamses and the McCarricks. These were the people with whom Mom felt most comfortable. "She could relax with Pat because they had known each other for so long she didn't have to be anybody," my father told me. At one of these long winding afternoons, Williams and his star quarterback Sonny Jurgensen negotiated Jurgensen's contract. Afterward Williams called to see if anyone remembered the terms they'd worked out. Both he and his quarterback had been too bombed to remember.

I had a simple and glorious life during elementary school. In the morning I walked up our driveway, through the woods and to the bus stop making sure to swipe away any spiderwebs that had grown across the path overnight. I attended private school through the third grade and then public school starting in fourth. The switch was made to accommodate another dip in the finances. I loved it. It didn't bother me that in public school we didn't have a separate room for science projects. Our science class arrived in a box every few months from the Fairfax County Depository.

I was hanging around with an entirely new class of kids. One friend's father plowed our driveway and worked in the filling station. Another friend's dad worked in a boathouse on the Potomac. My first girlfriend lived with her single mother, who delivered the mail. I think if Mom had spent time with any of these parents in their tiny suburban houses with mildewed basements she would have directed me to find other friends, as she tried to do later. But she never really interacted with my friends' parents, so she never had a chance to get uncomfortable with their modest world. Manuel drove me to their houses or I'd walk home with them after school.

I spent a lot of time as the surrogate child of the McDonnell family. They lived at the top of our hill. They had a son, Kevin, who was my age and three other kids who weren't much older. They didn't mind one more addition to their Irish clan. As I look over my composition books from elementary school, the trips I wrote about in big, uncertain letters are ones I took with them. To the beach, the ski slopes and Cape Cod, we all piled into their custom van carpeted with electric-blue shag. It had a refrigerator and an eight-track tape player and speakers in the back where we played marathon games of Monopoly at high speed.

The McDonnells had exotic things in their house. I didn't consider having an entire gymnasium or swimming pool extraordinary. But what I really coveted was their collection of kitschy items like the crossed swashbuckler's swords that hung over their fireplace. In the basement they had a real working slot machine. They also had a player piano and a jukebox you didn't have to pay to play.

In Kevin and his brother John's room it seemed you could get away with anything. They had their own television. In their room! Mom never let us watch television unless it was the news. At the McDonnells' we stuffed ourselves on *Dukes of Hazzard* and *Fantasy Island*. We played video games and kept score on an enormous blackboard that hung unevenly on the wall. I'd never seen one that big outside of school. We wrote out swear words in lavish block letters. Now those were words I could spell.

We courted peril everywhere, daring each other to do increasingly absurd things. Who would climb through Merrywood's third-floor dormer to retrieve the model airplane stuck on the roof? Who could run fastest down the rocky path to the churning Potomac River and not fall in? The swimming pool had no fence around it and in the winter it was never covered. Have you ever seen a frozen squirrel? We hadn't, so we walked out to the middle of the frozen brown ice to check out a squirrel trapped in distress. When we found an abandoned El Dorado in one of the neighbor's fields, I planned to drop a lit match in its gas tank. What stopped me? My innate good sense? Probably not. It may have been just a lack of ready matches.

How we didn't end up as a horrid statistic is a mystery. I discovered that Mom's ample stockpile of hair spray could be used to make blowtorches. She might have missed some of the mammoth cans, but who can keep track of such things when you're on the road so much. I took my fresh supply to the two-room basement meat locker where I had made my fort. In his memoir, Gore Vidal, who grew up at Merrywood twenty years before my parents bought it, wrote that he lost his virginity in those rooms. It's where I discovered increasingly dramatic plumes of fire could be made with compressed flammable gases. Years later, when we traded stories, Vidal told me he thought his discovery was more dangerous. Ultimately, he gave up girls and I pyrotechnics.

Sharpening the largest butcher knife in the kitchen with the abandon of a symphony conductor, I opened up a gash on my thigh. Did I really just do that, I wondered, looking down at my cleanly sliced jeans? At first, there was no blood. Then a bright diamond of crimson appeared in the surgical gash. I woke up a few moments later. I had passed out. I had bled through my jeans and had ruined the sofa cushion. I turned it over. A few months later, I was at it again and now have matching scars on both thighs. Both times, I was too scared to tell anyone what happened, so I just stayed up all night pressing at the wound. If you're going to raise yourself, you can't go running to mommy. The second time, I had a tennis tournament the next day and I was so woozy I could barely stand. My father, watching through the fence, shook his head as his sluggish son watched the balls whiz by. I don't think he noticed the hasty clump of Band-Aids on my thigh.

Toward the end of elementary school in 1980, Mom and I spent a lot of weekend nights at home alone while Dad was at the club. She'd be watching television while my friend Kevin and I would find ways to scare her to death. One of Jane's boyfriends had sculpted a black bust of himself and we'd put it in Mom's bed or behind the curtain or in her toilet. Then we'd wait. You could hear her scream on the other side of the house.

Dad was at the club so much because whatever renewed happiness Mom and Dad found in the '70s had started to disappear by 1980. They snapped and picked at each other in front of us. "The boys imitate you and that doubles the problem," Mom wrote Dad at the time. "It is especially hard on John who now thinks the way of life is to *ridicule everyone.*"

I'm not sure I ridiculed everyone. I think I mostly ridiculed her. In school I wasn't acting out as much as I had when I was younger. My grades were quite good. I had girlfriends. I was popular. At home I was a little shit to Mom. It wasn't that I swore at her or disobeyed particularly, I just found it terribly clever to make fun of her. I was looking for attention and showing off, but it was a sport all of the Dickerson men played. "I may have had problems with her," remembers Elizabeth, "but it was so hard to watch her when you were mean to her."

I am not sure why I did it. I certainly resented being an ornament at the front door and hated enduring her efforts to fix my spelling, my posture or otherwise make me presentable. In retrospect some of it looks like *Lord of the Flies*–style bullying that young boys do when no one stops them. We reduced her to saying things like, "People pay money to hear me talk." When she said that we laughed.

I think my brother and I also wanted to puncture the image and her pretense. We wanted to connect with a person, but she was a persona. She was a long way from the appealing girl who failed her steno tests in 1951. In public she had to be Nancy Dickerson and at home she kept a brave face, followed her lists to keep the house in order and struggled to never let anyone down. When she got home she couldn't relax. She was desperate to find out if everything had gone as planned while she was away and to plan for her next absence. She never let herself just be and she didn't have much time to anyway. After a while she forgot how.

When Mom and Dad held the party for the Reagans in January 1981, they put on a happy face. I don't exactly know how they did it. The party was a smashing success, but four months later the papers reprinted rumors that both of them were having affairs. I went away to camp in June of 1981 and by the time I made it back in August, Dad was gone.

Mom kept the notes Dad wrote when he moved out of Merrywood: "Good luck. Thanks for Mike and John and thanks for putting up with me," read one. Another letter was longer:

July 27, 1981

Dear Nancy,

You have been superb about so many things during our marriage. You may think I am unaware of all the unselfish and thoughtful things you have done for me and the children. I am aware and I deeply appreciate everything. I have been too critical but I have always meant it constructively. We may be two people who meant well but couldn't always make our good intentions understood by each other. I have been proud that you were my wife and I have been proud that men and women admired your brains and beauty.

I am very sorry that we ended the way we did. I will always love you, in spite of what might be said or done out of bitterness. I hope we can be helpful to each other in trying to build new lives apart in a way that we couldn't seem to together.

Chapter Thirty-two

Mom and Dad split just as Mom was trying to relaunch her career. After writing her autobiography, she spent the last years of the 1970s giving speeches and working on about one documentary a year. They were always on serious subjects. *We Will Freeze in the Dark* tackled energy policy. *A House Divided* reported on life in Congress after Watergate. For a PBS show on the crisis in the Middle East in 1980 she interviewed Egyptian President Anwar Sadat and Israeli Prime Minister Menachem Begin. Half of the effort she put into these programs went into raising money for them. She had to scrape together funding each time and pitch herself anew. She signed on with Merit cigarettes as an analyst when they sponsored a public opinion poll to upgrade their image as the smoke of the smart set. She agreed to host a televised debate on energy policy even though the program was funded by an oil company. Fifteen minutes before airtime she walked off the set when she learned that the oil company was going to air a fifteen-minute video before the debate promoting their views.

By 1981 she didn't have to scrape anymore. Bill Moss, a former business partner of Dad's and a wealthy Texas oil man, funded Television Corporation of America. The papers suggested they were having an affair.

Mom bought a Georgetown house as an office and set up shop with two other producers. Through 1981 and 1982 she worked day and night on a special commemorating the tenth anniversary of

Watergate. Much of the world seemed to have forgotten her television career. In the papers very few people referred to her as a journalist. "She hated being referred to as a 'hostess' in the newspaper or as a 'socialite,'" remembers Francine Proulx, whom Mom had hired back as her assistant. When Cassie Mackin, an ABC reporter who had covered the 1972 presidential race, died in 1982, the newspapers claimed she was the first newswoman to report from the floor of a convention. Mom had been first—Mackin had been the first for NBC. Mom had Francine call the Broadcast Pioneers Library to make sure they had the correct historical record. "She was far more like a diva the second time I worked for her than the first," remembers Francine.

At about this time, Mom reviewed three books written by women in the news for the *Washington Post*. Mom generally praised the one by Judy Woodruff, but the two shots she takes tell us more about her than Woodruff. "At times, however, Ms. Woodruff's sense of her own cosmic importance is second only to that of Henry Kissinger. One begins to feel that certain events at the White House . . . would never have occurred if she had not been there personally to witness them." That's not very generous and it's an extraordinary act of chutzpah coming from a woman with such a healthy view of her own influence.

But what made me drop my coffee cup were Mom's criticisms of Woodruff's views on balancing life and family. "When [Woodruff] talks about the difficulties of combining career and motherhood it wears one out just to read about it. Honestly, it's not quite as enervating as she makes out." In her notes for the review Mom remarked, "I did the JFK assassination with a five month old baby and *three* teenagers." She sounds like those parents who talk about how many miles they had to walk to get to school.

Woodruff and her husband, Al Hunt, didn't have the servants Mom did. One of their children has spina bifida. And when Mom wrote the review, at least four of her five children were in open warfare with her.

This was the woman I knew—hard and unforgiving. And this was the woman in evidence when a *Washington Post* reporter interviewed her about her Watergate program. The piece ran under the headline "Dickerson's Return—The 'First Lady' of Network News Looks to the Future with A Watergate Retrospective." It begins with a vinegary scene.

> *Nancy Dickerson is smiling but the smile is very tight and forced. Actually, Nancy Dickerson is very ticked off, very ticked off indeed.*
>
> *She gets up from her desk, a willowy, well-tended auburn-haired lady in her mid-fifties, looking very chic in a black and white checked Bill Blass suit. She paces the floor, then rather pointedly closes the door of her office, lest her executive assistant or assistant producer, working down the hall over-hear what she has to say.*
>
> *Why is Nancy Dickerson ticked off? Well, she reminds {the reporter that} the reason she had agreed, finally, to do the interview was to publicize her documentary . . .*
>
> *This is what she had agreed to talk about, she reiterates. She feels deceived, she says, and strongly suggests the reporter may have misrepresented himself.*
>
> *"I've refused numerous requests for interviews, because I don't want to talk about my personal life," she declares.*
>
> *"All these people you've been talking to," she goes on, "my friends, my ex-husband, people I worked with at NBC, asking them if the show is a comeback for me, asking if my emeralds are real . . ."*

Did Richard Lee, the interviewer, trick her? Maybe a little. But Mom had built her career on her personal life. They *always* asked about her personal life. She should have deflected his inquiries easily. Instead she got self-righteous and combative. I can hear Mom say: "Don't you know who I am?"

If I had been Richard Lee, I'd have thought she had serious issues. She did. She was in the middle of a very ugly divorce. Everyone knew that Dad had upped the ante. As the *Washington Post* had reported, he filed for divorce on the grounds that she had committed adultery with Bill Moss. She worried the reporter would focus more on the gossip than the Watergate show that she hoped would free her from the last tough ten years and launch a new stage in her career. In addition to her career angst, her youngest child was sulking, rebelling and pressing accusations at home.

Half a year later, in the spring of 1983, after the show had aired and was praised by critics, Michael and I were vacationing with Mom at John Gardiner's Tennis Ranch in Arizona. We were waiting to go to lunch outside our bungalow while Mom took a phone call.

She ran out of the house, her arms flailing.

"I won a Peabody!" she yelled, "I won a Peabody!"

My brother and I looked at each other and then at her. We started hopping around and running in circles.

"I won a Peabody! I won a Peabody!" we shouted. We had no idea what a Peabody was, but it clearly made you go insane. Mom explained that it was a very big deal—such a big deal that our teasing couldn't diminish her joy.

Mom's company's first show had won the highest award in the television news business. It was like her first drink of water in ten years. But Mom was not gracious in victory. She had produced the show with two other producers in Washington. Mom never talked about it as a team effort. One of her co-producers, Bill Carpenter, was so ticked off about it he called the papers. The day after the *Post's* television columnist wrote that Mom alone had won a Peabody, he ran a correction in his column: "Let's make one thing abundantly clear: William Carpenter was co-executive producer (with Nancy Dickerson) of '784 Days That Changed America—From Watergate to Resignation,' the syndicated show produced by Television Corporation of America here that just won a George Foster Peabody Broadcasting Award . . ."

While Mom was having her professional success, our relationship was disintegrating. Weeks after she won the Peabody, I moved out. I was in eighth grade. For the months after that we corresponded by letter.

Dear John,

This is a note to tell you I admire you and that I love you very much. Being 15 is sometimes exasperating because you're in-between—no longer a kid and not yet old enough to drive.

Up until a few months ago you and I had the normal usual family problems but we were friends. Not so long ago you and I were often the only ones at home on Friday and Saturday nights and we had a good time and laughed. Now things are different and it's difficult to talk about them. I've been told that you question that I love you. Have no questions. I love you and Mike more than anyone in the world—and your sisters too.

Perhaps it would have been easier if I was a nurse or a bank accountant. There would be less publicity but also less money and besides doing what I do is all I know how to do, and it's as you know essential for me to work to earn money.

Being my age has its confusion and complications too. And I also have trouble saying what I feel sometimes. But I have no confusion about you and Mike though the divorce has put a strain on these relationships with me. Never forget that I want you with me as much as possible.

Love, Mom.

She was stabbing at the problem. It reminds me of the letters of tentative advice her parents wrote her when she was deciding whether or not to marry my father: heartfelt, but off the mark. Mom was trying to sum up what had gone wrong with us. It's confused more than disingenuous. She thought the "publicity" was the problem and that she was compelled to earn a living. She had to make money to be sure, but she worked because she loved to. That's why it was natural for her to write that she loved us more than "anyone" in the world, but not "anything." She would have worked just as hard at her job had she been wading in bullion. In fact, she did. But it's easier to face your parental guilt if you can blame it on the mortgage. I know; I do it all the time. I type in the basement behind the closed door instead of going to the park because I want to work. I love to work. It's easier to justify if I can convince myself that I have to.

I don't remember the letter, but I do remember that our relationship was so sour that when I stayed with her at Merrywood while Dad traveled for a week, I unpacked my clothes and laid them out next to the door of my room as if I were going to leave at any minute.

I was totally independent and so proud of my own new world that I preferred the three rooms of our Georgetown townhouse to the rambling bounty of my childhood home. To not care about Merrywood was, of course, a way I could assert my independence. I thought I had it all figured out.

Then I screwed up. If my relationship with Mom was bad, it was about to get worse.

In November of 1983 I was caught breaking into my friend Kevin McDonnell's father's computer system. If in the first act of child development, you are brought back into the store bawling to return the stolen jawbreaker, then this was the second. I had to own up to the fact that I had snuck around reading his e-mail.

I was ashamed. The McDonnells had taken good care of me over the years. I had lived at their house for long stretches while Mom and Dad were away.

Kevin had given me his dad's e-mail address and told me that his server at the office had games on it. I was off. Well, I was off as fast as you could be back in the age of wood-burning modem speeds. You logged in through modems that looked like mouse ears at 300 baud. That meant if you wanted to read an e-mail—which was itself an exotic new thing—you selected it, made dinner, mulched the garden and came back when the file finally opened. That limited my game playing, but connecting to another computer by phone was novel and exciting. All I did was read Inbox e-mail. It gave me an early exposure to the deadening ass-covering and passive aggressiveness that takes place in so much corporate e-mail. How could people generate so much talk about meetings and people interfacing with each other about concepts, frameworks and strategies?

The problem was that each time I read one of the e-mails sent to Mr. McDonnell it shifted it to another box. It would show others that he had read the e-mail but he didn't know he had. I imagine many of his co-workers began to think he'd been drinking. Too many instances of Jack saying he didn't get the e-mail, and they started checking his desk for a fifth of Scotch.

Mr. McDonnell went to Kevin and Kevin dimed me out instantaneously. A family meeting was scheduled. It was excruciating. "I know more about computers than you ever will," Mr. McDonnell said to me, which both frightened me and made me think, *How do you know?* It turns out he was right and his computer expertise has made him worth more than I'll ever be. (I should have stuck with computers.)

Mom did not see my blundering exploration as a version of her own thirst for discovery as a young girl. Instead, she was anxious that I be taught a lesson because she was sure that Dad was poisoning me while she wasn't around. I, of course, had an ally in Dad. He didn't want to be too heavy, perhaps because he'd already seen me mope around and beat myself up using the superego he and Mom had given me.

I recognize that it was important for everyone to scare the paste out of me because we live in a world of laws, but I pray that this is the worst thing my children do.

The computer incident became a cause for great concern in the household of my other good friend, Robert Albritton. His father was the chairman of a prominent bank in Washington and owned one of the local television stations. They flew me to Snowmass in Colorado on their private jet every year and put me up at their grand slopeside house. Robert and I played with computers constantly, programming our own games and running our own one-phone-line bulletin boards. (Imagine America Online with only one customer.) We became so proficient, Atari computers hired us to work together at the Consumer Electronics Show in 1982 presenting their computers in Las Vegas. We were both members of the Atari Youth Advisory Board, which meant free computers and a trip to Palo Alto for days of high geekery with prototypes.

But after Mrs. Albritton heard that I read Mr. McDonnell's e-mails, the fun was over. Unlike the McDonnells, who frightened me but then gave me a hug, Mrs. Albritton banished me from her son's company. Mom used the opportunity to teach me yet another lesson, which, since we weren't seeing each other, she put in a letter:

Barbie Albritton feels that you never were rude, hostile, etc. before and that this is something new that coincidentally occurred with your new lifestyle and moving in with your father. Other people feel the same way. They have told me so. It is one thing to choose to live with your father: that is acceptable but it is not acceptable to coincidentally start acting rude and cool and sharp because while you may think you are "cool" or whatever the word is that describes what you want to be, others do not perceive you to be like that. To reiterate—and sum up: it's okay to move into Georgetown with your father, but it is not O.K. to change your attitude and behavior in a way

*that offends others. You, like everyone else in the world, want friends; the
way you are acting you will lose friends.*

I love the "other people feel the same way" construction. She's
bluffing. I know that trick—you make a hunch sound like it's widely
informed reporting. Reporters use it with sources all the time to make
one interview seem like several and therefore make their assertions
seem well informed. *I'm hearing this from a lot of Republicans on the Hill.*

I did not enjoy being lectured to, so when Merrywood was sold in
1984, I refused to go to her party saying goodbye to the house she'd
lived in for twenty years.

Mom moved into a charming townhouse in Washington and
repeated Merrywood's decorating scheme on a smaller scale. When we
communicated it was usually about money. I sent her spreadsheets
and she complained about either my expenditures or my accounting
practices. This was a very dark time.

I would see Mom once every six weeks or so for a sullen dinner
full of long pauses where all you could hear was the clinking of cut-
lery. I would only become animated when Mom's housekeeper walked
into the room. Mom wrote one of her oldest friends, Charlie Bartlett,
and scolded him for having lunch with me and Dad one day when we
ran into him at Pisces. She accused him of picking sides in the
divorce.

I spent high school being very normal. I played sports moderately
well, dated girls and got middling grades. Computers were far more
interesting than schoolwork and so in the summers after ninth and
tenth grade I worked at a computer store called the Byte Shop. I had
found the job on my own; I walked a few blocks from school to the
store with a handful of the newspaper profiles about my activities
with Atari and they hired me.

By eleventh grade I had further embraced the cliché of thousands of other children of privilege. I dropped the computers and
spent more time on girls, sports and Bob Dylan. My parents decided
that while my grades might have actually been getting better, I
needed something impressive on my resume. They called on their
contacts to see who might have a place in their office for a young
boy who was good with computers. The point wasn't for me to earn

money but to develop a relationship with a senator or Cabinet secretary who could later write me a college recommendation.

I later discovered that one of the people Mom wrote to was Vice President Bush, whom she'd known since he was a congressman. He and Barbara had played tennis at our house regularly.

March 16, 1986 (self-typed)

Dear Nancy,

I loved your letter, but the news is not the best. Here's why. We have been inundated with internship requests and Mary Ann Fronce in my office, who ably handles this for me, advises that every slot has been filled. For some reason the early "demand" has been unusual this year.

I showed Mary Ann your good letter about that computer whiz; and she pledges to keep her eyes wide open. Sometimes kids drop out at the last minute.

Hope all's well with you.

George Bush.

I found the letter in the middle of covering the George W. Bush White House for *Time.* At about that time the former president had called his friend, *Time* columnist Hugh Sidey, to tell him that a story I'd written suggesting Barbara Bush was unhappy with the way her son's 2004 campaign was being run was "complete bullshit."

I finally found a job working that summer in the mailroom of Senator John Warner of Virginia. When I wasn't sorting mail I was working the auto-pen. That was a revelation. I suppose if I had stopped to think about it, I never would have thought a senator signs each piece of correspondence, but when I saw the machine, which is designed to make it look as though he has, I had an "ah-ha" moment about deception in Washington.

What would have happened if I had worked for Vice President Bush? Would I have met his son, the future governor whom I wound up covering so closely? As it turns out, Mom was a part of our first introduction. I switched over to covering the Bush campaign after he beat John McCain in the Republican primaries in 2000. On my first trip, the governor was on the plane with Montana Governor Marc Racicot. I introduced myself to Racicot.

"Are you Nancy Dickerson's son?"

I hadn't been asked that in ages.

"Yes."

Governor Bush turned around from his own conversation.

"Did I know that?"

"I don't think so."

"A great lady.

Chapter Thirty-three

In the spring of 1986 Mom's relationship with Bill Moss was ending. She attended Washington parties on the arm of Virginia Senator John Warner, Texas Senator John Tower or former FBI director Bill Webster, but she had no regular beau. One evening, the wife of the Canadian ambassador called in a panic. She needed an extra woman to fill a seat. Mom was reluctant to go out alone, which made her look like she might not have been able to get her own date, but as a favor she said yes.

The wife of the Canadian ambassador repaid the favor. Mom was seated next to John Whitehead, the new deputy secretary of state. Whitehead had come to Washington after a long career at Goldman Sachs in New York, which he capped with a successful tenure as its chairman and senior partner.

"I didn't know who she was," remembers John. "If you had said the name Nancy Dickerson to me that wouldn't have meant anything."

That probably drove Mom insane. At an earlier part of her life she would have shown him those polling results: *But look, 85 percent of the viewers in the Midwest know me.* But if she'd done that, she would have had to admit that she had no idea who John Whitehead was. As a lifelong student of Washington, she wasn't quite sure what Goldman Sachs was either.

"We talked the entire dinner," he remembers. "She was charming and bright and I don't remember who was on the other side of me at dinner but I never talked to her. I just talked to Nancy."

Mom was doing commentaries once a week for the local Fox station and the two started having dinner every few weeks at Nora, a restaurant down the hill from her house.

She was smitten. She made lists of pros and cons about Whitehead in order to evaluate whether he was really interested in her. These lists were not much different than the ones little Nan wrote when she was twelve. When Mom thought one of her longtime friends might be trying to put the moves on Whitehead, who had just emerged from a divorce, she swatted her back. "I asked him to play tennis once," says Nina Straight, laughing. "And that was the last time I did that. I just wanted to play *tennis.*"

Whitehead was a former master of the financial universe, but Mom loved tweaking him for misunderstanding Washington folkways. When he testified in front of the House Foreign Affairs Committee about Iran-Contra, he was asked about President Reagan's claim that the Iranians had moderated their terrorism against Americans as a result of the secret arms sales. He said: "I don't like to differ with my president but I believe there is some evidence of continued Iranian involvement with terrorists."

The response made the front page of all the major papers: "Whitehead: I don't like to differ with my president." Mom collected some of the more choice headlines and had them engraved onto a plaque for him. Silly boy, didn't he know senior administration officials were not to contradict their presidents in congressional hearings? But privately she called her friends to say how proud she had been.

When they courted, Mom enjoyed a healthy dating double standard. She didn't like it when John went out with other women, but she didn't see anything wrong with continuing to date other men. Once when John was out of town, she attended a State Department dinner with Bill Webster. When she got to the dinner, there was a problem. Whitehead had come back early from Poland and was seated next to Mom. At the end of the evening he asked her if she would like a ride home.

"Yes," she said without hesitation. It wasn't until the two of them were halfway to her house that she revealed to John that she'd come

to the party with Bill Webster and hadn't told the former FBI director she was leaving.

By the end of 1988, as the Reagan team prepared to leave town, Mom
and John had been dating for four years. By this time, some of his visits to
watch the evening news lasted long enough to catch the *Today* show the
next morning. Like teenagers, they made the bed and he hastily left so
that Mom's longtime live-in housekeeper wouldn't find out.

But with his tour at the State Department over, John wasn't
thinking about bringing Mom back to New York. Having been married twice before, he was a little nervous about another try. Mom was
devastated. She enlisted reinforcements. Mary Jane Wick, one of their
mutual friends, called him. "John Whitehead, you are the dumbest
man in the world if you're going to leave behind a woman who is very
much in love with you," she said. He was about to go to Israel, so he
left Mom a voice mail. "I left a message saying 'I would like to marry
you. Please let me know.' I don't think we'd ever talked about that
before. I was smooth as gravel."

Mom was over the moon. Hours later, a fax was delivered to his
hotel room in Israel: "Yes (with conditions)." At age 61, she had gotten what she craved so desperately: security and love, and because of
his stature she was among those present again. She didn't even have
time to honeymoon because just days after their wedding she and
John flew to Poland to meet with Lech Walesa.

In the eight years since her split with Dad, Mom had been
obsessed with money. The sale of Merrywood had left her with considerable assets but in her files from that period are pages of green graph
paper with careful lists of her expenditures. After marrying John she
could relax, and she started to. It was as if a switch had been thrown. I
no longer had to debate with her about every rent or tuition check. In
1990, when I asked to spend the summer of my junior year in college
studying English literature at Oxford, she readily agreed. She even
offered to fly me and my girlfriend Anne McKeehan to New York for
a few days before I left for England. Anne and I had been living on
limp deli sandwiches and watery keg beer at UVA. Mom treated us
like royalty. We stayed in the swank apartment of then treasury secretary Nick Brady, and because John Whitehead was on the board of

Lincoln Center we got tickets to see the hot new play *Six Degrees of Separation*. We lunched with her at La Grenouille, the fanciest restaurant in the city.

While I was in Europe I sent an accounting of my school costs and received a letter from her doing the same:

> *Darling:*
> *Since you tabulated your costs, let me respond in kind:*
> *$315 Anne's ticket*
> *$180 money to you*
> *$50 cash in NYC*
> *$60 two John Guare books (and now Lincoln Center has asked us to give a dinner party which I couldn't refuse!)*
> *$70 tickets to Radio City Music Hall.*
>
> Plus *dinners and gifts et cetera and gifts to the Bradys for their apartment.*

Well, she hadn't changed *that* much. Dad on the other hand flew over for a weekend and he showed me London, his favorite city. He took me to his tailor, favorite restaurants where the waiters knew him by name and the Portobello market, where fabulous characters polished their silver picture frames and first edition volumes. We stayed up late drinking—he Dewars and me Jim Beam. We traded stories but we did not return to any of our old complaints about Mom. We too had both moved on.

I returned from England full of tweed, European pressings of Bob Dylan albums and a determination to be some kind of a writer. I had broken my fancy fountain pen at Tintern Abbey while reading Wordsworth's famous poem. I took out my notebook from my back pocket. That was the kind of thing a writer would talk about as a pivotal moment in his first book someday.

I returned to the University of Virginia to complete my English degree. But I wasn't sure whether I wanted to go into the law or find some way to embrace the writing life. I knew one thing: I wanted to live in New York. I didn't have goals. I had an area code.

The calendar entry for Friday, March 15, 1991, reads "Mom

comes down." I'm sure I wrote that sometime in January of that year when she told me she was going to come to Charlottesville for a visit. She should have known better. I only understood two units of time: the dates of my holidays for Christmas and spring break and the dates of my assignments, which included a very large thesis on Joseph Conrad. Every other appointment could be moved around or excused or I could talk my way out of missing it by claiming that I'd been hard at work, which I had been.

So I forgot that she was coming, or at least I'd like to think I forgot. Why would I have spent the entire night drinking if I knew she was coming for lunch? Yes, I'd spent weeks in one of the library cubicles and needed to celebrate, but surely I must have known that enjoying Southern Comfort from the bottle was not adequate preparation for a visit from your exacting mother.

I collapsed into my bed on the morning of March 15. I had no classes on Friday and my thesis wasn't due for a month, so I could get some rest before going back to the library that night. Plus, I didn't feel so hot.

Suddenly, I was taken by a most urgent business and ran to the lavatory down the hall. My housemates in the television room found this very amusing. They were even more amused when a woman appeared at the front door, wearing a leopard-skin skirt and some kind of hat that you could sled on.

They all pressed down their bedheads and welcomed her with big smiles. None of them had met my mother, but there was no mistaking this woman who had come for bunk inspection. They were gleefully anticipating what would happen next. I emerged from the bathroom feeling like I had knitting needles in my brain and socks on my teeth. There's nothing more confusing than being hung over near your mother when she's dressed in leopard skin.

"I have the flu," I said quietly, leaning against the wall.

My roommates in the other room barked.

I didn't care.

"But I have brought B. A. Bentsen."

Mom had brought the wife of Texas Senator Lloyd Bentsen. She sat in the driveway in the chauffeured car that had brought them from Washington. Presumably Mom wanted to show me off to her friend. The only friend who would have been impressed by my condition at that moment would have been a doctor.

Mentioning Mrs. Bentsen was not relevant. She might as well have said, "I have a box of topsoil in the trunk."

"I'm sorry mom, I just don't feel well."

She let me off the hook. Later Mom and I laughed about our brief encounter in the hallway.

"You smelled like a distillery," she said. She was mellowing. At an earlier time she would have called an ambulance and berated me while waiting for its wailing sirens, full of rage at being shown up in front of her friend.

As my senior year ended, I had no job prospects, no novel yet written and so I prepared to cave for money. Investment banks were looking for analysts. They would pay a great deal. The firms made it easy for you. If they liked your resume they would fly you up to New York and take you out and make you feel rich before you'd gotten your first paycheck. The guys doing the recruiting were just out of school themselves, so it all felt like fraternity rush again.

Anne got one of the jobs. I was struggling to get one. The fact that I'd taken no finance, statistics, accounting or anything else remotely having to do with business didn't matter so much. She'd been an actress and studied art history and she'd gotten the job. They just wanted people who could think.

It turned out I couldn't fake it. I went to the interviews and told them how much I wanted to work at their bank and they kept talking to me about literature and government—the two subject areas most heavily represented on my resume. Hoping to show them how smart I was, I lit up when I talked about those subjects. This, I wasn't clever enough to figure out, was a great way to show that I'd been mailing it in about investment banking. Thank goodness those recruiters were smarter than I was. If I could remember their names, I would put them in the acknowledgments.

When I started to moan about being jobless Mom stepped in. John Whitehead could get me a job at Goldman Sachs if I wanted it, she said. But if he went to bat for me, I'd have to take it. I didn't want it, and I think I was mature enough then to not turn down the offer just because she was making it. I think I'd actually learned that a life in finance would ruin me. But I couldn't go to New York with no job and I wasn't going to ask her to pay my way up there while I looked.

I needed some kind of job while I figured out what kind of writer I wanted to be, so Mom sent a resume to an acquaintance, Joe Quinlan, who did something with turning magazine pieces from *Time, Sports Illustrated* and *Fortune* into television shows. Joe planned to hire a new secretary so that his existing one could start working on television production. I said yes, and at $16,000 a year, I earned nearly a third of what Anne was making on Wall Street.

The day before my graduation from the University of Virginia, my whole family visited the house where I'd had my hungover exchange with Mom. I lived in what had been the house's library with a grand picture window and a wall full of bookshelves.

"Are these all your books?" Mom asked in amazement.

"No, they belong to the itinerants who live under the bed," I said.

It was a sign of how far apart we still were. She'd missed, or I hadn't showed her, my interest in books and learning. She continued to be shocked throughout the weekend. At my graduation dinner my friends made fun of my frantic obsession with schoolwork and long stretches in the library. When they announced at commencement that I had graduated with distinction she turned to my siblings in wonderment. It was as if she'd just learned I was a champion ice fisherman. (Which, in fact, I am.)

Mom seems to have missed the basics. Sure, I had shut her out, but she also didn't have any real curiosity about me until my studies received public validation—the shelves of books, the toasts and the graduation honors. I was having flashbacks to my childhood. It felt like she was impressed when other people could be impressed. I wanted to move to New York to be with Anne but the weight of that old grievance made me brace myself. I would be back in the same city with Mom.

Chapter Thirty-four

Joe Quinlan, my first boss in New York, was an angel. He did two wonderful things. He didn't treat me like a secretary (though many of the other people we worked with did) and he helped me try to become a reporter, which often meant I was too busy to do my job for him very well. I owed Mom for the job, but I was only a secretary, so I didn't owe her much. I hadn't let her call in any big favors so I didn't feel like I was giving in. She did, however, supplement my income, and I'm not sure how I lived with this. I think the fact that I lived with two other guys in a 500-square-foot two-bedroom apartment helped convince me I needed the money to survive. When faced with hard realities, my pride eroded.

In 1992, Joe let me attend the Democratic convention in New York and the GOP convention in Houston working for *Time* magazine. It was a huge coup. There I was, working for the country's largest newsmagazine on the floor of a national political convention. My position: assistant to the assistant for the chief of correspondents. I was an errand boy.

I spent most of my time soaking up the atmosphere and trying to get up enough courage to stop one of the delegates and ask him a question. If I was going to be a reporter I'd have to learn to talk to people I didn't know. I had no idea how to go about it. I'd approach them, they'd look at me like I was trying to convert them to Mormonism or hand them a pamphlet about weight loss, and I'd chicken out.

One of my jobs was to escort executives from the magazine's workspace to the seats inside the convention hall. It was amusing theater. The magazine executives and editors would arrive at their seats and nod gravely at the speakers. Some had been reporters long ago and thumbed empty reporter's notebooks as if trying to get in touch with their past glory. They would hang out for a few minutes and then, because political conventions are essentially dull, they'd ask me to escort them to the exit so they could go off to exclusive dinners.

As I walked one executive back to *Time*'s workspace, he assumed I was one of the interns—the children of other executives hired during their college summer break. "Whose son are you?" he asked as we walked through the stadium's inner hallway.

"No one's," I said.

Living in New York near Mom was less irritating than I'd imagined. She was very generous. She invited Anne and me to plays and black-tie dinners. It was a strange juxtaposition to eat spaghetti every night for two weeks and then sit next to Katharine Graham at an Asia Society dinner.

Mom went to endless dinners where people were honored with awkwardly shaped awards. John Whitehead has extraordinary energy and drive and served on twelve different boards—everything from the Brookings Institution to the International Rescue Committee. They also traveled constantly. She flew to Pakistan to visit refugee camps in Karachi and then she was off to China for a week with Henry Kissinger.

Mom loved it and John, but even for her it was too much. A frantic pace in Washington, the town she knew so well, might have been fine. She knew the rules and how the town worked. But each trip with John was a new emotional experience. Mom's diary entries from those times often end with a single word: "exhausted." She was booked every minute of the day and she felt rootless. Finally, after a year in the city, she found her salvation in the Ladies' Lunch Group. A once-a-month gathering, it was made up of Lesley Stahl, former White House correspondent and co-host of *60 Minutes;* Diane Sawyer, the ABC anchor; Peggy Noonan, the Reagan speechwriter and author; Joan Ganz Cooney, the founder of the Children's Television Workshop; and later, *Vanity Fair* writer and author Marie Brenner.

In her diary from 1992 she writes: "Nice Day because the group met. These women truly make my life; they are basically so NICE and so smart and so savvy and so bright and serious and amusing. . . . We are not bitchy—just very bright." This is the first new material in Mom's journals since the divorce, and there's a change in her voice. She sounds like twelve-year-old Nan again, writing on those Morton's Salt pages.

Mom had never had a collection of girlfriends, certainly not professional ones. "She told us she never had friendships like this because she didn't trust other women; they were too competitive," says Brenner. There was no sisterhood among the few women in the business when Mom was on the air. "On the campaign trail nobody mixed," remembers Marlene Sanders, one of the early female correspondents for ABC. "She was with a producer and I was with mine; we barely acknowledged each other. We didn't have conversations. This is the way it went on all the trips. There was just too much competition." With the lunch group Mom could be reminded that she had been a somebody and that she still was a somebody—a woman who was more than just the wife of a great man of the establishment. "It was like she was thirsting for friendship," says Lesley Stahl.

I joined the ladies' group for lunch—the first male guest—in early 2006 at the same corner table at San Domenico where they'd started with Mom almost fifteen years earlier. We immediately began talking about the Bush administration and the war in Iraq. Each of us contributed a little bit of news—conversations we'd just had with friends and sources. It was some damn good gossip, but as they explained the rules to me, "What's said in the group stays in the group."

It was easy to see why these women were Mom's lifeline. Perhaps the greatest gift they gave her was the space to simply be herself around them—or at least as close as she could get. Mom spent her whole life maintaining a public face, from Nancy Hanschman to Nancy Dickerson, and when she moved to New York, she took on a new one: Nancy Dickerson Whitehead. It was perhaps her hardest role yet: onstage but subordinate. During one trip to China with Kissinger, Mom was asked to leave a private briefing with local officials. After all, she was just a spouse. It was like she was back in Washington again in 1950 going to dinner where her companions only wanted to know what her date thought. "It's as if I'm *only* Mrs. Whitehead," she wrote in her journal. "Not Nancy Dickerson."

At the Ladies' Lunch Group she was Nancy Dickerson again. In fact, she could be more like Nancy Hanschman, her most authentic self. So when they had lunch a few weeks before the 1992 election it was easy for her to confess to them how nervous she was to have been chosen to host the PBS election night coverage. The assignment had come out of the blue and was her biggest live television job in twenty years.

"They had given her mountains of briefing books and they'd just made her more scared," remembered Peggy Noonan.

I was surprised to hear that she'd admitted to anyone that she was scared or vulnerable. But I could see how seriously Mom took the assignment from her endless pages of preparatory notes. She had been as diligent as she had her whole career.

But studying could only help her so much. One of the things that had made Mom so nervous was the "experimental format." Lots of analysts and commentators—from rap stars to polling experts—were scheduled to appear throughout the evening so the operation looked like a waiting room at a car dealership. She would have to coordinate it all while keeping viewers updated on the latest numbers.

When Mom arrived in the green room, an enormous vase of flowers was waiting for her with a note. "You did it first before any of the rest of us. You'll be wonderful tonight." It was signed by the members of the Ladies' Lunch Group.

Chapter Thirty-five

Mom's life in New York appeared to have everything she could want. She lived in a town house overlooking the East River filled with artwork by Degas, Picasso, and Maillol. Her clothes and jewelry were exquisite and she displayed them nearly every evening at dinners, plays or award ceremonies with New York's most exclusive and famous names. She adored her husband.

But she was not working. At age sixty-six it was the one thing she wanted that she could not buy.

"Unless you work people don't respect you. Don't talk to you. I should apply myself," she writes in one 1993 journal entry. "I am happiest when working." In other entries, she's edgy. "At dinner for Mrs. Thatcher everyone was in a joyous upbeat mood," she writes. "Mrs. Thatcher was terrific. When she saw me, she mentioned Bill Blass and clothes, a point that really did not suit me very well, particularly since I like to think about the substance of matters. However, Mrs. Thatcher spends a great deal of time on her hair and clothes and all of those accoutrement. And, so I guess I am not as irritated as I might be. However, I did have a discussion which she seemed to have forgotten about the Falkland war. Never mind, I just did not want to be considered a fashion expert only."

Even lunch with the group became painful. "Lunch with Group," she writes in March 1993. "I invited Pam Harriman. Afterwards everyone went off to work but me. I hurt. I must get work. Now I *busy myself* with charity work. It's no substitute—I realize it's important, but I've worked since age 12 and I can't suddenly become pro-bono—especially since the world still judges women by the amount of money they earn. Is there something wrong with me? Do I knock everyone? I'm not big on anyone at this moment. *I must get a secretary."*

In April, she met with an old friend at the William Morris talent agency. "He and two assistants listened politely as I told them about job possibilities," she wrote in her journal. "They were very polite but not enthusiastic. They were rather bemused by me but still, very pleasant."

I was looking for work too. I was still a secretary hanging around the newsdesk at *Time* trying to make friends and pick up an assignment.

At about this time, Mom and I started talking on the phone almost every day. She still read at least three or four papers by noon and constantly fed me story ideas. We were friends. We found the same passion in work. At least I wasn't treating her like a fashion expert and, to her credit, she wasn't treating me like a secretary.

"Mom, I'm not a reporter anywhere," I would remind her.

"Yes, but you can start pitching them stories."

To her credit, I don't remember her embracing the easy temptation to tell her Rayburn story. If she had launched into "When I was your age . . . ," I would have hung up.

I was trying my own scheme. While I was a secretary, I worked as a researcher for Jonathan Beaty and Sam Gwynne, two of *Time's* correspondents working on the BCCI banking scandal. I helped them with their magazine stories and then became their researcher on their book about the bank. Gwynne and Beaty were investigative reporters, a crazy and wonderful breed. They taught me how to be a reporter and they trusted me—they had too much material not to. There was always another angle to follow and another lead to mine. This was before the Internet and before newspaper databases were cheap enough for any reporter to use. *Time* still kept clipping folders of old newspaper and magazine stories. Reporters usually ordered a few folders for whatever story they were working on. I ordered them by the boxful. I unfolded each clip and read. Each name went into a database and each connection onto a vast chart. BCCI was the bank of choice for several international terrorists. The U.S. government had used it to fund the mujahadeen in Afghanistan and to hide money exchanged as a part of the Iran-Contra arms-for-hostages deal. It was the black hole bank to which every conspiracy after 1975 was linked. It was heaven.

Beaty and Gwynne even let me interact with their sources. They introduced me to the detective and former beat cops investigating the case for the Manhattan district attorney. I spent hours on the phone with lawyers chasing after the bank's money. A little network of us beavered away through the documents. When we'd found something, or thought we had, we'd pick up the phone. These revelations usually came in the middle of the night, which meant a lot of groggy phone calls with one person galloping through a set of facts and the half-asleep one saying, "Wait a minute, slow down, what are you saying?"

I also babysat a terrorist—or that's what he said he was anyway. One of the sources was a Jordanian who had worked for the bank's black operations, the portion that ran arms and drugs. He was legit to a point; after that he was a con artist. It took us a while to figure that out. I spent a lot of time smoking cigarettes and listening to his stories while he was in New York. One night I joined him for dinner in Little Italy with the detectives investigating the case for Robert Morgenthau, the Manhattan district attorney. They pressed him for information but he was vague. He tried to get money for the documents he said he had implicating U.S. officials. He was arrogant and bombastic. He was the kind of clever character who made people want to wring his neck. Suddenly one of the detectives got ready to do just that. The source is now serving time in a U.S. prison.

After hanging around the newsroom I was given my first official assignment for the magazine reporting on the financing of the first World Trade Center bombing. I had never officially reported a story before in my life but after all of those months of listening to Beaty and Gwynne and talking to their sources, I had a good idea of how it was done. I convinced a local bank manager to give me a little scoop and then stayed up all night typing a file to the *Time* writer who produced the story. That week I got my first byline and decided I would be "John F. Dickerson," because it sounded fancy. And it was a tribute to my grandfather, Frederick Hanschman.

I had lunch with Mom the next week and handed her an early

copy of Beaty and Gwynne's book on the bank, which had a generous acknowledgment to me. "I had lunch with John, Friday," she wrote in her journal. "He gave me a copy of his page galleys of *The Outlaw Bank* and I cry each time I read the paragraph about him. He's a good person, working too hard (as I did at his age and he should), he still has loyalties to his father . . ." Ten years after the divorce she still kept score.

Though I had my first byline, it took me a few months before I was hired as an "editorial apprentice." I wasn't given a leather smock but the job title made it sound like I might be. The editor who gave me the good news told me "they weren't too happy that we're hiring another blond white guy." It would have been better if I had been a woman, he told me.

I signed up for every story I could put my hands on, reporting all night in my windowless interior office. An editorial apprentice is one level above secretary. You don't have to answer the phones or get coffee but you're expected to take every assignment.

Mom and I kept up our phone conversations. I would call and she'd listen to my take on something. She'd offer hers and we'd kick the idea around.

I didn't know it then, but she was the first of my warm-up partners, the people you talk to when you're a journalist to sharpen your ideas. You muse, you joke and you poke around at an idea until you figure out exactly what you think. They are the people you call before going on television to see if what you're about to say makes sense. If your idea doesn't fly in conversation, you move on. You trust them enough to let them see you confused and stupid and wrong backstage so you can look poised in front of everyone else.

Occasionally she would tell me a story from the old days, but mostly we'd talk about what was happening in the world. We'd sometimes yell at each other and slam down the phone. It was just like when I was fourteen, but our disagreements were about Bill Clinton and Bosnia instead of my allowance and whether I could watch television. Unlike when I was fourteen, we were usually back on the phone by the end of the day.

I wrote stories and faxed her my rough drafts. She seemed to get a vicarious satisfaction through our conversations—for the first time we both seemed to have an equal passion about the same topic. She tried to drop little writing lessons into the margins of the pieces she edited: "Signal the differences with a 'warning sentence,'" she advised in a story I wrote about the prosecution of the first World Trade Center bombers.

At the end of 1994, she seemed less tense and agitated. I'm not sure what resolved her unhappiness about her lack of work. She still wanted to return to television, but she had found other interests. She became more engaged in her charity work. She joined the board of Covenant House, which took in troubled teenagers, and recruited Hillary Clinton to open a chapter in Washington. She became so involved she rode with the van that trolled the streets of New York in the middle of the night and brought homeless kids to the shelter.

In five years, she'd settled into her life in New York and was feeling more confident. Her journals sound less tortured. She stops writing about how unhappy she is and more about the world around her.

"Tonight was the United Nations Association Dinner in honor of the President of Korea, Mr. Kim. Or was it Lee? They're all either Kims or Lees and it is somewhat irrelevant because no matter what you say, they bow their heads, put their hands together and look toward the floor so there is very little eye contact and even if you had said Mr. Smith as opposed to Mr. Kim or Mr. Lee, it doesn't seem to matter much one way or the other."

Not politically correct, especially for the wife of the chairman of the Asia Society, but Mom had regained her sense of mischief. Her life as Mrs. Whitehead was finding a balance as more people in her husband's setting made a fuss over her. "I was seated next to the speaker of the evening, Larry Summers," she wrote of the future treasury secretary. "He made an immediate hit with me because he said that you remember some things in life more than others and he could always remember his mother saying that I was the most intelligent reporter on the air. Lesley Stahl said to the table, 'Get that man's autograph.'"

In the summer of 1995, John went on his annual Outward Bound trip. It made Mom nervous, so to distract herself she offered to take Anne and me to London and the Cotswolds while he was off roughing it.

We were not. We stayed at Claridge's, where the butlers have butlers. Anne and I went over a few days early. When Mom arrived and joined us for dinner, we debriefed her on our travels. As I talked, I saw Bill Moss, her boyfriend from the period of my parents' divorce, across the dining room. I knew it would be awkward for Mom, so I whispered that he was headed our way. She glanced at him and ducked under the table. Anne and I moved in over her on the banquette until Bill walked past with his current date.

Over the next few days we toured museums, tidy country gardens and the low green countryside. When she appeared for a hike in her ironed sweat suit and tennis shoes I figured we'd have to pay some kind of fine. Ye Olde English countryside cannot abide such aesthetic discontinuity. But Mom gamely ambled over the stiles and side-stepped the manure archipelagos. "Hello, Mr. Sheep, do you mind if we pass through?" she said to a small ambling flock. I lost track of her for a second and turned around to find her petting a cow. When she wasn't playing Jane Goodall to the Holsteins, she recited from a copy of the Norton poetry anthology I had given her. She explained tha Edward Burling, a famous Washington lawyer, memorized poetry in his later years to keep his mind sharp. We stayed up late drinking English bitters and smoking cigars.

She kept the thank-you note I wrote when we returned:

Dear Mom,

Late yes, but as you know the creating of journalism makes such demands on one's time. The promulgation of lies and half-truths being such weighty labor. What's late are my thanks for a wonderful trip and an experience I'll never forget. You're a great companion as well as a generous mother. Also thanks for inviting me to dinner with the foreign policy brain trust. I was awed and delighted to be included.

I meant it. We had fun of a very particular kind I'd never had with Mom. She was just easy. She wasn't acting or playing a role. Anne and I didn't confect diversions to steal away from her. She was good company. She was at ease.

The guests at that dinner she had invited me to at her Sutton Square house included U.N. Ambassador Madeleine Albright, and former secretaries of state Cyrus Vance and Henry Kissinger. We talked about Russia, China and the Middle East and how Clinton was perceived throughout the world. It was the first one of her high-wattage dinner parties I'd been to since leaving Merrywood. I didn't have to answer the door, thankfully. I was at the table. I talked and I asked questions, acting maybe a little too much like a journalist. It was the first time I was among those present.

In January 1995 I was assigned to cover politics in Washington. That fall I married Anne, who by then had left investment banking for independent film production. We made everyone travel to Charlottesville, where we had gone to school, and into the foothills for dinner at James Monroe's house. For the first dance we waltzed, shocking our guests, and no one more so than Mom. In a snapshot of our first steps she has her mouth open like she's in the dentist's chair. She had tried to teach me to dance once in sixth grade on the Merrywood landing. I ran away screaming. Anne and I completed our show, quietly practiced for months at dance class, and I then danced with Mom for the first and last time.

When I started covering the 1996 presidential race from Washington in the fall of 1995, I put Mom to work for me. At one dinner she asked Kissinger if he'd talked to Colin Powell about a run for the 1996 Republican nomination. "He had not heard from Colin Powell," she wrote in her journal, "a question I asked him because John Dickerson is interested to know."

In October 1995 I was in New Hampshire covering the Republican primary debates when Mom called. She had just been to Kissinger's for dinner with Newt Gingrich. The Speaker of the House had spent the evening wondering aloud whether he should run for president.

This was extraordinary. Kissinger was publicly backing Bob Dole, the party front-runner, who believed Gingrich was trying to undermine his candidacy. It would certainly cause problems for Kissinger if Dole found out he had hosted Gingrich.

I gave the news to the *Time* writer and he wove it into the top of a campaign story. I asked him to leave my byline off the list of reporters at the bottom of the piece so that I wouldn't burn my source, but Mom and I were busted even faster than we'd imagined. Someone with a good heart at *Time* wanted to make sure I got credit for my scoop and put my byline back on the story without telling me. At a luncheon in honor of Vance on November 21, 1995, Kissinger approached Mom. "You and John Dickerson got me in trouble," he said. She recounted the rest in her diary: "I questioned it and denied it because I am very careful about what I tell John Dickerson. After the lunch was over, Kissinger was leaving early, and I stopped him and said that John Whitehead would divorce me if he thought I was leaking things to John Dickerson. Kissinger said that Bob Dole had seen John Dickerson's byline in Time magazine and had called him, Kissinger, to complain. But then, Henry said, that he had got into much worse trouble than that in life. I pointed out that I had nothing to do with it and he put his hand on my shoulder and said, you are my friend and I said I was [his] friend and that was the end of that." She was spinning Kissinger and her diary.

Ten years later, I was waiting backstage to appear on a panel with Gingrich's old press secretary, Tony Blankley. He asked me if I was the one who had written about the dinner between Kissinger and Gingrich ten years earlier. Kissinger had called him to yell at him. He thought Blankley or Gingrich might have leaked the story. I blamed the whole thing on Mom.

Chapter Thirty-six

———

I was reporting a piece on tax reform in January 1996 when I checked my messages at the office in Washington. John Whitehead had called. Mom had suffered a heart attack. When I called him back he was vague. There were complications and she'd been throwing up all night. She was still in intensive care.

Anne and I took the first shuttle to New York. As we stepped out of the elevator on the intensive care floor, a gurney of tubes and machines and frantic doctors flew past, but I could make out Mom's face at the end of the blue hospital gown.

When Mom was wheeled back she was just a few patches of flesh and hair underneath all the tubes. She wasn't just unconscious, her whole body seemed to have been turned off.

There were machines piled on machines and haphazard tape keeping in her breathing tube and IV bags of slowly dripping fluid.

The heart medicine they'd given her had caused bleeding in her brain. That's what all the throwing up was about. It was apparently a possible side effect of that drug but the doctors missed it. While they scratched their heads she had a kind of slow stroke. This mistake unleashed a torrent of ass-covering and confusion. Administrators arrived and apologized profusely to the powerful Mr. Whitehead, who they thought might sue them into oblivion. He never did. We were all too focused on trying to remove the need for all the beeping mechanical hardware.

We didn't put much stock in what the doctors said from that

point forward. They continued to confirm our worst instincts. They were utterly clueless. No one could explain what had gone wrong. They knew there had been bleeding but they didn't know how much. When we asked how this could happen they disappeared into a vague haze of terminology and blame shifting. I remember thinking: "Jesus, they're spinning us."

I can't remember any of the doctors' names because there were so many. Whenever we needed an answer, the doctor who could provide it wasn't there. This went on for weeks. It was like they had all colluded in this enormous buck-passing scheme or they'd been taught the dodge in medical school: When you don't know the answer or the truth makes you look incompetent tell the patient Dr. Falusi will be there, even if you have to make up a name.

We focused on the last magical doctor's name we'd been given because the previous doctor had told us he would have the answers. It's amazing what grief and worry will do to you. We got stuck in a cycle. We'd get a name, believe he was the answer, get disappointed and then cling to the next name.

Finally we stopped muttering doctors' names to ourselves and started focusing on the tests. The CAT scan would be back soon telling us how much of her brain had suffered. Over the hours Mom's friends started to arrive. Each member of the lunch group—Diane Sawyer, Peggy Noonan, Lesley Stahl, Marie Brenner and Joan Ganz Cooney—did a tour through the stuffy windowless nook where we waited. Another friend, Kathy Greenberg, was there as much as the nurses.

The intensive care unit at the hospital didn't really have a waiting room. There was a wide place in the hall with sticky pleather chairs. I don't remember whether other families were waiting for other mothers or a sick boy. They must have been, but you get a kind of blindness at hospitals, blocking out everyone else. My recollection is that it was just us, the Dickerson-Whitehead vigil. You could only take short trips into intensive care and once you got in to see her there wasn't much to do. She was completely out.

Despite the strain, Mom's friends stuck with us. There were moments of occasional levity. Diane Sawyer arrived one morning with a basket overflowing with food. When Lesley Stahl saw it, she said:

"Wait, it's my people who are supposed to bring the food to these things."

"Score one for the shiksa!" said Diane.

We were hanging on to the CAT scan results but we got a string of opaque interpretations. It looked like some of the brain was damaged, but it was unclear how much. So we went back to focusing on the doctors. My least favorite was someone I'll call Dr. Unhelpful who was supposed to be very fancy and famous. The women from the luncheon group all seemed to know his name. We held out hope for him. He would give us the straight story.

He was a failure. There was damage, he said. How much he couldn't be sure. Could he guess? No. Was it permanent? He couldn't say. Was there a time frame in which we might be able to make a next judgment? He wasn't sure.

He went to medical school for this? Because we had put so much faith in Dr. Unhelpful he seemed doubly disappointing. He might have been telling us all that he could. There might be very little you can tell at that early stage about the brain damage. But it still felt like he was the meter maid and we were trying to talk our way out of a ticket. He seemed to be in a rush to get away from us.

When Diane and Lesley arrived just after our first frustrating encounter, they stopped to talk to him. As my brother and I watched the conversation, he seemed remarkably less dismissive. Through the glass windows of the hospital doors it looked like we were watching them on television. They were pros. They would get the story out of him. It was a hopeful moment.

They returned. We turned our faces up to them.

"Well?"

"Nothing," said Diane.

"It was frustrating," said Lesley.

I can't remember how many days we stayed in the hospital in that first haul but we learned nothing more about Mom's condition. She was transferred to the fanciest private room, which meant a less sticky brand of pleather on the chairs.

The 1996 GOP Iowa caucus was not far away. It was my first campaign. I was twenty-seven and covering Lamar Alexander, the former governor of Tennessee, who was a distant contender for the nomination. Mom had insisted that I keep a campaign journal and at the time I wrote this: "My weeks are spent with Lamar and end at the hospital in New York where I sit in a one sided conversation with my mother." Mom couldn't say a word for the first few months and she couldn't move her left side. Her head had been shaved and the stroke had twisted her face. Even when she slept, her face looked like it was in a permanent wince, like someone had raised their hand to smack her.

I had only been in pleasant refined places with her in my life, rooms with fresh cut flowers and newly dusted surfaces. You felt like you were breathing air with more oxygen. In the hospital I hated to breathe. There were smells you couldn't flush away, the stench of steaming overcooked carrots and the synthetic blast that came with each new set of gloves or fresh tubes or instruments torn out of their sanitary packaging.

My brother set up a voice-mail box at his office and John Whitehead left daily updates. At the end of every day I'd call from the campaign bus or hotel room to see if John had left a message. Sometimes there was a major development—they had removed the breathing tube and she could breathe on her own or the swelling would go down in her brain. But a lot of times there was no progress. He tried to make us all feel like she was getting better anyway. "Nancy rested a lot today, which was good for her," he'd say or, "Nancy didn't open her eyes while I was there but her friend Kathy Greenberg spent the entire afternoon with her, which Nancy must have enjoyed."

In March he told us Hillary Clinton had visited her and that Mom had enjoyed it. Later, I learned John had oversold the moment—Mom had slept through the visit, but his efforts were human and wonderful and they worked. If nothing else we knew she was in his great hands. Everyone noticed the change in John. I interviewed Treasury Secretary Robert Rubin, John's old colleague at Goldman Sachs, during Mom's illness. After our interview Rubin mentioned that John had been known for his toughness and focus, but Rubin now saw tenderness and affection that seemed at odds with his image and reputation. Lesley Stahl remembers seeing John at a party during Mom's illness. He talked of finding an even greater kind of love after she became sick. "He had this deep emotional connection to this little girl that she had become," says Stahl.

By April, after months in the hospital, Mom went in and out of consciousness but was able to say a few words. We cheered for the slightest signs of advancement. "This week John said she was able to name the book she wrote, which to me is a sign of serious progress," I wrote in my journal. A longtime friend who had a drinking problem at the time came to visit and she scolded him for reeking of gin. When people asked how she was doing she would say her old line: "All the better for seeing you," even if the questioner was an orderly. As Diane Sawyer would say later: "She was hardwired for courtesy."

Even if a lot of the time she didn't answer questions or she mumbled, we saw little blasts of recognition as pinholes in the shade: They'd just keep multiplying until we could connect with her.

Then one day, while her nurse ran to get some clean sheets, Mom, who had been asleep, tried to get out of bed. Her left side was still paralyzed and she fell from the bed onto her face. My journal:

> I went to visit Mom last weekend. It was the first time I had seen her since she tried to walk and fell. The left side of her face had been smashed in the fall and her skull had been bruised and was bleeding. She had massive reconstructive surgery to fix the left side of her face which one doctor said was "pulverized." She had a three inch piece of her skull removed to wash the blood from it. Her head now is zippered together with staples. You could tell how well she was recovering from the first head shaving by the progression of the short little hairs. Now her head has had to be re-shaven and to an even greater degree. For a woman who was once so beautiful, Mom looks like shit.

In June as I was off with the Dole campaign I called in to the update line. Instead of John's voice it was Mom. Mike was staying with her and he'd coaxed her into saying a few words. "This is Nancy. Mom. I'm okay." The words were faint but they were there.

On my twenty-eighth birthday I called her at home. She'd just left the hospital after seven months. She could talk, but the conversations were mostly monologues by the caller interrupted by her questions, which were usually off topic. I gave her a rundown of my campaign travel.

"Where are you?"

"I'm driving away from the airport."

"Oh."

"Do you know what day it is?"

Silence.

"It's July 6th."

"Oh my God, it's your birthday."

Another time she heard from one of her nurses that I was going to be on C-SPAN. She asked them to dial my number.

"That's wonderful," she said.

"What?"

"It's wonderful."

"Oh, the C-SPAN thing. Yes."

"Just tell them everything you know and what you don't know, make it up. They won't know."

Was that how she did it? That August I spent a week with her while John Whitehead was traveling. I jogged along the East River at the end of the day and when I came home she would hear the door and ask her nurses to bring her down to greet me. She thought I was her husband John. That had always been their routine when he came home. Her third-floor office had been transformed into a wardroom with an adjustable hospital bed and crude folding chairs for the around-the-clock nurses. The books on the shelves were shoved aside to accommodate the amber pill vials and facial wipes and endless paperwork that accompany the desperately ill.

She was sixty-nine before she got sick, her high cheekbones were still well defined and she seemed to step out of the shower into Chanel suits. Now, under the white hospital sheets, she was softer and rounder, the medication swelling her face. Her nurses dressed her each day in the same frowsy sweat suit. She tried to recapture her morning routine, spreading the five newspapers before her as she ate breakfast, but she couldn't read. She'd hold the *Times* and stare at it hard, trying to make out the editorial page. It was often upside down.

When she had recovered a little, her past became our therapy. It was embarrassing how little I knew. This is my journal entry from that period:

> *These past weeks were the first time I'd ever really focused on much of what she did. She was in pictures with Kennedy and Jackie Kennedy and Lyndon Johnson I'd never seen before. She also did the Today show which I didn't know. Her career was really in its prime in the sixties. For my entire adult life she's been in the decline of her career. Certainly one of the great ironies of Mom's position is that it forced me to pay attention to her career and accomplishments at just the time she can't tell me anything about them and at the time when I, covering a campaign, need that advice the most . . .*

When I discovered a cabinet full of photo albums I spread them out on the oriental rug. It was like I had just discovered a friend's family trove—the faces are familiar but you know nothing about the experiences they're having. It's one thing to know your mother is famous in theory. It's another thing to see pages and pages of glossy photographs of her with the key historical figures of the last thirty years.

I showed Mom some of the pictures but got little reaction. So I showed her some pictures the *Time* photographers had taken of me at work on the campaign trail.

"That's Dick," she would say, pointing to a picture of me interviewing Lamar Alexander.

"No, that's me." She had called me by my father's name, or maybe she really thought it was my father.

After a while she learned the tricks toddlers do: to say yes or repeat the right words as if she understood what was being said. And for a few rounds of questions I'd let the trick work, pretending along with her that she knew what we were talking about. But then I had to test her.

I'd point to a picture of Nixon. "Who is that?"

"Michael."

My brother. Sorry Mike, I'm sure she didn't mean it. A few months into her therapy, I mostly gave up on the identification drills, happy enough that she was talking and interacting. Sometimes, she would check her watch and look around confused.

"What time is it?"

I would tell her.

"I've got to get to work." Then she would drift away.

Then, one day, a surprise. We looked at a picture of her with Jack Kennedy near the Ohio clock in the Senate. He was a senator at the time, leering—I think it's fair to say—at the young Ms. Hanschman, a clerk for the Foreign Relations Committee. I joked, mostly to myself: "He's giving you the big eye."

"He gave every pretty girl the big eye," she said, as clear as can be and, I'm certain, with a knowing smile.

I didn't know whether I was more shocked that she'd uttered a clear sentence or that it had been Kennedy's indiscretions that had brought her back.

Mom's days were remarkably busy. She went on walks with her nurses, and speech and occupational therapists made regular visits. She also had a full schedule of doctors' visits. The medication she took for her heart thinned her blood, which caused problems with the weakened blood vessels in her brain. Each time the balance faltered she was off to the hospital again.

Toward the end of my extended stay she had a visit with Dr. Unhelpful, who had been so opaque in those early days at the hospital.

I told Mom about the upcoming visit.

"I don't like him."

"I know. When he says something you don't like, say, 'You're terribly glib.'"

"You're terribly glib," she repeated.

He was glib. He was pleasant enough, but he talked to her in that condescending sing-song voice. I tried to explain some of her latest developments. "She recognized President Kennedy in the scrapbook."

It was pathetic. I was spinning, trying to show that she was making progress in the hopes that he would somehow jump at some fact and tell me she was going to get much better, that the walls were going to come down.

Dr. Unhelpful moved past my little attempts. He'd seen that kind of unsubstantiated hope before and he wasn't having any of it. But he was interested in the campaign trail. He asked me about Dole.

"You're terribly glib," Mom said to him.

But he wasn't listening. He was ignoring her to give me his theories on the presidential campaign. People had once ignored everyone else in the room to talk politics with her and he couldn't have cared less. I guess I should have recognized that as his diagnosis. She wasn't going to get too much better.

Why did Dr. Unhelpful irritate me so? I had spent a lot of my life not giving Mom her due. As a teenager I would have been delighted to see someone talk past Nancy Dickerson. Of course, she wasn't Nancy Dickerson anymore. She was now the opposite of that person, a child in a grown woman's unsteady body struggling to form a few rehearsed words.

Mike came through town on business during my weeklong stay and the three of us had lunch at the house. We sat in on her occupational therapy and teased her like we did as kids. She couldn't use her right hand very well so the therapist made her pick up grapes one by one and tried to teach her to play checkers. This was hard to watch. When I was a kid, Mom and I sometimes played checkers on a big fuzzy rug in the library with pieces the size of butter plates.

Perhaps it was because Mike and I were there, but the therapist said she'd done as well as she ever had. She couldn't handle the grapes but she moved a few checkers pieces at the right time and in the right direction, though she had to do it with her left hand. Her right was just a soft useless claw. We decided that our teasing had helped, so we gave her more of it. There was a certain comfort in being able to tease her again because if she weren't sick, that's what we would have done. It made us feel a little normal. So we taunted the hell out of her to get her to do things. During lunch that day we behaved like teenagers. We all had a little plate of grapes to keep her therapy going, and Mike and I threw them at each other. They bounced off the antiques and imperiled the Daumier miniatures and the Corot hanging on the wall. We knew the idea of them rolling someplace they might never be found would get a rise out of her.

And then we went through the old litany: her tennis game, her performance in those commercials, the time her chair collapsed beneath her on Thanksgiving.

"Oh, you kids," she said smiling slowly.

As we kept at it, her right hand moved toward the grapes.

"It has as much Vitamin J as orange juice," I said, repeating her commercial gaffe.

She pinched a grape with her mangled fingers.

"And as much bread as watermelon," said my brother.

We tried not to look at her, but we knew she was concentrating hard. She moved her arm quickly and threw the grape at me.

It's the greatest thing I ever saw Mom do.

Chapter Thirty-seven

———

Mom was well enough to make it to a 1996 Christmas lunch at the "21" Club. When she moved to New York, she had transformed her Christmas tradition that had started at Merrywood to fit her new town. She would plan marathon days that started in a private room at 21, followed by a march to see the Christmas show at Radio City Music Hall and ending with a chartered bus ride across the river to watch the New Jersey Devils play hockey. When she was sick, lunch was about all she could handle. We were all a little uncomfortable. Some of us doted on her too much, patting her as if she were on fire or talking to her like a toddler. Others had an extra cocktail, including a family friend who got up to speak and referred to John Whitehead as "Nancy's great lover." Mom loved it, and she was so moved to see us all there in our suits and holiday dresses that she stood to speak. Though she was unintelligible, it was okay. We had duplicated the joy of her favorite time of year for her.

It was the last time she was together with the family. The next year she went downhill. The medications she was taking had to be continually adjusted and in the fall of 1997 they were losing their effectiveness. She went back into the hospital at the end of the summer and on October 15 she was given last rites.

Mike and I flew up to New York. She was unconscious. Earlier that day John had signed the papers instructing doctors not to take extraordinary measures to keep her alive. The ink smeared from his tears. We were waiting for her to die. Mike, Anne and I got drunk together at dinner and went back to see her after midnight. We told her it was okay to go.

She went.

The next day, Saturday, I called AP and Reuters and told them she had died and I filed a brief story to the *Time* obit page:

To: obit
From: Dickerson
Msg: Fil
Slug: Nancy Dickerson Whitehead

Pioneering newswoman Nancy Dickerson Whitehead died this morning. She was the first woman news correspondent for CBS television, the first woman to report from an anchor booth and the floor of a political convention, the first woman at NBC to anchor her own newscast and she was my mother.

Mom had two funerals. In New York, John Cardinal O'Connor presided over the service at St. Patrick's Cathedral, which spilled out onto Fifth Avenue. There were so many boldfaced names lining the pews, an account in the paper would have looked like an ink stain.

The Washington ceremony was more intimate, held in a modest chapel deep inside Arlington National Cemetery, past the graves where the tour buses linger and hard to find, like one of those secret nooks Mom would have known about. First Lady Hillary Clinton spoke, remembering how Mom talked up the city to her when they'd first met. Her eulogy was simple, personable and warm. She delivered it without notes and had perfect pitch, a quality none of the pundits were ascribing to her at the time.

Years before she got sick, Mom asked Peggy Noonan, Michael and me to give the eulogies at her funeral. It was so perfectly her way, arranging the one event that she would not be there to orchestrate. Peggy was a real friend. (Mom's journals are peppered with little paeans to her: "I adore Peggy. Such a wild, witty nice girl. She enhances my life.") Of course it would all work out that Nancy Dickerson would have the most famous modern speechwriter deliver the eulogy at her funeral. Peggy had so perfectly eulogized the

Challenger astronauts and the soldiers at Normandy for Ronald Reagan, and she captured Mom too—her elegance, discipline and her gallantry but also her complexities and hidden parts:

"She had a good life. For all that she was a complicated little pirate; she had some struggles along the way deciding what things she really wanted, really needed. She was wordly, navigated well in the world, knew the ropes. And yet she said her rosary every day. She was a secret sayer of rosaries, a sneaker into churches in the middle of the day, a friend to ministers and Jesuits and do-gooders of all sorts."

I was unsettled about my eulogy. It had been a draining few days as we raced from vigil to death to ceremony. Seeing Mom's body at the funeral home was also a mistake. There was no closure. She looked like hell, her lipstick was fire-engine red and her makeup looked like it had been applied by a madman.

I was trying to order my feelings and judgments under the deadline of the coming service, but it wasn't the shrinking time that frustrated me. It was the expectation. I wanted to get this messy and fraught and wonderful story right. I sat at Mom's desk in New York and typed. Summing up her life late at night staring out over the East River, I was a mess. I typed; I paced; I swore and I banged the table.

I started to have the familiar self-dialogue I recognized from my work deadlines. I thought about what a person giving up on the task would think. *Why was I putting myself through this? I could bail and not give the eulogy. Mike could represent the family. Plus, I was speaking on the same podium as Peggy Noonan, for goodness' sake. That was no act to follow. Fewer words would be more tidy and respectful.* It was a curious experiment. I couldn't even convince myself to start *thinking* about not playing my role at the funerals. Was it out of loyalty to Mom, because she had asked me to speak? No, that didn't seem like what was going on.

The frustration, the fevered dialogue and the pushing, poking at phrases until words lost all meaning and every paragraph seemed out of order—these were the familiar fevered acts of this life we had both chosen. I had signed up to tell her story long before she ever asked me to give her eulogy, because I had signed on to a career of telling stories. I was experiencing the life I had chosen while trying to explain her desire to live the same life. I had a story—her story, my story, our story—and I would have had to tell it even if everyone had told me not to. This was not the kind of epiphany that required a sound track; just the opposite. Strip away the fancy reasons for being a journalist—the beauty of the craft, the necessity of a free press, the duty to inform—and there's a personal drive we shared: If you've got something in your hand, you're going to show it to people.

You just do the work. The tribute to her was not just in getting the story right, but also in *trying* to get the story right—the inescapable process. I spent the rest of the night writing this:

This is the toughest assignment Mom has ever given me. Where do you begin talking about a woman both tender and brave, both willful and soft, who has achieved so much and among whose achievements you would like to count yourself. How do you survive a mother?

I know what she would have done. It was a trick Edward R. Murrow taught her. Start your lede with this, she taught me: "J. C. listen to this." She typed J.C. rather than Jesus Christ on her Smith Corona because as a Catholic she knew the first amendment doesn't trump the second commandment. On campaign planes she couldn't use a typewriter; she'd get airsick, so she'd repeat that line over and over again in her head as she wrote and memorized what she'd say when the plane landed. We used to joke that it was as much of a prayer that someone would listen as it was an exclamation to get you started.

They used to call her Nan when she lived at 7013 Cedar in Wauwatosa, Wisconsin. In junior high, she was editor of the Hawthorn Echo like her sister before her and she loved to go to dances. She was competitive in both. She wrote in her eighth grade journal: "Today we voted for the five highest girls to be queen of the Valentine Day dance. I was second. Sally Wood, to whom I'm now not speaking at present, was first." When she went to college she stole her sister Mary's argyle socks and cut a locket of her hair to keep. She wanted her life to change the world. And she wanted to have fun. And she did both.

I came along after she'd lived half of her life. Being pregnant wasn't the kind of thing you talked about as a newswoman at the time. So, I was hidden under the anchor's desk and viewers were surprised to find that she was on the air Friday and I arrived on Saturday.

Perhaps that's why I'm in the business now. But one need not follow in her footsteps to admire her stride. Anyone might be attracted to a profession for which Mom had such passion. She wanted to do it all, grabbing at every experience she could and picking up every interesting bit of this and that along the way—scribbling it down urgently on bits of paper. It was all part of the story. The story she wanted to tell.

She wanted to help people see. See what was going on in the world. Why? Because she thought it made the world a better place when people knew. It was her first lesson that you should love what you did and that each day you should try to make the world a better place. That's what she believed she was doing, whether it was reporting on Martin Luther King's march, or working for Covenant House, or raising us. She made the world a better place.

She had a big and messy Irish heart. The right song or line of poetry could make her cry. But she could also hold wounds in that heart and never show it.

She was a tough lady in a brutal business and it was very cruel at times. A few hours before she was to interview President Nixon on air she watched a television commentator explain why she was unqualified to participate. After all, she was only representing PBS and Sevareid, Smith and Chancellor were men of stature from the three networks. It could have been devastating but instead she set her teeth. The next day's New York Times lead editorial mentioned her questions and not the others'.

But it wasn't just in work that she was tough. No one can hurt you more than your own son and I did as I pushed away the woman who'd sung lullabies and combed my hair and taught me to spell my name by painting it with nail polish on my mirror. I could be awful. But she never stopped loving me.

As we get older we unbind ourselves from our parents. We move out, we move away. But as I got older those binds were re-wound. She never once suggested I get into the business, but one day I looked at my office and it looked like hers—piles of papers and newspaper clippings, lists of committee chairmen and shelves of books underlined for only the first forty pages. And almost every day we talked about politics and stories and writing. Sometimes I'd fax her my copy and she'd edit it, and she'd get it wrong, and we'd yell, and we'd argue and we'd slam down the phone, and it was glorious. The two of us started to tie those binds back together.

Then she got sick. And the talk was broken. Days before the Iowa caucuses. My first campaign: her eleventh. Those new binds evaporated.

And it didn't matter.

We had more important things to do. We had stronger stuff to exchange. It was a chance to love back. To stroke her hair as she had mine as a sick child, to read to her as she had to me, and on the night before she died to sing her that old Irish lullaby "Toora Loora Loora" the way she had to me when I came into the world.

That Irish heart saw a lot of its love returned over the last 19 months. From her friends who kept vigils at the hospital to those praying at Holy Trinity church in Washington to the love of her dear husband. That love fed her and it fed all of us.

I don't know what kind of news bureau they have where she is. But I'm guessing that to be all-knowing you need some good reporters. Mom was happiest when working, so she's probably already filed her first few stories. And she'll probably use the lede she used in all of her other stories. Jesus Christ listen to this—but finally she'll be able to say it out loud and to Him in person.

There is more I would like to say and more I would like to show you about this wonderful lady, but you can almost hear her saying: "The speaker has gone on too long."

So goodbye, Mom. God gave you to me for 29 years. And you gave me a lifetime of gifts. I loved you very much and I hope I make you proud.

Chapter Thirty-eight

A couple of months before Mom got sick, she wrote in her journal about a party Joe Quinlan gave to celebrate my marriage. His broad New York apartment was full of my *Time* colleagues, many of whom had helped me get a job as a reporter.

"I went to a party tonight for John and Anne McKeehan Dickerson," she wrote. "Bonnie Angelo who works with John and whom I've known for more than 40 years was there. John spoke and he really does have a knack to be amusing as well as witty. He spoke just so properly, not over-doing anything, but in great gratitude for his start at *Time,* without over-doing the case."

We had repaired our relationship enough that she didn't need to boast, even to her journal, about feeling proud of herself or vindicated that her son had chosen her profession. She was happy because I was in for a life of work that she had known and enjoyed. She knew I would spend my time in good company too, even if I wouldn't always be in hers. At the end of the journal entry, she wrote, "There is no more amusing group than people in the press."

She was right. I do have an amusing life in the press. I wish I'd spent a little more of my time in her company though. I miss her. I miss the newspaper clippings she'd send with her notes in the margin or the phone calls in the morning after she'd looked at the papers. *Did you see that story in the* Post *today?* Mom would have been a fiend on the Internet. Then she would have called and said, "Did you see that story in the *Jerusalem Post* or the *Times* of London?" She had taken a few computer lessons, writing the new terminology in her deliberate block letters on the small pages of a spiral pad just as she had the terms from her voice lessons forty years earlier. The last dinner we had together she asked me to explain the "world wide web."

It has been ten years since Mom's stroke and I still have little darting instincts when I hear an anecdote from the Kennedy or Johnson administration. I want to ask her about it. I hear a piece of news and I think: *I've got to tell Mom about this.* Mom's phone number has gone out of my head, but I still reach for the receiver. And then there are the echoes of our life together repeated in mine, the memories I'd forgotten until I watched my own child mesmerized by a cameraman who has come to the house to videotape me.

I wish she'd seen more of my career. It might have been a way to pay back her sacrifice in her currency if she could have seen me standing in the East Room asking questions at presidential press conferences. She would have enjoyed the White House Correspondent's Dinner in April 2004. President Bush was making fun of himself, as every president does at those annual affairs. "In my recent press conference, John Dickerson of *Time* magazine asked the question about what I considered my biggest mistake. It's an excellent question that totally stumped me. I guess looking at it practically my biggest mistake was calling on John."

For the rest of the night, colleagues, friends and the famous who didn't know me approached me to share my fleeting moment of fame. Lesley Stahl ran into me as I walked out of the dinner. "Your mother would be so proud to see you if she were alive," she said. When I was younger, that wouldn't have mattered. It does now, because I am so grateful to her.

Watching her old clips, I'm impressed by Mom's talent. She was clever and she hustled. And when the camera was on and she was at her best, she was really good: at ease, tough and authentic. She wasn't perfect. Journalism wasn't perfect back then either. She got too close to her sources on the dance floor and at her parties, and it affected her stories, but it's the kind of mistake I know how to make. And she was tough enough that when I've had to pose uncomfortable questions to presidents, first ladies or cabinet secretaries, I've more than once taken a little strength from knowing how in the same spot she would barrel right ahead. *I wouldn't have asked if I didn't think it was a fair question.*

I also miss the awful parts of Mom, the woman who couldn't get past her own judgments and who needed regular public acclaim to live. At my wedding, her toast was about my life in the press. She was more focused on my life in the newsroom than the life I was start-ing with a woman I loved. She could be nasty and throw tantrums more violent and impetuous than those of my one-year-old daughter. She was mean enough to a few people in Washington that her name still makes them want to lash out at her.

I miss those rougher parts because I think I understand what made Mom that way and I think that part of her was softening. She drove back from my wedding in Charlottesville with our family priest, quizzing him for two hours about the choices she'd made in her life, searching like she was on deadline for his guidance about how to live the most charitable and best life for her remaining years.

As I wrote this book and learned about those parts of her life that I didn't see or that she kept hidden, I kept thinking, "I'd like to meet her." If she'd lived longer, Nan would have kept coming out from under all the roles Mom played. Before she got sick, when she met with the Ladies' Lunch group, maybe she got as close to being herself as she had in a long time. Peggy Noonan, in her eulogy, made it clear she'd seen Mom at ease behind the immaculate suits and the white gloves she wore to church. "She had a gaiety you could hear in that laugh she got when she heard something that was true and sharply stated. It was a surprising, almost burly laugh, and when I heard it sometimes I thought I was hearing the authentic sound of Washington in the '50s and '60s . . . a Washington of both dignity and sauciness, of high-mindedness and no small amount of stylish mischief."

With her lunchgoing friends, she could wonder out loud about her regrets and the way she'd ordered her life. She was vulnerable in front of them and practiced tiny acts of love and closeness with an abundance she never had before.

My female colleagues wonder if Mom's challenging career caused our difficulties. One took me out to lunch to quiz me in the hopes she wouldn't make the same mistakes with her kids. I wasn't much help. Mom and I had some ugly years, but I know so much now about how difficult it was for her. I'm in awe that the entire Dickerson family didn't fly apart in a messy flaming accident earlier. She was a first-run working mother, a pioneer in a tough and brutal business who chose to work for her career and not for financial support. There was no tradition, no literature, and she had no peers to help her figure out how to pull off those complicated tricks. And she did it all in the spotlight, which was both judgmental and deeply luring. She didn't get everything right. She got some things very wrong. But I find myself measuring her by the same standard she talked about when she wrote her autobiography. "Try, try, try, try—the one thing that attracted me to anyone or anything was that they cared and tried." She tried.

I don't think, given the way she was wired, she could have found the joy she found at work by staying at home and doing the hard work of raising children. Other women are wired differently and can't imagine the same rush from any other source. Other men are wired that way too. And plenty of constant stay-at-home mothers have hectored their children into ruin.

If Mom had shelved her career, as her mother and her sister had suggested when she got married, she would have been denying who she was. She would have been miserable touring the rounds of luncheons and children's birthday parties, and that would have made us miserable too. I can't wish for her the same level of joy I get from my children, because to wish for that is to wish for a reordering of her DNA.

Our story should not be mined for any confirmation about whether a woman should choose work or family. Those aren't the lessons I was looking for. I have tried to figure out my role as a person and a parent, figure out how to get the balance right between achieving something durable in the public realm and doing something important and genuine in the private one. How do I avoid the anxiety, indecision and regret of getting that mix wrong? I don't see that task any differently for my wife just because she's a woman who works and is a mother. Not everyone holds that view quite yet, but Anne and I have a better chance at balance than Mom did, in part because of what Mom and other women did to allow women the

choice to shape a broader identity. Sometimes we look at our screaming children on the kitchen floor and long for Mom's plug-and-play
arrangement. Other times we blow off swish and important parties
just so we can bounce on our bed with our kids. It's having the choice
that makes us so lucky. It's enjoying both that makes us even more so.

I wish I could apologize to Mom. Now that I've seen all the internal bleeding in her journals and understand, as she put it, "her penchant for suppressing unpleasant things," I wish I'd given her a
break. I've seen now how insecure she was and it makes me sad to
have misinterpreted it. So much of what I thought was pride, arro-
gance and selfishness grew out of that vulnerability.

I am also sorry because I am the keeper now of all of her many
kindnesses that she didn't talk about. I've found the bill for the high-
priced wig she had made for her friend who was undergoing chemo-
therapy and the pictures of a trip to Ireland she took with a friend
who was dying of breast cancer so that she could see it before she
died. After Mom died, I expected the letters of tribute. What I didn't
expect was the letter from an older male colleague of mine who said
Mom had taken time out to help him when he was just a kid stum-
bling around the White House. Another colleague told a similar
story of being a girl reporter who Mom took to lunch to deliver a
"you-can-do-this-too" pep talk. ABC's Cokie Roberts tells the same
story of how Mom helped her when she was new in town.

All of the Dickerson children have gained the perspective that
comes with time. "I don't know how Mom did as much as she did,"
says my sister Ann. "She was juggling so much. I remember at one
point counting the number of servants that we had, and I got up to
seven. I feel so sorry for her and what she had to go through. I just
know how challenging my job has been with only four children, no
news job, and relatively speaking, no social life." My chastened vener-
ation for Mom comes not just from having children but from also living a life in the news. My children have kissed no presidents (though
President Bush sent them both letters when they were born). But if I
am not in the inner circles of Washington, I'm close enough to them
to know how hard it is to be both a good parent and a good reporter.

I don't begrudge Mom her devotion to work. How could I? I am
in the same business and I put it before everything else too a lot of

the time. I know what it's like to have opportunities that are too attractive to pass up. Presented with the same luring options Mom had, I would have almost certainly done the same thing. I've almost done it—taking the tantalizing job offer that would have made me a ghost to my children. I've assumed, as she might have, that I could make up the lost time with the kids on the back end. That's what Mom and I were doing when we were interrupted by her illness.

I wish my children could have known her. They've run into the playroom as I've watched tapes of Mom at press conferences or doing stand-ups. For a long time they confused me with President Bush, so they're suspicious of anyone in that box who makes me take out my notebook. When they stop and ask who that lady is, they don't believe me when I tell them.

Anne and I would have enjoyed the mischief of Mom's visits to see her grandchildren. The kids wouldn't be wearing the formal uniforms of my youth. Since my wife and I often dress our own children, everything is connected with Velcro. We don't have Merrywood-style help or the patience for buttons or snaps. If we're not having company, we let the kids eat dinner in the pajama tops they woke from their nap in. If we have company, we put on their pajama pants. I have inherited the British children's paintings from Merrywood, but they are the only things not smeared with yogurt, Play-Doh or other unidentified viscous liquid. I'm not sure Mom would have known where to sit. We probably would have taught the kids to yell "Granny!" the minute she hit the threshold and wrap themselves around her legs. She would have turned green. "Oh, honestly," she would have pleaded.

Some of Mom's old Washington friends have a similar reaction to the more textured next generation of Dickersons. When I interviewed them for this book they didn't want to talk about Mom's vulnerability or the moments they witnessed where she was not so generous or flourishing. I understand that, and I'm grateful, in a way, for their protective decorum. They do it out of friendship and respect, so I'm easy on them when I watch them squirm a little as I ask about the life behind the public image. They are of a time and a generation that kept lots of their lives locked away. I am a bit of a threat, not just to Mom's memory, but to their lives and choices. Why not let the dead sleep in peace? No matter what I may tell them about my search, I am the nightmare they thought they'd gotten rid of when their kids left home: the second generation child who embarrasses his parents in the newspapers.

And yet I don't forgive all of them. Some of these same people make up the Washington whisper class. They don't shy away from more bracing truths about Mom, they just prefer to pass them between themselves. One old friend of Mom's who was squeamish in an interview was less so when she asked another Washington denizen, upon hearing I was writing this book, "What will he say about the affairs?"

The full life of Nancy Dickerson can withstand the scrutiny. To look at the frailty, tenderness, nastiness, vanity, generosity, love, pride and humility all in proper proportion still yields a very impressive woman, and a more genuine one. Mom loved image and glamour and insinuation, but she also liked to know a true thing when she could find it. She would understand my need to search for the story because she had that same need. I went looking for my mother's story and found a woman who was compelled to find stories and tell them too.

Our first child, Brice, is named after his maternal great grandfather, a Tennessee teacher and football coach who was so beloved that his funeral was attended by nearly everyone in town. It's a tribute and not an expectation, a way to reach back across time and connect with a past we celebrate. When Anne and I had a daughter, we knew what her name would be. There were many Nancy Dickersons. And now there is one more. We call her Nan, just as Mom was called when she was a little girl.

Afterword

In the ten years since this book was published, I've not stopped being my mother's biographer. My children never knew her, so I tell them her story. I have also kept reporting on her life. When people hear my name, they press stories on me. They'd watch Mom on television every day after school because their mother said she was proof of what was possible for women. Veteran reporters tell me about how she gave them advice or looked out for them when they were starting out. I introduced my daughter to a retired senator, who, upon hearing there was a Nancy Dickerson in a new generation, told us of a date he'd been on with Mom in the 1950s. "She said, 'You're being naughty,'" he told us. "And you know what? I was!" He walked off, on the arm of a helper. My daughter, then ten, looked at me and executed what I believe was her first arched eyebrow.

I wrote *On Her Trail* to tell the story of the many Nancy Dickersons I discovered after she died. I have found one more—the posthumous parent—the one still sitting in the bleachers behind me.

"Your mother would be so proud." Almost everyone said this when I was named moderator of *Face the Nation*. Mom had been an "Associate in Production," on the very first broadcast of the show in 1954. The compliment is more powerful than they know.

When I was a kid I didn't like hearing that my mother would be proud. But my children remind me why. "Of course you're proud," my son says when I say that I'm proud of him. "You're my dad." They think it's a rule: A parent must be proud of his children. I could explain that I proved such a rule does not exist when I was about their age. Or, I could foreshadow the certain time in the future when I will clash with both of them as I did with my mom. But they raise a good point: what is it that makes a parent proud of his children?

As Mom's biographer, I have an answer. It is in the lessons they draw from the never-ending story I tell them about their grandmother.

I spent so much time thinking and writing about Mom's life, I filter my experiences through her, and the lessons that I take from her life—both good and bad—are easy to tell the kids because they are related to her. Grandma Nancy is what we call her in our house. That name sounds reasonable to the kids, though I smile, because I know we're pulling off a caper. Grandma Nancy conveys all the best parts of Mom's humanity. She would have loved our kids—my daughter has her mischief and will; my son has what she would call "a nice face," which was the term she used to describe someone with a good heart. But calling her Grandma Nancy would have gotten a rise out of her. It suggests a head handkerchief more than Chanel, or biscuits on the stove, not state dinners.

The kids, who are almost teenagers, would have learned to tease Mom the way I did when I was their age—asking her to join them in the kitchen to cook something or perform some (any) household task. I'd have told them to cool it. The circle would be complete.

In *On Her Trail*, I wanted to get across the complexity of Mom's life. As a biographer a second time to her grandchildren, I do the opposite. I simplify. The lesson of Mom's life is this: try. No matter how many times someone says no, or how embarrassed you are, or how much it hurts, keep trying. When you're told you're not smart enough, study harder. When they tell you a woman can't do it, show them that she can. When you are fired, build your own way to success. When you have no money and your marriage is disintegrating, hang on. Try. You will survive.

"Try, try, try," Mom wrote in her autobiography. "The one thing that attracted me to anyone or anything was that they cared and tried." She also sent this message to me and my sisters and brother when she thought she might not live long enough to see us as adults.

"I leave each of you all my love and the fervent hope that you will always try to do your very best—better than anyone might rightfully expect—and the hope that you will never stop trying."

So when I see my kids try and not give up, despite fear or failure or embarrassment, that is when I am proud of them. The problems they face are small. They live a life of privilege, but that doesn't make their fears any less real to them or any easier for them to overcome. When I watch them refuse to quit, I feel Mom nearby. I want to wink at her and let her know the message got through. They're listening. I was listening.

I am proud of them for the same reason Mom would be. That they have the capacity for grit suggests maybe they're going to be okay in life when the challenges will be bigger and we won't be around.

To try is all well and good, but not if it's only about you. That's a more complicated part of Mom's life. She was obsessed with her success. But she also practiced secret kindnesses. That's what the kids hear about from the people she helped or paid attention to. If she were as consumed with her ambition as my fourteen-year-old self thought, she never could have left behind so many stories.

When Mom wrote to me about trying, I was two years old. She was worried she'd die in a plane crash and leave us with no instruction about life. Even later, when I was a little older, her words didn't take. They sounded too trite back then. When I hear them today they guide my behavior far more than anything she might have said to me when I was younger. Now she makes more sense because I know how hard she had to try. I can see that one little moment—alone and scared in a dark jumpy plane, doubting herself. I also know what that letter meant for her, because I live a version of that same life. I am about the age she was when she wrote to me at age two. I have little people upstairs reading past their bedtime whose future now depends on me.

The artifacts Mom left me provide unexpected instruction, which I missed the first time around. When she wrote "always keep smiling and making people happy," I was too young to even read, but now I feel as if she's reminding me about some essential part of myself. It's a lesson to me, but more important, it is a prompt. I need to write my children the same kind of note for when they are older and need to be reminded of their essential selves. Someday my son will need to be reminded that on the fifth of May he put a jar of mayonnaise in the sink while we were making dinner and announced: "Cinco de mayo."

Another letter I found but had forgotten suggests that if I want to become a writer I should "keep a journal daily. . . . It's amazing how your perceptions change as you go along and are often vastly different from what you remember them to be at the time first experienced." That's true of my life and true of the way I think about hers.

But I didn't tell just heroic tales in this book. I tried to tell the whole story, something that stings a little as I re-read its candor against the nearly twenty years of missing Mom. But readers have rescued me from doubt because they have reminded me in their reactions to the book that Mom's qualities are more powerful for not being otherworldly.

When my kids are old enough, I hope they will read this book and learn about the more complicated Nancy Dickerson. Not all the stories are wonderful, but the complexity of her life puts what is wonderful in context and makes it more real. Those words about trying have weight for me because I know about Mom's struggles and failures.

Every parent tells the story of their parents to their kids, but few of us also share that story with the world. It ripples back to you in unexpected ways, like in a conversation I had with my daughter about criticism. I told her the story of how this book had been received. No matter how many lovely reactions I got, I said it was hard not to focus on the few who missed the point. The trick, I told her, was to focus on the only thing you could control: your effort. "Try as hard as you can, because you can't control other people. You can control what you do though. So don't worry about the rest, just don't stop trying."

She'd heard that sermon before so I wasn't expecting much of a reaction. "You mean like Grandma Nancy?"

'Atta girl. I hope so.

Index